Also by Barbara Isenberg

Conversations with Frank Gehry

State of the Arts: California Artists Talk About Their Work

Making It Big: The Diary of a Broadway Musical

Tradition!

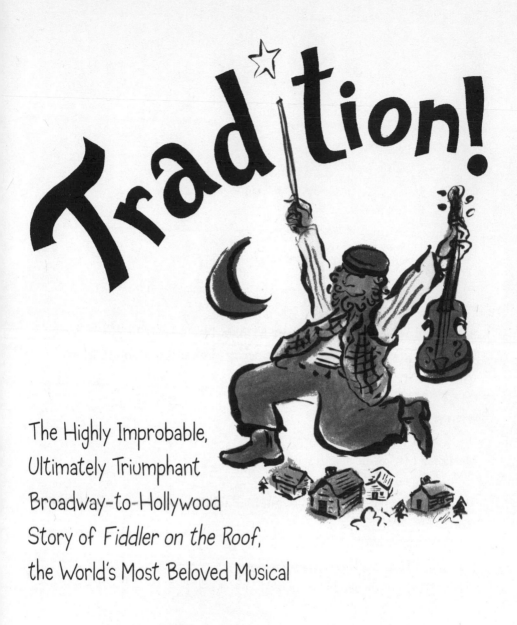

The Highly Improbable,
Ultimately Triumphant
Broadway-to-Hollywood
Story of *Fiddler on the Roof,*
the World's Most Beloved Musical

Barbara Isenberg

St. Martin's Press   New York

TRADITION! Copyright © 2014 by Barbara Isenberg. All rights reserved. Printed in the United States of America. For information, address St. Martin's Press, 175 Fifth Avenue, New York, N.Y. 10010.

www.stmartins.com

Designed by Steven Seighman

The Library of Congress Cataloging-in-Publication Data is available upon request.

ISBN 978-0-312-59142-7 (hardcover)
ISBN 978-1-4668-6252-4 (e-book)

St. Martin's Press books may be purchased for educational, business, or promotional use. For information on bulk purchases, please contact Macmillan Corporate and Premium Sales Department at 1-800-221-7945, extension 5442, or write specialmarkets@macmillan.com.

First Edition: September 2014

10 9 8 7 6 5 4 3 2 1

Contents

Part Three: The Movie

Part Four: The Phenomenon

Epilogue

Introduction

On September 22, 1964, after the long-awaited Broadway opening of *Fiddler on the Roof,* invited guests gathered at New York's swank Rainbow Room to celebrate. The first review that came in that night was from critic Walter Kerr, and it wasn't very good. But producer Harold Prince read it aloud to his guests anyway. "I can't resist reading this to you," he said that night, "because it's so irrelevant."

Apparently so. Nearly eight years and 3,300 performances later, *Fiddler* became the longest-running show on Broadway. Winner of nine Tony Awards, including Best Musical, *Fiddler* was *still* on Broadway when United Artists released Norman Jewison's film of the same name in 1971.

Rarely offstage, rarely on hiatus, *Fiddler on the Roof* has already been back on Broadway for four revivals, played London's West End four times, and remains among Broadway's sixteen longest-running shows ever. There have been stage productions all over the world—including fifteen in Finland alone—as well as in thousands of schools, community centers, and regional theaters.

Whether played by Zero Mostel, Chaim Topol, or a high school student in India, Russian milkman Tevye just keeps on worrying about his family, his God, and his poverty-plagued shtetl. Brides, grooms, and wedding planners would be bereft without "Sunrise, Sunset."

After half a century, Tevye and company remain unstoppable. Today *Fiddler* is a phenomenon, with sing-alongs, tens of thousands of Facebook "likes," and enough former Tevyes of all ages and nationalities to populate a dozen shtetls.

Why did *Fiddler on the Roof*, a musical based on nineteenth-century Yiddish stories, become such a hit? What is it that has kept *Fiddler* pertinent and meaningful to Jews and non-Jews alike for all these years?

Fiddler is set in 1905 Anatevka, a shtetl created first by the great Yiddish humorist Sholem Aleichem, drawing on the same Eastern European shtetl life that inspired his contemporary, artist Marc Chagall. It was the Aleichem stories that initially ignited the imaginations of *Fiddler*'s creators, while the show's very title came from Chagall paintings that also influenced the look and feel of the show.

Working without a producer on what librettist Joseph Stein has called a labor of love, Stein, lyricist Sheldon Harnick, and composer Jerry Bock began in 1961 to craft their musical. The three men were all Jewish, all descendants of immigrants from the Old Country. They wrote it as they would any other show, Bock told me years ago, but added "those embers that kept burning underneath."

When Jerome Robbins came in to shape and stage the show, they did what composers, lyricists, and librettists have always done—they rewrote. Stein turned out five drafts of the show's book, and the songwriters came up with about fifty songs, of which the show used fewer than one-third.

Their songs, dances, humor, and insights became *Fiddler on the Roof*, freezing time before pogroms, emigration, and Hitler destroyed a culture and way of life that had endured for centuries. It surely also revived interest in Aleichem, who died forty-eight years before *Fiddler* crossed a Broadway stage.

Fiddler was not typical show business fare in 1964. That year, the Beatles debuted on *The Ed Sullivan Show*, while *My Fair Lady* and *Mary Poppins* were hit movies. Both *Hello, Dolly!* and *Funny Girl* were already faring well on Broadway when *Fiddler* premiered in September.

Fiddler came of age in the sixties, when traditional American values were being questioned amid great social upheaval. The civil rights movement, Betty Friedan's *The Feminine Mystique*, and the Cuban missile crisis were all taking place. President John F. Kennedy was assassinated. Smoking was declared bad for your health. Nice girls took birth control pills, and nice boys evaded the draft.

It was also a pivotal time in world history, with the horror of the Holocaust only two decades before. Much as *The Diary of Anne Frank* is not just a Jewish story, neither is *Fiddler on the Roof. Fiddler*'s strong themes of family, tradition, repression, prejudice, and diaspora continue to evoke common ground for its audiences wherever they are.

Glenn Casale, who directed a 2012 production at the 2,200-seat Music Circus in Sacramento, told his actors to turn on the television and watch the heartbreak in Syria. This was his fifteenth *Fiddler* production, he says, "and every time I do *Fiddler on the Roof*, it coincides with something going on in the world. People losing their rights and losing their homes. That's what makes it timeless."

That timelessness is similarly captured in Norman Jewison's movie *Fiddler on the Roof.* The United Artists film received eight Academy Award nominations, including Best Picture, has a score arranged by John Williams, which won the renowned composer his first Oscar, and features music in its opening credits played by Isaac Stern, the most famous violinist of his time. The film that critic Pauline Kael once called "the most powerful movie musical ever made" has already been seen by one billion people, according to its star, Chaim Topol.

Production designer Robert Boyle created 1905 Anatevka in the villages of Yugoslavia, while cinematographer Oswald Morris shot through ladies' stockings to get the film's earthen colors and textures. Director Jewison, who had stood in snow up to his knees when scouting locations a year earlier, never encountered any during the entire shoot. Every bit of snow in the film is marble dust.

Jewison is candid about his challenges on the film. Among them: casting Tevye, dealing with that total lack of snow, getting phone poles out of his images, communicating with three hundred extras speaking many different languages, and even wrangling geese and pigs on the set.

Violinist Stern told Jewison that Marc Chagall's original fiddler on the roof was the artist's frequently drunk uncle, so Stern's violin had to be played a little off-key as the drunken uncle would have played it. Jewison asked actor Paul Michael Glaser to wear brown contacts to hide his blue eyes, and Topol's Tevye talked to a "God" that was in actuality a piece of white cardboard with a Jewish star on it, attached to a pole and hung from the camera (so Topol would always look at the same place).

Topol, an Israeli who brought his family with him to Yugoslavia, held Friday-night Shabbat dinners, often including Jewison, a non-Jew, among his guests. Jewison appeared in a documentary of the filming, clearly moved by what he was shooting, wiping away a few tears as he shot the scene where Anatevka's families prepared to leave the land they loved.

For so many people involved with *Fiddler* over the years, the experience has been a powerful one. Austria-born Theodore Bikel, a frequent stage Tevye, has a study filled with books about the period and often instructs his fellow actors about the world they are portraying. Los Angeles–based orchestrator/conductor Larry Blank, who has scored many productions of *Fiddler*, remembers attending the Broadway production as a child with his parents and grandparents, two generations of family members who fled Russia's pogroms for America.

David Wohl, who played butcher Lazar Wolf on Broadway in 2004, recalls watching two of the show's dancers, both Jewish, both from Argentina, dancing across the stage in a way that reminded him of how his grandmother from the Ukraine danced. And when Elaine Kussack performed as Tevye's wife, Golde, both on Broadway and in summer stock, she thought of her own parents from the Ukraine, and how her father had fled in a wheelbarrow to get to America. She says tearfully, "I never had to get in the mood because that was so much a part of my experience as a child, hearing the stories."

The English actor Henry Goodman, who played Tevye on London's West End in 2007, calls *Fiddler* "a brilliant combination of beautifully crafted storytelling and emotional manipulation. If the story doesn't get you, the music will, and if the music doesn't get you, the dancing will. It piles on so many layers of truthfulness, real humor, and compassion, there's no escape for the audience. It understands the rites of passage—bar mitzvahs, confirmations, weddings, death—and because it charts the individual and the community going through those rites of passage, it will always speak to people."

Librettist Stein liked to talk about his initial experience when he went to Japan for the show's first Asian production. "The Japanese producer asked me, 'Do they understand this show in America?'" Stein said. "When I replied, 'Why do you ask?' he said, 'Because it's so Japanese.'"

Stein told me that story in December 2001, when I was writing about *Fiddler on the Roof* for the *Los Angeles Times*. It was wonderful then to write about *Fiddler*, a groundbreaking musical with historic roots, contemporary resonance, and amusing, articulate people to relate its creative odyssey. Several years later, I remembered how much I'd enjoyed their many stories, and, I thought, "That's my next book."

Everything fell into place. Michael Flamini, my editor at St. Martin's, was as keen on the *Fiddler* story as I was, and so it seemed was everyone I contacted. When composer John Williams, who rarely does interviews, responded quickly and positively to my inquiry, I knew I was on to something.

As I interviewed people associated with the film and its diverse stage productions, I realized it was an opportunity for many of them to reflect on a time of great joy and meaning. Many times it was like a detective story, as I cobbled together bits and pieces from many sources, confirming stories that at first seemed mere conjecture (and in some cases, alas, were indeed conjecture).

I was unfortunately not able to interview Jerome Robbins, Zero Mostel, or set designer Boris Aronson before their deaths, but I was able to interview their assistants, family members, or former colleagues. While both *Fiddler* librettist Stein and composer Bock died in the fall of 2010, I had interviewed both men a decade ago for my earlier *Los Angeles Times* article.

After spending nearly three years with these people and their memories, I understand why so many of them made themselves available to me. It is my great pleasure to share with you now the story of *Fiddler on the Roof*.

Barbara Isenberg

Before we begin our story, let me add a quick note on the spelling of Sholem Aleichem, the Yiddish writer who memorialized his own humble dairyman as Tevye, the dairyman and patriarch of his famous stories and, much later, *Fiddler on the Roof*. Born Solomon Rabinowitz, a name which also has a few spellings, he wrote his Tevye stories under a pen name which loosely translates as "peace be with you" and which is sometimes spelled as Sholom Aleichem and sometimes Sholem Aleichem.

Most contemporary references to the author use the spelling Sholem Aleichem, and so generally will I. However, I left Sholom Aleichem in titles of books, plays, television shows, reviews, etc., although some were already Sholem. Even spelling was a challenge in Anatevka!

Without our traditions, our lives would be as shaky as—as a fiddler on the roof.

—Fiddler on the Roof

Part 1

BEGINNINGS

1

The Boys

In the fall of 1960, a friend sent lyricist Sheldon Harnick a copy of Sholem Aleichem's 1909 novel *Wandering Stars*, with the notion it might make a good musical. Harnick read the book, agreed, and sent it along to his longtime collaborator, composer Jerry Bock. The two men had written the scores for Pulitzer Prize–winner *Fiorello!* and the musical *Tenderloin* and were looking for a new project.

Bock was also intrigued by *Wandering Stars*, the sprawling tale of a traveling Yiddish theater company. So the two men took the idea to playwright Joseph Stein, with whom they'd first worked on the 1958 musical *The Body Beautiful*.

"I loved it," Harnick recalled. "I thought, Ooh, this is a musical, and when I gave it to Jerry, he said, 'Ooh, this is a musical.' So we gave it to Joe who said, 'Ooh, this is *not* a musical.' He said it was just too big a canvas; it would be too hard to reduce it to the stage and have it still be effective."

Body Beautiful, a musical about prizefighting, hadn't worked out, but Stein did like the idea of working with Bock and Harnick again. Since he, too, was ready for his next project, Stein came up with another idea. *Wandering Stars* reminded him of Aleichem's stories of Tevye the milkman, which his Poland-born father had read to him in Yiddish when he was a boy and which he thought had better odds as a musical.

Aleichem's Tevye stories pivot around the worries and wisdom of dairyman Tevye in a poor Russian village, or shtetl, where he is blessed with a skeptical wife and many daughters to marry off. In the closing years of Tzarist Russia, amid pogroms and poverty, the irrepressible, Bible-quoting Tevye deals with the untraditional courtships of his "modern" children and simultaneously confronts the political and social changes that threaten his beliefs, community, and traditions.

An incredibly popular writer first in his native Russia, then around the world, Aleichem wrote about three hundred short stories, five novels, and several plays. Born Solomon Rabinowitz, the writer used the pen name Sholem Aleichem, which translates as "peace be with you," and was revered as, among other things, "the Jewish Mark Twain." When Aleichem came to New York, Mark Twain reportedly said to him, "I wanted to meet you because I understand that I am the American Sholem Aleichem."

Few writers were as celebrated in their time as Aleichem, whose funeral in 1916 attracted more than a hundred thousand mourners and included a processional that ran through three New York boroughs. But forty-five years later, Stein had trouble finding English translations of Aleichem's short stories, which he finally came upon in O'Malley's Bookstore and passed along to his collaborators.

Bock, Harnick, and Stein all said that the more they read the Tevye stories and talked about the material, the more excited they became. "The writing struck a resonant tone with us, and we decided to have a go at it," Bock said. "I'm not being modest. We had no idea what would happen to this project. We would do this show, and if it works out, we'd do another. What was special about it was our personal connection to the material.

"I began to hear the music as I read the stories and remembered the lullabies and little melodies my grandmother would sing to me. It was almost as if I recognized and knew these people spiritually. For all of us, the people in the stories brought back early memories of our own families, and we felt confident about plunging into the material."

The "boys," as writers on musicals were often addressed, discussed their project fairly casually at first, then had their first formal meeting in March 1961 to discuss what was then called *Tevye*. And as they did, Bock took notes, writing down dates and progress in a small, black notebook he called "Tevye diary (beginnings)." By mid-July, he wrote, they had all read the Tevye stories and met a few times. Stein had sketched out a rough outline of the show, and they had begun negotiating with Crown Publishers for the rights.

Proceeding without a producer, they invested not just their time but also their money in getting those rights. "Everything else that we had done had been an assignment or a commission from a producer," said Harnick. "This one *we* decided to do."

Given their Broadway credits, they all felt it was a calculated risk. "We weren't novices," Stein said. "At that time, all of us were fairly well known in the theater."

Stein, for instance, was still employed as a social worker in 1942 when he met actor Zero Mostel, who gave him his first writing assignment—for fifteen dollars a week. Soon a prominent comedy writer, Stein was an alumnus of Sid Caesar's fabled *Your Show of Shows*, which also nurtured such talents as Mel Brooks, Carl Reiner, Imogene Coca, Larry Gelbart, Woody Allen, Mel Tolkin, and others. His first Broadway musical, the 1955 *Plain and Fancy*, about the Amish of Pennsylvania, was very successful, and there were several more before and after *Tevye*.

Bock, also a Caesar alum, had worked with Stein on the Sammy Davis Jr. vehicle *Mr. Wonderful*. Before they were introduced by their mutual friend, the actor Jack Cassidy, Bock and Harnick had also independently written assorted songs for Broadway and off-Broadway revues. The two men were brought together to form a songwriting team in 1957 by the music publisher Tommy Valando, and *Body Beautiful* was their first joint show. *Body Beautiful* ran just six weeks on Broadway—Harnick quips it would have run seven but there was a blizzard—but its score impressed the producer Harold Prince and led indirectly to their award-winning *Fiorello!* assignment a short time later.

In his outline for *Tevye*, Stein worked at turning nineteenth-century stories, written in Yiddish, into something relevant to an English-speaking, twentieth-century theatrical audience. The playwright worried that what might be "amusing" to Aleichem's audience "would be bewildering to ours; what was moving in Yiddish could become oversentimental, even melodramatic." His task: "to remain true to the spirit, the feeling of Sholem Aleichem and . . . tell the story of Tevye, his family, and his community in terms which would have meaning for today."

The shtetls of Aleichem's stories also reflected their time and place. Russian Jews had long struggled for survival, anti-Semitism was rampant, and pogroms were becoming more common. The situation worsened with the 1881 assassination of Alexander II, and between 1881 and 1914, almost three million Jews left Russia, most of them headed for the United States.

Adapting that world for the stage was one challenge after another. "They were isolated tales only connected to each other by the central character of Tevye," Stein has said. "So, it was a matter of constructing a total storyline—deciding which tales to use, what aspects of them to use, which characters to use. . . . The stories were monologues, written as Tevye saying, 'Let me tell you about what happened to my daughter. You won't believe it.'"

God is an offstage character in Aleichem's stories, and Stein made the most of that. "I don't talk to God, but I did feel the Tevye character would be clearer if he chatted with his best friend, who happened to be God," Stein said. "It's a friendship, like I have with my brother."

Stein was able to use many of the same characters who populated Aleichem's stories as well as several incidents. He honed in on Aleichem's three oldest daughters, Tzeitel, Hodel, and Chava, and their suitors, with the two youngest daughters relegated to the background and two other daughters with sadder stories discarded entirely. As proven by William Shakespeare's *King Lear*, Anton Chekhov's *Three Sisters*, and, much later, Julian Fellowes's *Downton Abbey*, the three-sister setup works well.

The playwright found that little of Aleichem's dialogue was usable, and he also had to beef up his central character of Tevye as the "moving force" in the plot. To give the story more contemporary meaning, he accentuated what he characterized as the "hostility, violence, and injustice" of the time and the way the people of Anatevka harnessed their "internal strength, dignity, humor, and . . . unique talent for survival" to deal with it.

The book writers, or librettists, on musicals are often underappreciated, and Harnick felt Stein was among them. Said Harnick, "Some of the critics praised him, but others said he had such an easy job—all he had to do was to quote the stories. But there were very few lines that he could use. There were some. But I would say that ninety-five percent of the show, he had to invent. It was all Joe Stein."

While Stein worked on his outline, Bock and Harnick turned to the score. They began their work on September 11, 1961, which fell that year on Rosh Hashanah, the start of the most sacred of Jewish seasons. The score moved relatively quickly, and within eight weeks, they were already starting their fourth song.

Bock and Harnick had a distinctive way of writing musical scores, explained Bock's friend and lawyer, Richard Ticktin. To start their songs, each would go off to work on his own, then send the other some suggestions. Bock might send Harnick tapes with "snippets of musical moments" or Harnick might send Bock "some lyric moments" he'd written up. Then they would mold their songs together.

The first song they tackled was for Tevye's dream, a dream the patriarch creates to persuade his wife, Golde, to let their eldest daughter, Tzeitel, marry the poor tailor, Motel Kamzoil, rather than the rich butcher, Lazar Wolf. It was a song they felt would stay in the show for plot purposes no matter what changes Stein made to the book.

The dream song did remain in the show, but the next two—"I'll Work for Tomorrow Today" and "A Butcher's Soul"—did not. Then, in November, Harnick received a tape of music Bock felt had "that authentic, folk Russian feel." It was, the composer admitted, "unashamedly sentimental."

It was the music for "Sunrise, Sunset" and, remembered Harnick, "as I continued to listen to it, the words just crystallized automatically. Jerry lived in New Rochelle and when we finished, we called his wife, Patti, down to the basement, and we played it for her. At the end, I looked at her, and she was crying. Then, a while later, I was in Bethesda, Maryland, where my sister lived, and when I played it for her, *she* was crying. I thought, 'We have something here.'"

Around that time, Bock invited Ticktin over to hear it as well. Again they went down to the upright piano in Bock's basement. "I was the only other person in the room and I was reduced to tears," Ticktin remembered.

"I said to myself, This is an extraordinary moment. If the book and the direction turn out as well, this was going to be an enormous event."

Fueled by such reaction, Bock and Harnick turned out song after song, some used in the final show but most not, their lyrics all indexed and kept in a thick, three-hole binder at Harnick's home on New York's Upper West Side. Among them were "Sabbath Prayer," the celebratory "To Life" and something called "Poppa, Help Me," which Harnick recently said even *he* doesn't remember. Flipping pages, Harnick called out to a visitor long-forgotten titles: "'Promise Me,' 'The Story of Jacob,' 'Baby Birds,' 'Brand New World' . . . Now, here's an interesting title: 'Why Jew, Why Gentile?'" He laughed heartily at that one.

To inform all those lyrics, Harnick read not just Aleichem but the Bible and books on Jewish, Russian, and European history. Very helpful was the interview-based 1952 book *Life Is with People: The Culture of the Shtetl*, which described such traditions as Sabbath meals and rituals, weddings, and prayers. In her foreword to the book, Margaret Mead introduced an "anthropological study of a culture which no longer exists," and that study was clearly useful to the *Tevye* team.

"When we read those accounts, it really filled in what was missing from Sholem Aleichem," said Harnick, whose parents were both born in Eastern Europe. "For me, the book brought back memories of the little synagogue I attended in Chicago, and I'd picture those gaunt elderly men in their shawls praying."

But their most useful source was clearly Aleichem. "It almost embarrasses me that when people read Sholem Aleichem, they see where I got the lyrics for 'If I Were a Rich Man,'" Harnick told a packed audience at New York's Lincoln Center in 2011. "I'm very smart. I know where to take from."

Bock, however, has said he didn't really feel the need to research klezmer or even Russian music of that period. Instead, unexpectedly, "the music that I hadn't been able to write with all our shows was something that I had silently deposited in my creative mind, and the opportunity to now express myself with that kind of music just opened up a flood of possibilities for me.

"I felt if we had to write fifty more songs, they were still inside me," said Bock. "I felt I had tapped a source that would not run dry, and I think that came from having nourished it without being able to express it all my life."

The final play script of *Fiddler on the Roof* is dedicated "to our Fathers." As the show's producer Harold Prince said several years later, *Fiddler* was "clearly conceived" by Stein, Bock, and Harnick "as a kind of valentine to their grandparents." For Prince, their "celebration of what they came from is present throughout the creation of the musical."

2

Forging Tradition

When it came time to find a producer, the authors turned first to Harold Prince, whom they had all worked with before and respected. But when Prince first read *Tevye* in 1962, he passed on it. He told the authors that he found it fascinating but "foreign"; it wasn't his background. He was German-Jewish, not Russian-Jewish, Prince said, "and I didn't feel the connection I felt years later with [the musical] *Parade* and German Jews in the South."

So Bock and Harnick told Prince they had *two* shows to offer. One was *Tevye* and the other was a musical called *She Loves Me* based on *The Shop Around the Corner*. As Prince said several years later, "Sheldon gave me a book about shtetls—I didn't know what they were—and after I read it, I was even less eager to go there. But I liked the *She Loves Me* idea, and I said, 'Yes, I'd love to do it.'"

She Loves Me also launched producer Prince's directing career. Born in New York and a theatergoer since he was eight years old, Prince was just twenty when he began his career working for free with legendary producer/director George Abbott. The first musical he coproduced was *The Pajama Game* in 1954, when he was twenty-six. Soon came such shows as *Damn Yankees*, *West Side Story*, and *A Funny Thing Happened on the Way to the Forum*, just the start of Prince's extraordinary career directing and producing dozens of award-winning musicals.

Prince meanwhile gave them smart advice on the show he had just declined. Get Jerome Robbins, he told them. First of all, Robbins came from a Russian-Jewish background, said Prince, but that wasn't the only reason for his suggestion. "I said, 'For it to be universal, you need a choreographer/director' because I thought dance was an easier language to understand than words."

Stephen Sondheim had also had a hunch it would be a good project for Robbins. "Steve asked me later if I remembered how Jerome Robbins became our director, and I didn't," said Harnick. "He reminded me that Jerry Bock and I had gone to Joe Stein's home in New Rochelle to play the score for a number of invited guests, and Steve was one of them. He liked what he heard and happened to be speaking to Jerome Robbins the next day. When Robbins said he always wanted to do something about Jewishness, Steve said, 'Well, now's your chance. I heard this terrific score.'"

The timing wasn't right for Robbins, however. In the early sixties, he was just coming off the film of *West Side Story*, which would win him two Academy Awards, and entering another busy time. In addition to dance projects, he had directed Arthur Kopit's *Oh Dad, Poor Dad, Mamma's Hung You in the Closet and I'm Feelin' So Sad*, which fared well, and then Bertolt Brecht's *Mother Courage and Her Children*, which did not. Along the way, he had given up work on two shows he'd hoped to do—*A Funny Thing Happened on the Way to the Forum* and *Funny Girl*—only to have both shows run into trouble and ask him to come to the rescue.

Yet Robbins did not decline the *Tevye* project. Rather, said Harnick, "Robbins said since he'd been asked to go fix *Funny Girl* and we had an offer to do *She Loves Me*, why don't we put this on hold and come back to it next year."

The writers agreed, in part because they still weren't sure of the financial viability of their idea. "I think it was a personal project for all of us," said Stein. "None of us had the remotest idea that this would be very successful. The cliché, it was a labor of love—this one really was."

Aleichem's short stories had been dramatized before. Aleichem had adapted some of the Tevye material for the stage himself in *Tevye Der Milkhiker: A Family Portrait in Five Scenes*, which opened at New York's

Yiddish Art Theatre in 1919 and was later adapted as a Yiddish-language film by the play's director and star Maurice Schwartz. In the 1950s, Arnold Perl adapted three Aleichem short stories for his play *The World of Sholom Aleichem*, and also wrote the play *Tevya and His Daughters*, which drew on many of the same Aleichem short stories that inspired *Fiddler*, but with different emphasis and style.

There had also been an earlier work adapting Aleichem's Tevye stories as a musical. Broadway playwright Irving Elman's drama *Tevye's Daughters* was described in *The New York Times* as "embroidered with folklore tunes." According to the paper's longtime Broadway reporter Sam Zolotow, several producers were interested in the property as early as 1949—including Norman Bel Geddes, Michael Todd, and even Richard Rodgers and Oscar Hammerstein II—but the work did not make it to Broadway.

Now it was Bock, Harnick, and Stein's turn, and after Prince's early pass on producing their show, they showed their Tevye project to other producers. "We were turned down by everybody because everyone thought it wouldn't have popular appeal," Stein recalled. "It was too ethnic, and 'ethnic' was a code word for 'Jewish.'"

The question they heard most, added Bock, "was 'When we run out of Hadassah benefits, what other audience would we expect to entertain?' In hindsight, it makes them look foolish, but this was our day-to-day travail."

They did have early interest from Arnold Saint-Subber, who had been raised by a Jewish grandmother and knew the stories in their original Yiddish. They brought one act to him and played the score, said Harnick, and while it made him cry, the authors didn't want to risk his not being able to raise the money.

They had better luck with television, theater, and film producer/director Fred Coe. They played the score for him on July 25, 1962, and in August, Coe sent them to play the score for director Arthur Penn. Penn later wrote them that he was too busy with other commitments, said Bock, "but he thought it was a very important show."

Coe hadn't heard of shtetls before, and the writers found his interest very encouraging. Coe was a Southerner, said Bock, "but, if you'll excuse the pun, he cottoned to the material, so much so that he started stead-fastly to raise the funds, which ultimately he could not. He met the same opposition as we had auditioning it—the parochialism of the subject."

Although Coe would later option the show, Robbins remained un-available for the next several months. So while they waited for Robbins, the Tevye project was moved to a back burner. Bock and Harnick took time off to write the score for *She Loves Me*, which Prince was direct-ing and producing, and Stein wrote the play of Carl Reiner's semi-autobiographical novel *Enter Laughing*. When their other shows opened on Broadway in the spring of 1963, they went back to *Tevye*.

In the summer of 1963, Robbins was finally available. Coe was busy with the film *A Thousand Clowns*, and it was time for Prince to step back in. He had refused to produce the show unless Robbins agreed to direct, Prince said, and Robbins refused to direct without Prince producing. Prince came onboard that summer, as coproducer, and negotiated an ar-rangement with Coe, who Prince said was "delighted not to be actively involved."

Robbins, celebrated for his work both on Broadway and in dance, brought with him years of experience choreographing and directing. He was choreographing on Broadway by 1945. By the time he did *Fiddler*, he had directed and choreographed *West Side Story*, *Bells Are Ringing*, *Gypsy*, and *Peter Pan*, as well as choreographed such shows as *On the Town*, *The King and I*, and *Call Me Madam*.

Robbins and Prince had worked together before, and, said Prince, "We always got along very well. Jerry and I had a good relationship. I think an awful lot of people didn't, but we did and I think it was because I was tough with him and strong. And I would not indulge him. I think that was interpreted as 'Hal's a good censor and I trust that.' After all, I was the only producer he'd ever had who was a director, too."

The authors did express concern about bringing in Robbins. Stein worried, "How would he work with this guy?" said his widow, Elisa Stein. Harnick, in turn, even asked Sondheim for advice. "Steve said to me, before I took the show, 'Jerry is very poetic. You have to listen very closely because *he* thinks he is inarticulate. But if you listen very closely, you will hear him describe in poetic terms what he wants.'"

Like Stein, Bock, and Harnick before him, Robbins was drawn to the material. Perhaps he felt a kinship because his family name was Rabinowitz. Jerome Wilson Rabinowitz was born on October 11, 1918, just a few years after the death of Solomon Rabinowitz, better known by his pen name Sholem Aleichem. Robbins also felt a kinship to the shtetl experience itself; his father, Herschel Rabinowitz, was born in the Russian village of Rozhanka, home to less than one thousand people. The Rabinowitz family and their neighbors, mostly Jews, lived in simple wooden houses not unlike the houses in the fictional Anatevka.

When Robbins was six years old, his mother took him back to that village, then part of Poland. The boy and his grandfather sang Jewish songs together and "there was comfort there," Robbins said on the PBS special, *Something to Dance About*. "It was what I belonged to. That was one of the reasons I wanted to do that show—because of that background I had."

Robbins talked with the show's authors about his family, his experience at six with his grandfather, and the Nazi destruction of Jews and Jewish life during World War II. Said Harnick: "He told us, 'Someday, if I have the chance, I want to restore that culture, put it on stage and give it another twenty-five years of life.' I remember the number twenty-five because he would be so pleased it is now close to fifty."

"It was a very emotional show for Jerry," said Maria Karnilova, a friend and colleague who was later cast as Golde in the show's original Broadway production. "As far as Jerry was concerned, this was *his* family back in Russia."

So it was that on August 28, 1963, Robbins sent a night letter cable to his friend and longtime colleague Ruth Mitchell, who would later serve as *Fiddler*'s production stage manager. Read the cable: "Dear Ruthie— I'm going to do a musical on Sholem Aleichem stories with Harnick and Bock. Stop. I'm in love with it. It's our people."

The authors had written almost a complete show when Robbins came in. But everything changed with the arrival of their new collaborator. Most important, the director guided Bock, Harnick, and Stein as the four men turned what Harold Prince called "a simple folk tale" into an American classic.

For Prince, "the original script was realistic. It opened with Tevye and his family at Sabbath prayers, concerned less with the community and still less with the larger world outside. It lacked size. . . . Great art transcends particular milieus. Marc Chagall, using the same shtetl, creates universal art. I reckoned Robbins would do the same."

Robbins did exactly that, pushing his collaborators to expand Tevye's world far beyond home and hearth. He set up a long preproduction period, using it largely to launch the discussion that would change *Fiddler* radically, from its opening number to its conclusion.

The very first question Robbins asked the authors, Bock recalled, was, "'All right, what is the piece about?' We were dumbfounded," said the composer, "because previously, on other shows, everybody assumed that everybody knew what the piece was about, and that's how we wrote it. But he was searching for something deeper."

Harnick said that Robbins acted like a district attorney, coming back to his authors again and again. "When he'd ask, 'What is this show about?' and we'd say, 'It's about this dairyman who has five daughters,' he'd keep saying, 'No, no, that is not what the show is about. If that's what this show is about, it's the forerunner of *The Goldbergs*. It's warm and it's funny, but it doesn't have the *power* the Aleichem stories have. Where is that power coming from?'"

Prince called it noodging. "I remember Jerry noodging them, and what Jerry noodged about was only one thing. He would not move until the guys did it, and he was right," said Prince. "Then, finally, Sheldon Harnick said, 'It's about tradition,' and Jerry said. 'That's it. Write that.'"

The authors first applied Robbins's dictum to the crucial opening number. "Robbins said, 'If this is about the way traditions were changing all over Europe, we need an opening number that shows the audience some of those traditions,'" said Harnick. "And I still remember his words—'It should be like a tapestry against which the entire show plays. If possible, after that, every scene should show or relate to the changing of tradition. That's what will give the show its cohesion and strength.' We finally understood why Aleichem stories were as powerful as they were."

Before Robbins came in, the show's opening number was a song called "We've Never Missed a Sabbath Yet." The first lines, sung by youngest daughters Shprintze and Bielke—later almost silent in the show—are: "Momma, Momma, we finished what you told us/Momma, Momma, can we go out and play?" The song continued about the rituals of getting ready for the Sabbath, cleaning the house, cooking the food, making noodles, plucking chickens, and baking challah.

Robbins could stand back and see the big picture, just as he had done earlier on *A Funny Thing Happened on the Way to the Forum*. On *Forum*, Robbins famously worked with composer/lyricist Sondheim to set aside that show's opening number, "Love Is in the Air," for the show-stopping—and show-defining—"Comedy Tonight." In both cases, the new opening number would make it very clear to the audience what the evening was about.

"Tradition" happened in chunks, not all at once, said Stein. The librettist would write "a piece of dialogue here to introduce the rabbi, another to introduce Yente, others to introduce various other characters. They were just bits and pieces of dialogue, and somehow it was put together with the song so that it worked."

While "Tradition" wasn't staged until many months later, merging music, lyrics, and dialogue was still complicated. While they were able to use some of the music from their original opening number, said Bock, "it came about through pain and tumult."

For Prince, "Tradition" changed everything. "It seems to me that, aside from the brilliantly metaphorical staging that Jerry gave the entire show, his main contribution was nagging—almost to a fault—the authors for a reason behind the musical," said the producer. "That opening number accounts for the show crossing ethnic and religious lines and becoming a huge success."

Getting one of Broadway's most formidable performers to inhabit Tevye didn't hurt.

3

Mostel and Company

Zero Mostel was starring in *A Funny Thing Happened on the Way to the Forum* when the musical ran into trouble en route to its Broadway opening in May 1962. *Forum*'s composer/lyricist, Stephen Sondheim, wanted to bring in Jerome Robbins, not Mostel's favorite person, and producer Prince knew their political differences could be a problem. So Prince stopped by Mostel's dressing room one night after a tryout performance in Washington, D.C., and asked the actor if he would be okay with Robbins coming in to work on the show.

It was a good question. It had been less than a decade since the terrible days of the House Un-American Activities Committee (HUAC), when both Mostel and Robbins had appeared before HUAC interrogators. Robbins had been a cooperative witness, naming names that included *Forum* costar Jack Gilford's wife, Madeline Lee Gilford. Mostel and many of his friends had been unfriendly witnesses and were later blacklisted.

Still, Mostel answered fast and positively. "Listen, Hal, I'm a professional and Jerry's a professional, and if he can help the show, get him," replied Mostel. "Besides, we of the left do not blacklist."

Yet it was hardly a friendly relationship. When Prince asked Mostel if he was willing to work with Robbins, said the producer, "Zero said, 'You didn't ask me to have lunch with him.' Whenever Jerry wasn't around, Zero would ridicule him in front of everyone, just because he felt guilty that he was working with him. But Zero knew Jerry would be incremental in helping to save that show, and he was practical enough to want the show saved."

Tensions on *Forum* were evident from the start. When Robbins was first addressing cast members gathered onstage, everyone was waiting to see how he and Mostel would greet each other. According to Tony Walton, *Forum*'s set designer, when Robbins got to Mostel, "Zero said, 'Hiya, Loose Lips!' Everybody, even Jerry, cracked up."

Mostel's nephew, the composer Raphael Mostel, cites family legend about a less amusing scene around the same time, when Mostel ran into Robbins at a restaurant. "He went over and put his hand on Robbins's shoulder and clamped down with a grip so strong that Robbins couldn't move. 'Why, Jerry, why?' he asked, not expecting an answer. Although to others in the restaurant it probably looked like a friendly gesture, Zero had incredible strength and doubtless wanted Robbins to feel the weight of his opprobrium in the most physical and painful way. I can imagine Robbins grimacing in agony and not being able to say anything because he needed Zero."

Mostel had spent a long time waiting for shows like *Forum* and *Fiddler*. Before the blacklist, he had been a successful comedian and Broadway performer, with solid television and film work. He had been on Broadway in such shows as Duke Ellington's *Beggar's Holiday*, and Billy Rose's *Concert Varieties*. Other theater roles included *Flight into Egypt*, *The Good Woman of Setzuan*, and *Lunatics and Lovers*, and among his films were *Panic in the Streets* and *The Enforcer*.

Not only did Mostel's being blacklisted mean he often got paid less than what he was promised, but good work itself was limited. While he "*could* sometimes work on Broadway—and more often off-Broadway—movies and television were closed to us," his wife, Kate, recalled, "and without that exposure it was hard to get the few well-paying jobs in the New York theater."

As the blacklist ended, Mostel shot upwards again. In 1958, he won an Obie for his off-Broadway appearance as Leopold Bloom in *Ulysses in Nighttown*. Then came Ionesco's *Rhinoceros* in 1961, and his first Tony Award, in 1961 for Best Actor (Dramatic). He was back to get a second

Tony in 1963, this time as Best Actor (Musical) for his performance as Pseudolus, the slave, in *Forum*.

It was when he was doing *Forum* that his old friend Joseph Stein visited him backstage at the Alvin Theatre with a script for *Tevye*, his new musical. When they first met years before, Mostel was doing a five-minute monologue for the *Chamber Music Society of Lower Basin Street* radio show. "I was unfamiliar with him, but when he said he had run out of his material, I suggested something," Stein said later. "He said, 'That sounds good. Why don't you put it on paper?' So I did, and for the rest of his thirteen-week contract, I supplied that monologue for him."

Mostel may have liked Stein's early radio monologues, but he wasn't particularly taken with the *Tevye* script. Without even hearing the score, he returned it to Stein with a note that said, "No, thanks."

But Mostel did not close the door completely on *Tevye*. Mostel's then-agent Toby Cole was at that time trying to interest him in Saul Bellow's play *The Last Analysis,* and Mostel was apparently not enchanted with that option, either. Yet he would not decline either one and kept both the *Tevye* creative team and Roger Stevens, producer of *The Last Analysis*, dangling for eight long months in 1963.

After Stein and Robbins worked on the script and sent it again to Mostel, the actor started to get more interested. Harnick and Bock played their score on the piano and sang for Mostel at their music publisher's office, and Mostel then sang them some of the old Yiddish songs he remembered from when he was a child. Later, the songwriters visited the Mostels, sang some more songs for them, and Kate Mostel felt "the show looked to us like it was going to be something special."

Mostel also had more than a passing interest in the subject matter. He grew up in an Orthodox Jewish family where his parents regularly read the Sholem Aleichem stories to their eight children. His Eastern European parents settled in New York early in the twentieth century, where his father, who worked over the years as a winemaker and kosher butcher, was a rabbinical figure who read and spoke several languages. Not long after Mostel's birth in Brooklyn on February 28, 1915, they moved for a while to a farm in Moodus, Connecticut, but they soon returned to New York City, settling on the Lower East Side.

"Having been brought up in a strict Orthodox household, he was really cognizant of Jewish customs and traditions, which Jerry Robbins was probably not," said nephew Raphael Mostel. "There were many times that Zero had to explain things, and it was pretty clear he was the one who really knew that culture. Robbins had to do anthropological research. Zero knew it in his bones."

While Mostel was putting off a decision, auditions began in the fall of 1963 for Tevye, as well as for the show's other parts, and many high-profile actors came by. In his 1971 book, *The Making of a Musical: Fiddler on the Roof*, Robbins's assistant, Richard Altman, lists such performers as Danny Thomas, Alan King, and Julius La Rosa. Other auditioners slotted into schedules for Robbins included Jack Gilford, Eli Wallach, Rod Steiger, Howard Da Silva, and Tom Bosley.

According to Kate Mostel, one contender, Walter Matthau, was in the middle of his audition, stopped, and said, "You know who you should get to play this part, don't you? Zero!" The reply, from the dark auditorium: "If we could get Zero, do you think you'd be reading for it?"

Bock and Harnick had wanted Howard Da Silva to play Tevye because they'd worked with him on *Fiorello!*, "and we loved his work," Harnick said. "When we said this to Jerome Robbins, he said, 'Howard's wonderful, but he's life-sized, and we need someone who is larger than life."

Who could be more larger than life than Zero Mostel? Nobody, as far as Prince was concerned. "I said you have to have Zero because I know he'll be brilliant, and I shoved Zero down their throats. Maybe I'm exaggerating, but I know Zero wasn't anyone's first choice but mine."

Prince considered Mostel both "a presence" and "creative and economic insurance," and was apparently willing to wait for him; Mostel was offered a contract in October 1963, but he didn't actually sign it until much later. On October 25th, Robbins even sent him a handwritten note saying, "I want you so very much for the show. . . . Please don't make me do this without you. Please. Sincerely, Jerry Robbins."

Mostel eventually agreed to do the show, of course, and Prince was relieved to find that the relationship between Mostel and Robbins was better than it had been on *Forum*. "This time around, the situation was easier," Prince observed. "By *Fiddler*, Zero just did the work. They were not friends, ever. They were just working together."

Mostel and Robbins "did the show out of respect for each other's talents," said Tanya Everett, who was later cast in the show. "They hardly ever talked. We knew it was important because if they put their personal feelings aside to do this project, they really believed in it."

The first person cast, however, was not Zero Mostel but Austin Pendleton. Jerome Robbins had cast Pendleton in 1962 as overmothered young Jonathan in the actor's first New York show, Arthur Kopit's *Oh Dad, Poor Dad, Mamma's Hung You in the Closet and I'm Feelin' So Sad*. It was now September 1963, and Pendleton's agent called to say Robbins was doing a musical called *Tevye* and had suggested that the actor audition.

At first, Robbins wanted him to audition for the part of the revolutionary Perchik, but after Pendleton had read for Perchik a few times, the director asked if he would also read for the tailor, Motel. At that time, said Pendleton, "Motel was sort of a bland role, but I didn't want to say, 'No, I refuse, it's Perchik or nothing!' So I read for the part of Motel also."

Pendleton, who would later become a notable director and playwright as well as performer, made his Broadway debut in *Fiddler*, and he did so as Motel. Just a few weeks after the director decided to cast Pendleton as the tailor, the actor ran into Robbins on the street. "Jerry greeted me with, 'Oh, listen, we're going to rewrite the part of Motel. I have an idea of what he should be like now that I know you're going to play it.' He told me Motel was going to be 'really scrappy, utterly tenacious, and he's going to fight Tevye.'"

With Pendleton in place, Robbins went on to cast two other people he had worked with before and respected. The actress and dancer Maria Karnilova was cast as Golde, and Robbins's first mentor, the choreographer and director Gluck Sandor, was cast as the elderly Rabbi.

While Karnilova is generally thought of as a dancer and was a charter

AUDITIONS FOR *FIDDLER ON THE ROOF* ONSTAGE

Agents and performers alike sent notes asking for auditions, and *Fiddler*'s creative team wound up seeing hundreds of people. Director Jerome Robbins kept at least thirty typed lists of names, and audition call sheets listed one prominent actor after another.

For Tevye, audition times were scheduled for the following:
- Jack Gilford
- Eli Wallach
- Rod Steiger
- Howard Da Silva
- Tom Bosley

Other notables:
- Gene Wilder auditioned for Motel
- Jon Voight read for Fyedka
- Mercedes McCambridge, Nancy Walker, and Lee Grant were all considered for Golde.
- Other people on audition lists, sometimes for no part in particular, included Red Buttons, Sam Waterston, Ron Rifkin, Vincent Gardenia, Joseph Chaikin, Penny Fuller, Dixie Carter, Jessica Walter, Tony Roberts, Louise Lasser, Ron Leibman, Jean Stapleton, Charlotte Rae, Elliott Gould, and Charles Durning, and many of them came back again and again.

member of the American Ballet Theatre, Robbins well knew that she had already played several Broadway roles. There had been her turn as strip-tease artist Tessie Tura, the "Texas Twirler" with ballerina dreams, in *Gypsy*, which Robbins had directed and choreographed. She had also worked with him in Irving Berlin's *Miss Liberty*, and, even earlier, in the musical *Stars in Your Eyes*.

"I still think of her as the best Golde we ever had," said Harnick, who had worked with her earlier on the Broadway musical revue *Two's Company*. "When she auditioned, we saw that her look was absolutely right. She was just the right age, and there was a peasant quality about her. She *was* Golde, and Robbins realized it."

For Yente the matchmaker, Robbins eventually chose Beatrice Arthur, who would later become a household name as television's Maude. At that point, she had several off-Broadway credits, including Lucy in *Three Penny Opera*, a revival of *The Gay Divorce*, and the long-running *Ulysses in Nighttown* with Mostel.

Yet Arthur had to audition many times before she got the role. She was the strongest candidate, Harnick recalled, "but there was something very contemporary New York about her, which is why Robbins kept bringing her back."

Her problems continued after she was hired, as well. "Jerome Robbins didn't like her at all," said Elisa Stein. "He wanted a Molly Picon type, and he argued with Joe to cut down her lines more and more."

When the authors told her that her role would not get any larger, "I began to dread seeing her coming because she'd follow me around saying, 'You know, this is Yente speaking. Yente really wants to sing such-and-such at this moment, or say such-and-such,'" said Harnick. "But she was wonderful in the show."

Arthur did not have great memories of working with Robbins. "The man was a genius, but he really wasn't a very nice person," the actress said during her 2002 Broadway show, *Just Between Friends*. "Actually, he was the only director who ever made me cry. He was really a *dreadful* human being."

Casting the show's more than three dozen parts kept Robbins and his creative team busy from October 1963 through February 1964. Agents and performers alike sent notes asking for auditions, and the creative team wound up seeing hundreds of people.

"Everyone wanted to be in *Fiddler*," recalled Sammy Dallas Bayes, the show's dance captain. "Anybody auditioning for a Jerry Robbins show, whatever it was, knew it would be remarkable and a success on Broadway. He had that reputation."

Voluminous audition call sheets listed one prominent actor after another. There were at least thirty typed lists of names noting, for instance, interest in Gene Wilder for Motel, Jon Voight for Fyedka, the Russian suitor, and Ron Rifkin and Leonard Frey for Perchik. Besides Beatrice Arthur, Mercedes McCambridge, Nancy Walker, Charlotte Rae, and Lee Grant were all considered for Golde. Other people on audition lists, sometimes for no part in particular, included Red Buttons, Sam Waterston, Vincent Gardenia, Joseph Chaikin, Penny Fuller, Dixie Carter, Jessica Walter, Tony Roberts, Louise Lasser, Ron Leibman, and Jean Stapleton, and many of them came back again and again.

Week after week, cast hopefuls trekked in and out. On February 29th alone, Elliott Gould and Charles Durning were among the two dozen men who turned up to audition between 11:00 and 1:15, for five to ten minutes apiece.

"It was a pressured time," said Sandra Kazan, who auditioned ten times before she was finally cast as a villager and understudy for daughter Hodel. "There were such good people associated with the show, it was something you ended up really wanting. There was no doubt I was right for the show, but so were a million other young girls with dark hair who looked like they could have come from the shtetl. I think Jerry was at every audition, but I didn't think he knew what he wanted; he was noodling around, trying to find it."

When it came to casting Tevye's three daughters, not every member of *Fiddler*'s creative team was looking for the same thing. Bock and Harnick wanted actors who could sing, while Stein and Robbins were looking first for acting ability.

Joanna Merlin, who was eventually cast as Tzeitel, Motel's bride, had met Robbins earlier when she'd auditioned for *Mother Courage*. The actress was called back four times before they hired someone else, but Robbins made it clear that he liked her work. When he called her to audition for *Fiddler*, he wasn't even put off by her saying she really wasn't much of a singer.

Like Pendleton, Merlin started out auditioning for another part—the second daughter Hodel who sang "Far from the Home I Love." "I came in again and again, and there was no way I could sing it," remembered Merlin, "but he didn't give up. He even had me work with Sheldon Harnick and Jerry Bock on the song."

Again and again, the actress auditioned. When she returned for her seventh audition, the exasperated director said he wanted to go with her to her voice lesson and listen to everything she sang there. So one rainy day, Merlin and Robbins went together to her singing teacher's studio. When Merlin got to "Irma La Douce," which she sang in a "chest" voice rather than in a soprano voice, Robbins stopped her. "*That's* the song you should sing at your next audition," he said.

At her eighth and final audition Merlin sang "Irma La Douce," and this was not the Joanna Merlin that Bock and Harnick had heard before. The two men stood up, and said, "She's got a chest voice. She can play Tzeitel."

Merlin remembered that day forever, and not just because she finally was cast in *Fiddler*. It was November 22, 1963, and when she walked out on the street, people were running and screaming that President John F. Kennedy has been shot. Back in the audition hall, someone rushed in with the same news, and auditions stopped. That night, all Broadway shows were canceled.

Tanya Everett, cast as youngest daughter Chava, made her Broadway debut in *Fiddler*, but Merlin and Julia Migenes, cast as middle daughter Hodel, both had prior Broadway experience. All three Broadway suitors—Pendleton, Bert Convy (Perchik), and Joe Ponazecki (Fyedka)—also had New York theatrical experience.

While the three couples and everyone else had to look as if they belonged in 1905 Russia, it apparently didn't matter if they were Jewish or not. Many were not, but by the time Robbins was done with them, they probably knew more about Jewish rituals than most Jews.

For his design team, Robbins brought together people he'd successfully worked with before, including lighting designer Jean Rosenthal and costume designer Patricia Zipprodt. For set designer, he chose Russian-born Boris Aronson, who had designed sets and costumes for Robbins's 1952 *Ballade* and whom he felt would be perfect for *Fiddler*.

Rosenthal had lit both dance and theater projects for Robbins, including *West Side Story* and *A Funny Thing Happened on the Way to the Forum*, and the two got along well. Before she died in 1969, the designer had worked on more than three hundred shows, operas, and ballets, many with Robbins, and Robbins dedicated his landmark ballet, *Dances at a Gathering*, to her memory. Writing an appreciation in *The New York Times*, writer Leo Lerman said of Rosenthal: "She not only lit a show, she illuminated it."

Costume designer Patricia Zipprodt had worked with Robbins most recently on both *West Side Story* and *Oh Dad, Poor Dad*, but the director had a pointed question for her regarding this new project. He asked her if she was Jewish, and she said she was not, she told Frank Rich in a video interview for the New York Public Library. When Robbins then asked her why she thought she could do *Fiddler*, she replied, "Well, I did *Madame Butterfly*."

But Zipprodt also knew she needed to know more. She reviewed books, historical photographs, and Chagall paintings, but that was just the start. Aware of the large number of Orthodox Jews who had left Eastern Europe and settled in Williamsburg, Brooklyn, she visited the factories where they worked, their homes, and their synagogues. Every Saturday for months, she went to an Orthodox Jewish temple to observe what people wore, then had lunch with the rabbi and other members of the community where she'd pepper them with questions about how their grandparents dressed.

When Zipprodt discovered that shtetl residents were often so poor they probably had little more clothing than what they wore or recycled, she had to improvise. She gathered together old fabrics which she thought could handle not just an "aging" process, but also all the dry cleaning required for eight shows weekly. Then she "aged" clothes by bleaching out the color as well as using such tools as a vegetable grater, sandpaper, and electric brushes.

While Zipprodt's costumes for *Fiddler* were to bring her the first of her three Tony Awards—the other two were for *Cabaret* and *Sweet Charity*—they proved to be very expensive. After all the bleaching and aging, Zipprodt would show her results to Robbins. Then, said Prince, Robbins would tell her to do it all again, after which they were returned for his approval, "which came reluctantly."

Part of the problem, of course, was Robbins's inability to make decisions. Rich told the designer that Stephen Sondheim once said of Robbins that "Jerry is like the person who comes into a men's store and says, 'I like that shirt. I want to see it in seventy-five colors before I decide.'" Her reply: "If you could see the pile of sketches from each show—they get higher each week."

Robbins was similarly demanding with set designer Boris Aronson, who he may have tortured most of all. According to his wife and assistant on *Fiddler*, Lisa Jalowetz Aronson, "Jerry worked best when he had things in front of him, onstage, where he could add or eliminate things. On a sketch, it was much harder for him to make up his mind."

Robbins would come up with an idea during a meeting, she added, and Boris Aronson would work on that idea. But by the time the designer came back to show Robbins what he had done, "Jerry had changed his mind, and we had to start all over. This went on and on."

It must have been particularly upsetting to Aronson, who had lobbied hard for the job. *Fiddler* was set in a Russian shtetl around the time of Aronson's birth, as the son of a rabbi, and the designer had worked on an Aleichem play for the Yiddish Art Theatre soon after arriving in New York. He "felt a kinship with the writer," wrote Frank Rich in *The Theatre Art of Boris Aronson*. "When Aronson heard that a musical was to be adapted from Sholem Aleichem's stories about Tevye . . . the designer did something he had hardly ever done before in his Broadway career: he actively sought the assignment."

When Aronson had an exhibition of his paintings and set designs at Storm King Art Center in Mountainville, New York, perhaps an hour outside Manhattan, the designer made sure Robbins went, said his widow. Harnick, who went with Robbins up to Storm King, said later that their excursion clinched the assignment for Aronson. "I remember Robbins looking at Boris's set for the play *J.B.* He said, 'This is the perfect set because it is a beautiful piece of sculpture but as a set, it is incomplete and won't be complete until the first actor steps on the stage.'"

Aronson got the job, but as his great admirer Prince said later, "Jerry drove Boris insane. He knew what he wanted when he saw it, but he didn't necessarily know what he wanted *until* he saw it. So he would send Boris back and back and back. Jerry made Boris fiddle with the roof of Tevye's house eighty million times. I think Boris was driven quite crazy by Jerry because he did not know how to articulate what he wanted or what was wrong. The end results were swell, but it was tough for his collaborators."

4

The Fourth Author

Robbins's dance card was very full in the fall of 1963. Almost simultaneously, he was casting the show, selecting and meeting with its designers, and continuing work with the authors to keep them focused on the idea of traditions changing. If he wasn't in a meeting, he was somewhere doing research, looking at films of the period, or writing long notes to his collaborators and, a great deal of the time, to himself.

Rehearsals did not begin on January 1, 1964, as originally expected, but on June 1st. Robbins wanted more time. Prince found him extremely "gun-shy" at the idea of starting rehearsals on January 1st because he didn't feel he was ready yet, and they postponed rehearsals for six months.

With six extra months, there was more time to shape, rethink, and rewrite the show they would take into rehearsals, and the director used every minute of it. Robbins knew that once rehearsals began, time was limited. "You get on a toboggan slide," said Harnick. "You go into rehearsal, and the next day you open in New York. There's just so little time . . . he wanted to try and head off any problems, anything that he could solve ahead of time."

Robbins became the show's fourth author, reviewing and changing its parts again and again. Often, too, he'd sit with his notebook of lined yellow paper, writing to himself every thought he could about who Tevye was, what the show was about and how it should look. His notes for

Fiddler are replete with questions he had about his musical, his hero, and the drama inherent in that hero's struggle between "his traditions and the questioning of it." Tevye asked "why" again and again, and so did Robbins.

Not long after he agreed to take on the show, Robbins spelled out for himself very clearly what he hoped to put onstage. "The play must celebrate and elevate the life of the shtetl and its peoples," wrote the director. "We must keep the guts, flavor, humor, color, smell, sound, gesture, and cadence of the life but make the audience see it as a work of art and therefore seen and felt and heard in a new way that reveals and illuminates the material above the realistic and the expected."

In page after page of notes, Robbins reminded himself that "we must keep away from the sentimental," avoid "hearts of gold" type expression and not be "compassionate to the point of nausea." Moreover, *Tevye* should not be a conventional Broadway musical. Rather, he saw it as "more a combination of an opera, play, and ballet—a form [like that] of *West Side Story* . . . as much of the material that can be musicalized, should be."

Both shows also reflected Robbins's interest in the visual arts, observed Robin Wagner, scenic designer for the 1989 Broadway show *Jerome Robbins' Broadway*. "*Fiddler* wasn't the first time that Jerry used the work of an artist in envisioning the look of a show. On *West Side Story*, Ben Shahn was the inspiration for set designer Oliver Smith," said Wagner, who worked with Smith early in his career. "If you look at Ben Shahn's drawings, you see Oliver's set. The *Fiddler* set is based on the paintings of Marc Chagall."

Citing the "fantasy atmosphere" of Chagall's paintings, Robbins acknowledged in his notes that Chagall's paintings came closest to his own vision for the show. The director appreciated the great modernist's "free and nonrealistic choice of color and form," his depictions of shtetl life, and, perhaps most important, the way the artist "translated and elevated the material above the limited appeal of those who recognize its sources and revealed and endeared it to all people everywhere. This is also our job."

In much the same way Sholem Aleichem kept the world of nineteenth-century Russia alive in his prose, so did Chagall bring his native Russian village of Vitebsk to life again and again on canvas. Indeed, the same day Robbins wrote out his philosophical notes about Chagall, he also sent a cable to the artist asking if he would be interested in designing the show's sets and costumes.

Chagall graciously declined, saying he was too busy, but Robbins didn't relinquish his notion of a Chagall-like look for the show. Boris Aronson, his choice as set designer, not only knew Chagall but earlier in Berlin had published a thirty-page monograph about the artist. For Aronson, Chagall was "a philosopher, a storyteller, and someone who helped keep traditions alive."

Robbins gave Aronson extensive notes early on, which covered everything from sets to colors. In terms of color, for instance, the director wanted "Chagall simple-naïve-buoyant-primitive-childlike-charming-delightful to look at." Aronson was urged to "combine elements of fantasy and reality."

"It was difficult to figure out a style," recalled Lisa Jalowetz Aronson. "They wanted Chagall, and Boris wanted to do his own style of painting. He did feel 'it is Chagall, after all,' but he also didn't want to imitate him."

It was a fine line. Harnick recalled that when Aronson showed Robbins his first sets, "Robbins was laughing. He had to tell him, 'Boris, I want *a flavor*. But this is Chagall. I also want Aronson in these sets.'"

Robbins was particularly taken with Chagall's many colorful images of violinists, however. In his early notes to Aronson, the director referred to a "musician" who started the show, established its tone, and was essentially its guide. Robbins's fiddler wove in and out of the action, sort of a "magician" figure who knew the future.

Paul Lipson, Mostel's understudy and, later, successor, credits Robbins with the fiddler's development. "It was amazing how many things it meant to different people, but it seemed obvious to me that the fiddler pretty much represented the spirit of the Jewish people in the shtetl," Lipson told Mostel biographer Arthur Sainer. "Regardless of what would happen to the characters, you would play the music and that certain spirit was always with them."

Chagall appears to have felt similarly, writing in his memoir that the

TITLES THAT CAME AND WENT

- While the rooftop fiddler eventually contributed the show's title, that took a while.
- Joseph Stein's first draft, dated October 17, 1961, was called *The Old Country*.
- When the show was first announced in *The New York Times* on August 20, 1962, writer Sam Zolotow said it was a new musical, "tentatively named *Tevye*."
- The title Stein's son Harry Stein remembered best: *Not So Long Ago, Not So Far Away*.
- The one librettist Joseph Stein, composer Jerry Bock, and lyricist Sheldon Harnick had hoped for, said the lyricist, "because it meant a lot to us," was *Where Poppa Came From*.

Hasidic Judaism of his family was a powerful influence on his work, and many of his paintings of Jewish culture drew on the notion that one could communicate with God through music and dance. Fiddlers were often present at Hasidic festivities, and among Chagall's best-known images were those violinists perched on roofs. Chagall's Uncle Neuch played the violin, and as a child, Chagall thought for a while about becoming a violinist himself.

While the rooftop fiddler eventually contributed the show's title, that took a while. Stein's first draft, dated October 17, 1961, was called *The Old Country*. When the show was first announced in *The New York Times* on August 20, 1962, writer Sam Zolotow said it was a new musical, "tentatively named *Tevye*." The title Stein's son Harry Stein remembered best: *Not So Long Ago, Not So Far Away*.

The one Joe Stein, Jerry Bock, and Harnick had hoped for, said the lyricist, "because it meant a lot to us, was *Where Poppa Came From*. All of our fathers came from the old country, and we wanted to dedicate this to our fathers."

Who came up with the final title? Bock said Robbins wanted a "more evocative title." Actor Pendleton also recalled being at a party with Robbins "when he told me Boris was designing it and said, 'I'm going to make it like Chagall. In fact, I think I'll call it *Fiddler on the Roof.*'"

Harnick, in turn, tended to credit Hal Prince, recalling that one day the producer came to the writers "and said, 'I've got to have a title. We have to announce the show, and we need to have something to sell it.' We said we have a list, and Hal said, 'Show me the list.' He looked at it and said, '*Fiddler on the Roof.* I like that because it suggests there's music in the show. It's a musical. That's the one.'"

As he shaped the show, Robbins also drew on books, films, and other research. The director brought in not only Aleichem stories but also books on Jewish history and proverbs, the Talmud, and such resources as Hyman E. Goldin's 1941 book *The Jewish Woman and Her Home.* There were reprints from magazines and journals about such things as rural Jewish occupations in Lithuania, shtetl life, and Jewish dances.

His screening choices included such films as the 1933 Yiddish-language film *Laughter Through Tears,* which was based on an Aleichem play and which Robbins considered so useful he rented it twice. Others on his viewing list included the 1938 Russian film *The Childhood of Maxim Gorky,* the 1938 Polish film *The Dybbuk,* and the 1937 Yiddish language musical drama *The Cantor's Son.*

While Lisa Jalowetz Aronson recalled she and Boris also looked at films at the Museum of Modern Art, the set designers would often join costumer Patricia Zipprodt at Robbins's apartment on the Upper East Side to look at films about shtetl life. Aronson also hired a photographer to shoot stills of some scenes that the designer could later use in creating set details.

Aronson's files for the show include movie stills that featured such things as close-ups of windows, tables, and low fences. There were photos that show men's peasant caps, women's shawls, hairstyles, and the way children looked. Others showed interiors and exteriors of houses, crowd scenes, even a man pulling a cart not unlike Tevye's along rough, unpaved streets.

While they saw the movies together, recalled Lisa Jalowetz Aronson, "Jerry didn't want Patricia Zipprodt and Boris talking about costumes or colors when he wasn't there. Robbins just wanted one voice, his own." Robbins "got so upset that Boris was influencing me, he wouldn't let us talk to each other," Zipprodt said once. "So we met secretly."

Robbins excused lighting designer Jean Rosenthal from such rules, Lisa Aronson said. "Jerry got along well with her because he'd worked with her on ballet. She was helpful because she knew how to talk with him."

Dance scholar Dvora Lapson sent Robbins letters and books on Jewish religious and wedding dances. She also kept the director informed as to when he might visit Hasidic weddings like the one he would later recreate in *Fiddler*. And he didn't go alone. The show's authors, designers, and cast members were often on his guest lists. Costume designer Zipprodt, for instance, would join him at Orthodox Jewish ceremonies where he might study the dancing while she had an eye on what people were wearing.

"He was like a man obsessed," recalled Harnick. "He managed to get us invited to Hasidic weddings so he could observe them. We saw the tradition of the velvet rope down the middle that divided the men from the women, which he used in the show. The tradition of women wedding guests lifting the chair with the bride and men lifting the chair with the groom also turned up in *Fiddler*."

Joanna Merlin and Austin Pendleton, *Fiddler's* bride and groom, also got dragged to Hasidic weddings with Robbins. "It was something he wanted us all to witness," said Merlin, whose own parents were both born in Russia. "You became infected with the music, dance, spirit, and joy, and the whole atmosphere was really charged."

Robbins had already been taken with Hasidic dance and ritual for a few years. When the director was in Israel in 1959 with his *Ballets: U.S.A.*, he ran into photographer Arnold Newman, and the two men did some touring together. They were visiting synagogues in Jerusalem one Friday night when they came upon a Hasidic temple where congregants "felt that the way to pray to God was through the joy of dance and singing," said Newman. Many of the Hasidic worshippers started singing, dancing, and clapping their hands "and Jerry got excited. Finally, he jumped out of his seat and ran down and joined them. . . . He came back after they stopped—sweating, all excited, flushed—and he said, 'One day, I'm going to make a ballet out of that!'"

Long before they began rehearsals that June, Robbins knew that tradition would be key to the entire show, not just the opening number. "The amazing thing is that even though it was being reconstructed and deconstructed, he could see it all together," said composer Bock. "He envisioned the piece starting in a circle and ending in that circle being broken and splintered in different directions. I'm certain that affected our writing constantly."

It also affected the set design, wrote Frank Rich in *The Theatre Art of Boris Aronson*. The circle idea was accentuated by Aronson's use of two concentric turntables, Rich explained, with the smaller turntable placed asymmetrically within the larger one. Boris Aronson had been inspired by a sentence in Aleichem: "Tevye's family is like a small circle within the larger community of the town of Anatevka."

Using the circle that began in "Tradition," the director then concluded the entire show "with the breaking up of that communal circle, to symbolize the dispersal of the Jews who were forced out of Russia by pogroms." It was, wrote Rich, "one of the most moving final curtains of the American musical theater."

Led by Robbins, the collaborators created "something magical," Rich later recalled. "As the community dispersed, the scenery was gradually pulled away in increments, so that by the time Tevye is leaving, the setting is almost bare. You see Tevye alone onstage, the turntable moving slowly as he exits. It created an effect of destruction and loss without announcing it."

"Robbins, in his remarkable, creative way, connected all this," said Bock. "Working with him became a new adventure for us because up to that point, we were working without that kind of guidance or interest, much less commitment."

With Robbins at the helm, Prince, too, saw the size he felt the original lacked. "I suppose no man is indispensable," said Prince, "but on *Fiddler* I think Robbins was."

"I think my father considered it the most fruitful collaboration of his life," said Harry Stein. "He did say that for all the *tsuris* with Robbins, they all appreciated that it would not have been remotely what it was without him."

5

Rehearsals

One snowy night early in 1964, Robbins invited several people over to his place to hear the *Fiddler* score. Everyone was seated in the living room as Bock sat down at the piano and Bock and Harnick sang what they'd written so far, including their brand-new opening number, "Tradition."

"'Tradition' had not been in the script that I had earlier, and the first time I heard it, I wept," said actor Pendleton. "I thought earlier that this was going to be a small-scale, sweet little musical, kind of a low-key, domestic story about Tevye and his daughters. But when I heard that opening number, it was so moving, I didn't believe it. It just took the show to a whole new level."

Stein's book, too, was evolving, and that spring there was a reading so everyone could hear the script, then go off and think about it. And nobody thought harder and longer than Robbins, who now had a good opportunity to see what other changes he might suggest or encourage. By early April, he was sending off some very long, very comprehensive requests to his songwriters and to his book writer.

On April 3rd came more than three pages of notes for Stein, a stern list of instructions that began with the assertion, underlined, that "forty pages of script must be cut. . . . No arguments on this—this is fact." Robbins knew that could mean cutting entire scenes, and he wanted it done before they started building sets and doing staging. Stein should make it clear dramatically that Tevye was "a man in the state of transition," trying "to keep his traditions and still follow his heart." The writing should be stronger about the daughters, their suitors "and their stories." Robbins took the show apart by scenes, asking for less repetition here, extensions or trims there.

The next day, it was the songwriters' turn. Robbins told Bock and Harnick that "the score is wonderful but it did not fuse with the show the way it should on the basis of our reading. One reason is the over-length of the book which prevented musical continuity. You must find the places to play things in song. This also must be vital places and not divertissement."

There was more. The score was "too one-dimensional. . . . Though most of the songs are charming, even the charm wears thin. Missing in the show is the toughness, tenaciousness, robustness, virility and hard core resilience of the people. . . . If every song is sweet, sentimental, sad, touching and nostalgic, all will come off as Second Avenue."

Robbins complained that Tevye had just one fully realized musical moment, his first song, Golde had none, and the two together had none. Even with new songs, he worried, the show still seemed to him "too ethnic and too one-note Jewish."

The director wanted them to concentrate more on what he called "the musical dramatization of Tevye's struggle between tradition and his daughters' unorthodox behavior and needs." He wanted more work on the theme of change, more choruses for the song "To Life" and some trims on "Sunrise, Sunset." There were also "far too many slow songs. Far too many minor songs that wail."

Just a few days before the start of rehearsals, Robbins asked once again for a postponement. There were contracts, bookings, actor salaries, and more, but Robbins "decided we weren't ready," said Prince, and sent the producer a telegram refusing to start rehearsals.

"I never had a telegram before from Jerry," said Prince. "We talked all the time. It was offensive and crazy, so I sent back a telegram saying, 'Please tell Mr. Robbins to send me a check for what I have already spent of the investor's money, and we'll postpone for a week.' I got a phone call from Jerry, crying practically, asking, 'How can you do this to me?'

whereupon I replied, 'How can you do this to *me*?' We went into rehearsal on time."

On the first day of rehearsals, Prince called to say he was coming over to take a look, and stage manager Ruth Mitchell tried to dissuade him. "She said, 'Don't come, I beg you,'" remembered Prince. "I went immediately. Jerry was enthralled with the Actors Studio at this point, and they were improvising scenes in which the actors were saying things like, 'What do you mean, you won't sell me a book? I walked into your bookshop because I want a book.' I asked, 'What's going on?' and learned Jerry was trying to show them what it would be like to be a black man in the South going into a bookstore where blacks were not allowed. I thought it was crazy."

Crazy maybe, but not surprising. Prince had previously seen Robbins dabbling in what he called "method" directing. In *West Side Story*, for instance, the Jets and Sharks would each stay with their own kind away from the theater as well as onstage. Since the character Anybody's was rejected by both gangs, the cast similarly rejected the actress playing her. Prince observed that she lunched alone.

The second day of *Fiddler* rehearsals, Mitchell again told Prince not to come, and again he ignored her request. "I went, and they were all sitting on the floor," said Prince. "The exercise this time had them in a concentration camp, which was well after the life of this show, but that made them committed to the seriousness of the project, which was very smart. I copied the idea when I did *Cabaret* two years later."

Another reason for the exercise may have been the high preponderance of non-Jews in the cast. Some knew little about anti-Semitism, much less shtetl life, and the director wanted his actors to know more about both. "I wanted to make a shtetl out of them," said Robbins. "I told them to think of the Jews in Anatevka as though they were a theatrical company trying out a new show out of town," Robbins told Robert Kotlowitz of *Show* magazine. "Each person was trying to build something in common with his neighbors. In doing it, each person was an outsider to the rest of the world."

Many cast members were primarily villagers, but Robbins wanted everyone in the village to have an identity. The director talked with each of the actors playing villagers and asked them to pick their names. Sandra Kazan, for instance, chose Freda, the name of her mother, who had come from Poland.

Rehearsals didn't begin with a big read-through around the table the way they usually did, since Mostel wasn't there. Rather, they rehearsed several scenes that Mostel was not in. That included the opening scene after "Tradition," when Tevye's family was preparing for the Sabbath.

The scene featured Golde and her daughters setting the table. "Jerry restaged that scene all in one evening, compulsively, time after time, maybe twenty times, until he was totally clear that everything was in focus," said Pendleton, whose character, Motel, also appeared in the scene. "He would block the scene, the cast would run it, he would be dissatisfied, and he'd block it again. Sometimes he'd interrupt it and start again. Other times he'd let us go all the way through it, then reblock. This went on for *hours*."

Pendleton felt some of the obsessiveness was justified. "It was the first scene he staged, Zero wasn't in it, and it was the most complex because you have to establish all the relationships in that scene," the actor said. "He wanted to do that by showing the way each of the daughters helped the mother set the table. And he wanted it perfectly timed so the audience would be looking in exactly the right place at every moment."

Choreographer/director Jerry Mitchell, who earlier worked for both Robbins and *A Chorus Line*'s Michael Bennett, noted that perfectionism goes with the job. "We come from a very disciplined form—dance. Dance isn't about talking. It's about doing. Dance is about standing at the bar and repeating it until it's right. There's no in-between. You will do something until it's perfect. That's the discipline a dancer is born with, and as you become a director, you take that discipline with you."

As might be imagined, that sort of discipline is better to give than to receive, and Robbins often had cast members in tears. "Jerry was a genius, but also a troubled soul," recalled Tanya Everett, who played daughter Chava. "He could zero in on someone's weakness to bring out something in them that was painful. When we were out of town with the show, he got Bea Arthur to a point where she couldn't stop crying. She was ready to leave before we got to Broadway, but she really believed in the show."

Robbins had never been an easy man to work with. "He would just pull the flesh right off your bones," said dancer and actress Helen Gallagher, who had worked with him in *High Button Shoes*. "He could be mean, mean as a snake!"

The two strongest egos on this show, Robbins and Mostel, denied any fighting during *Fiddler* rehearsals. Interviewed shortly after the show opened, Mostel told *The New York Times*' Barbara Gelb, among other things, that "Jerry is a very strong director who knows what he wants and fights for his principles." Robbins, in turn, said differences were part of the rehearsal process. "I felt Zero's interpretation in some scenes was too broad, and he felt my interpretation of his role was too straight. We worked it out."

Bock, Stein, and Harnick all talk of continual rewrites on both songs and scenes once Robbins decided the show was about the dissolution of traditions, and he wanted every scene to respect that. Bock recalled rewriting nine songs and Stein has spoken of writing five drafts of the show.

With the show's new emphasis, said Stein, "a fresh story needed to be created, to hold the isolated tales together. This became the saga of the community . . . finally breaking up and scattering to different parts of the globe. . . . The new structure of the play required the creation of new scenes and new dialogue."

It also required patience. The director would take a scene, say he liked it very much, then ask, "Can you change it?" said Stein. "I would write it from a different point of view, and Jerry would say he liked it better the other way."

Songs changed for various reasons. For instance, the first song for Tevye's three oldest daughters was originally something called "To Marry for Love." But when they got into rehearsal, the song didn't work for the three actresses cast as the daughters. Julia Migenes, who played the middle daughter, was a singer, said Harnick, but Tanya Everett, the youngest daughter, was a dancer, and Joanna Merlin was primarily an actress. Undeterred, Bock took some of the melody from the original opening number "We've Never Missed a Sabbath Yet," and in just a few days, the songwriters recast the song as "Matchmaker, Matchmaker."

TEN SONGS THAT WEREN'T USED IN THE FINAL SHOW:

- We've Never Missed a Sabbath Yet
- I'll Work for Tomorrow Today
- A Butcher's Soul
- Dear Sweet Sewing Machine
- Promise Me
- The Story of Jacob
- Baby Birds
- Brand New World
- Why Jew, Why Gentile?
- Poppa Help Me
- To Marry for Love

Similarly, said Harnick, Tevye's first song was originally not "If I Were a Rich Man," but "That's Life," which was essentially a tale of woe about his lame horse. Among its lyrics: "What a horse! What a day! What a life!/So you'd like to be lazy and fat, of course,/Well, it's your rotten luck to be Tevye's horse/and it's God who decides/how our life is gonna be/whether you and I agree or not!/Giddyup! Move along! . . ."

"That's Life" was never in the show, however. When the authors played it for Robbins, said Harnick, "he loved it," so they were surprised when he said he didn't want it in the show. "We thought it was because Tevye was supposed to sing it to his horse, and Robbins was afraid that a real horse might misbehave onstage. But we found out that wasn't the reason; he knew that he intended to have stylized shtetl houses around the proscenium, and the proportions of a real horse would make the stylized houses look strange."

To replace "That's Life," the songwriters soon came up with the showstopper, "If I Were a Rich Man." Bock and Harnick had gone to a benefit for the Hebrew Actors Union, said Harnick, looking for performers who seemed right for the show. They found one—a man named Zvee Scooler, who was cast as Mordcha, the innkeeper, in the show (and, later, as the *Fiddler on the Roof* film's rabbi). Then, as an unexpected bonus, they were in the audience as a mother and daughter came out and did a Hasidic chant, unaccompanied and wordless.

Both Bock and Harnick were very taken with that Hasidic chant. The next morning, recalled Harnick, Bock called to say he'd been up all night writing something he wanted Harnick to hear. So the two men met at their publisher's office, "where Bock played me 'If I Were a Rich Man,' using the phrase 'dedededum.' Then, when I went to do the lyric, I thought what Jerry had written was so charming, why don't we leave it in in a few places, so we did. I didn't know how to do the chant, so I had to invent syllables that sounded like the chant.

"When we got into rehearsal, Zero asked, 'Do I have to do that?' and I said, 'No, not if you know them.' So he said, 'I grew up with this,' and he would invent his own Hasidic syllables. Now I've heard people do it all kinds of ways. They use my syllables, they use their own, they use something that sounds more Hasidic," said Harnick.

At a production meeting after rehearsals had started, Harnick was worried and suggested they shorten the song and end on what he called "a high comic moment." Mostel strongly disagreed, however, telling Harnick, "You don't understand this man. This is not about jokes. This is not about the comedy. This is about a man who is deeply religious and who wishes he had the opportunity to go to synagogue and really have a good seat by the Eastern Wall, but he can't afford it. He's exhausted every evening, but he comes home and he tries to read a little of the Bible, and he falls asleep. That's this man, so you mustn't change the ending of it."

Mostel also asked Robbins if he could work out the number on his own. Robbins agreed, and Mostel's interpretation has long been copied by one actor after another. According to Mostel's dresser Howard Rodney, "because of Zero's crippled leg, he sat on his wagon, or bench, he always sat. . . . But every [subsequent] Tevye with two good legs would do the same thing."

Mostel had been injured in a bus accident several years earlier. He was getting out of a taxi in front of his house when a bus hit him and his leg was pinned between the curb and the front wheel. The actor spent four months in the hospital, had five operations, "and for the rest of his life his leg gave him trouble," said his wife, Kate.

Mostel refused to have his leg amputated. "They said he might die of gangrene, and he said he'd take the chance," recalled his nephew Raphael Mostel. "They did an experimental skin graft which was successful." His doctor, who later gave a lecture on this new procedure, asked the actor if he would agree to participate anonymously in the lecture, and Mostel agreed. "Zero was behind a white curtain as the doctor explained the procedure and then was to stick out his leg. For maximum dramatic (and nonanonymous) effect, Zero instead stuck out his unblemished good leg and then, with his loud, unmistakable voice, boomed from behind the curtain, 'Oops. Wrong leg.' Then he put the patchwork one out."

After each performance, his dresser Rodney "would massage his bad leg with special creams and lotions," reported Kate Mostel. "The operations had left it with almost no feeling, so Zero couldn't tell if he'd injured himself onstage. And the circulation was so bad that the leg would be hot until Howard massaged it back to its normal temperature."

"Very few people realized how much pain he was in after that," said his nephew. "He self-medicated—alcohol and pain pills. Offstage he was walking around with a cane because he needed to, although he carried it off as simply an affectation. Onstage no one had any idea he was incapacitated in any way. It was worse in *A Funny Thing Happened on the Way to the Forum*, which was so physically demanding; there were times when he had had to run offstage to collapse so as not to do so in front of the audience. For such a large guy, Zero was an incredibly graceful dancer. But the dances Zero did in *Fiddler* were done mostly with shoulder and very little with the feet."

His bad leg apparently didn't much hinder his stage jokes, either. "He would chase me around the stage, trying to show me his leg," recalls actress Everett. "It was so grafted down, there was hardly a leg left. And he would make faces at me, and I'd try not to break up laughing. Then he'd congratulate me later for not laughing—'That was a good acting job, Tanya,' he'd say."

When it was nearly time to leave for Detroit, Robbins finally staged "Tradition." "We had rehearsed for eight weeks and people kept saying, 'Jerry, when are you going to stage "Tradition"?'" said Pendleton. "Then finally, in the middle of the final week, he said, 'Oh, all right.' And he staged it in like an hour and a half."

Pendleton was one of the few people who was not in the number and could observe that staging. "He just came up, right there, with all those gestures that are still being performed when the show is done," said Pendleton. "Everything the number was and has been ever since, he came up with in that hour and a half. I think he wanted to be full of the whole show before he staged that number."

This was different than earlier stagings, Pendleton said. "In the early weeks of rehearsal, when he'd stage something, he would take hours and hours. Then, a couple days later, he'd stage it all over again. The further along rehearsals went, the more swiftly he was able to stage things, but he would still restage. 'Tradition' he never restaged."

Harnick didn't get to rehearsals too often because he was rewriting constantly, but he made sure he was there the day Robbins staged "Tradition." "Everybody was there—the cast, Joe Stein, Jerry Bock," he said. "We watched Robbins, like a great sculptor, begin to put all the pieces together. He would say to Joe, 'Give me a line here, I need a transition from this section to this section,' and he would tell the person who wrote the incidental music, 'Give me some incidental music here.' He was just taking all these pieces and melding them into this wonderful number."

Then came the final night of rehearsals, the show's "gypsy" run-through for friends and family. There were no sets or costumes. There was just a piano, no orchestra, and the fiddler balanced on a chair, not a roof. "The reaction was noncommittal, polite at best," said Robbins's assistant, Richard Altman. "We couldn't help feeling disappointed and a little concerned by the overall coolness."

When the cast got to Detroit, they shared feedback from friends about the run-through, and the consensus was that the show had problems, said Pendleton. One of *Fiddler*'s child actors had gone out into the lobby at intermission and reported back to her colleagues. "The word on the street from the child actor mafia was thumbs-down," said Pendleton, turning his thumbs down. "They said, 'It's no *Sound of Music*.'"

Part 2

BROADWAY

6

On the Road

hrough the summer of 1964, the show traveled first to Detroit, then to Washington, D.C., shedding lines and songs that didn't work, adding new ones that did and testing it all on theatergoers. Stein found the out-of-town tryouts "enormously helpful because you have people who can tell you what is working and what isn't—the audience. . . . You won't get that unless you go out of town."

Fiddler's first paying audience was in Detroit's 2,000-seat Fisher Theatre. Designed by the architect Albert Kahn and built originally for movies and vaudeville, it opened in the fall of 1928 with banana trees, a goldfish pond, and live birds. The theater was remodeled in 1961 for live theatrical productions and soon boasted the largest subscription audience in the country, making it a very attractive starting point for Broadway-bound shows.

The *Fiddler* company left New York for Detroit on July 21st. *Fiddler* was booked at the Fisher for five weeks, but only three and a half weeks were covered by subscription audiences. And what that meant, Sheldon Harnick explained, is that they'd have to drum up business on their own that last week and a half. In other words, he said, "We could die in Detroit."

They didn't, of course. The show was too long, and the second act needed a lot of fixing, but that's what going on the road was for. Indeed, some reassurance came as early as the first preview. Librettist Stein was standing at the back of the theater when people were coming out for intermission, and he heard a woman on the phone tell her husband he should have come and skipped his card game. "This is a very wonderful show," she said. "You won't believe it. In the middle of everything, they have a pogrom!"

With just a few previews before opening night on July 27th, the reassurance helped. Early on, they caught the first problematic song, which was "Dear Sweet Sewing Machine," an ode in the second act to the new sewing machine that newlyweds Tzeitel and Motel hope will keep them solvent. Robbins had some trouble with the song during rehearsals, and it didn't fare particularly well in Detroit, either. Starting with previews, when Joanna Merlin and Austin Pendleton finished singing the song, there was hardly any applause. Figuring the orchestra was too loud, Robbins asked the orchestra to play softer, but the result was the same. Nobody could figure out why, in Bock's words, it got only "one applaud."

When Robbins decided to cut the song, Bock and Harnick asked him what he thought went wrong. Robbins replied that when Tzeitel and Motel got married at the end of act one, their story was resolved. "We move on to the second daughter, Hodel, in act two, and the audience wants to follow *her* story," said Harnick. "It's too late to give Motel and Tzeitel a new song. The audience doesn't want to hear it."

But they did want to hear every word of *Fiddler*, apparently even at its original length of nearly four hours. "On opening night, we ran very long—I think we started at eight p.m. and ended at a quarter to twelve—and people were leaving before the end," Harnick remembered. "The only encouraging thing was that they were walking up the aisle backwards. They wanted to see what was happening up to the last minute."

The lyricist was worried about the show, he said later, but he didn't know how much until after the opening performance, when he joined several people from the *Fiddler* company at a nearby restaurant. After a few minutes at the table, he suddenly got up and went to the men's room. "I went into one of the stalls, and I thought, 'Either I'm going to be physically sick or I'm going to faint, I don't know which.' Then I sat down on the john and began to perspire. Water just poured out of me. I was in there for what seemed like ten minutes—I suppose it was four or five minutes—but by the end of that time I was soaking wet. For the first time I realized how scared I had been."

Prince had his own worries. Everything was expensive, he lamented, given the eight weeks' rehearsal, costly salaries, and sizeable expenses everywhere. They capitalized at $375,000, but spent $450,000. The difference, he wrote in his 1974 memoir, *Contradictions*, was his problem. Said Prince: "Before the curtain went up in Detroit, I was out of pocket $75,000."

The best piece of luck they had in Detroit, said Prince, is that the newspapers were on strike. But a few of the reviewers' negative comments made their way to radio, and a review in *Variety* was pretty awful. In his opening-night review, published July 28, writer "Tew" began with the following sentences: "Everything is ordinary about *Fiddler on the Roof* except Zero Mostel. He's extraordinary."

The critic worked his way through the creators and cast, disparaging one and all. "None of the songs are memorable," he wrote, and "many of them sound alike." He found the dancing "pedestrian" and said supporting cast members "give professional performances within the limits set by the lacklustre book." Boris Aronson's sets "are serviceable, rather than spectacular. So are the costumes by Patricia Zipprodt, and lighting by Jean Rosenthal."

That review was the first published comment on their show. When Tew called the show "ordinary," the company's morale was "all but destroyed," according to Richard Altman, Robbins's assistant. The *Variety* review was "a blanket condemnation, and being the only critical voice to be heard so far, it cast a feeling of doom over the entire company."

The review, added Pendleton, "was just four or five paragraphs long and totally dismissive, and, of course, everybody was very depressed. We knew everyone in New York was reading that. People were calling me saying there was a rumor that Jerry Robbins would be fired, which I don't think was ever true—I'd like to have seen someone get him out of there!

"The night of the review, we all went to the bar across the street as we always did. Everyone else was at tables drinking, and Jerry was standing alone at the bar. I asked him, 'What are you going to do?' And he said,

'Ten things a day.' And that's what he did. All that time in Detroit and in Washington, he kept cutting and heightening and shaping."

As would be repeated in New York many weeks later, the first review seemed to be the worst of them. The day after *Fiddler*'s opening came a review written by the *Detroit News*' drama and music critic, Jay Carr, that was unpublished because of the strike but read on radio and TV. It was more positive, calling *Fiddler* "an uncommonly fine musical."

The critics unanimously felt the show in Detroit was too long and should speed up. But as Carr wrote, while it should tighten up, it still contained "enough freshness, inventiveness, verve, and emotional impact to make it a theatrical evening worth anyone's while."

Peter Bellamy, drama critic at the Cleveland *Plain Dealer*, thought the show "has heart, pathos, bittersweet comedy, and tenderness. The opening-night audience was most enthusiastic." But Bellamy didn't like the score much. For him, Harnick's lyrics were "acceptable but not memorable" and Bock's music had "a sameness." Concluded Bellamy: "There isn't a hit or catchy tune in the score." (Bellamy did have a kind word for Austin Pendleton, however, noting the actor grew up in the area, and his mother, Frances, had acted at the Cleveland Play House in the mid-thirties.)

Like so many shows before and after *Fiddler*, the out-of-town tryout gave the show's creators a great chance to improve their show without New York critics and theater patrons looking over their shoulders, and Robbins took advantage of that. Song and scene casualties mounted. Robbins scrapped "If I Were a Woman," which Hodel and Perchik sang, replacing it with a scene where the couple danced holding each other, breaking another tradition.

Before they left Detroit, they also got rid of a scene where Tevye read a letter from a relative in America that led into a big song about people enjoying life in Anatevka. That song, which Stein would later call "the peppy Anatevka," essentially said that America might be nice, but they were content being in Anatevka. Later, when the letter-reading scene and ensuing song were dropped, they slowed the song down and turned it into the powerful good-bye to Anatevka now at the end of the show.

But along the way, the show felt "fractured," said cast member Sandra

Kazan. "We didn't know how it would come together. Once I saw Joe Stein approach Robbins very tentatively with a tiny piece of paper in his hand: 'Is this a better line?' It seemed a show put together with Scotch tape.

"Detroit was wild in terms of the show being in disarray," Kazan said. "It was not coming together, there was this huge cast and Jerry kept changing things minute to minute. But when we were all disheartened, Maria Karnilova, who had worked with him before, would say, 'You all don't know what you're talking about. This will all come together, and it will be a hit.'"

Prince, too, was convinced he had a hit on his hands. "I was never worried once I saw it onstage," said Prince. "It seemed irresistible. When the news got back to our investors, I did the unprecedented thing of sending a note to them saying, 'Don't believe a word of those reviews. We are a huge smash and will run forever.' And despite those reviews, the word from Detroit was so incredible that we had long lines in New York from the get-go."

Robbins, however, wasn't taking any chances. Altman has written that in Detroit "there were rehearsals every day, including matinee days, with no days off, not even Sundays when there were no performances." By the time they got to Washington, said Altman, "the company was completely exhausted." People were limping, some rested on the floor off-stage between scenes, "and the backstage area assumed the atmosphere of an army field hospital."

Altman noted a new Actors' Equity Association ruling came about later, too late for *Fiddler* rehearsals, which said actors had to get one day off a week, whether the show was in rehearsal, on the road, or on Broadway. Observed Altman: "Although the ruling barely missed affecting *Fiddler*, it never occurred to Jerry to give his people time off."

Robbins devoted considerable time in Detroit to a long ballet in the second act. In the number, Tevye went mad over his youngest daughter Chava's decision to marry the Russian Fyedka, a non-Jew, and the stage was full of people and scenery. "It was a huge production number, with trees flying in, two turntables going in different directions, and people with big pushcarts going on and off," said dance captain Sammy Dallas Bayes. "It used the whole company."

The "Chava Ballet" had been the subject of what Tevye understudy Paul Lipson called "countless hours of backbreaking rehearsal." Everett, who played Chava, recalled all the time costume designer Patricia Zipprodt spent creating and testing a skirt "so it moved almost like I was flying." And Robbins had set designer Boris Aronson thinking about that ballet as early as fall of 1963, when the director described how Tevye's "world is collapsing around him . . . the traditions he has lived by crack apart under the impact of Chava's action."

But Robbins's ballet, which ran more than ten minutes, wasn't working. "We found that the show died after that," said Stein. "We were all worried about it. We urged Robbins to cut it, and he did. He kept cutting and cutting it. Finally, it was down to that tiny little crossover called 'Chavaleh.'" The new number ran about two minutes, with dancing.

"Mr. Robbins said always have more material than you need," said dance captain Bayes. "He said never be afraid to throw anything away, and he did that constantly. The show was very big and overloaded in Detroit. The main thing that happened from Detroit to Broadway was that he was looking for the simplest, most honest way to tell the story."

In some ways, Detroit was a reminder of the time the show's four authors had spent learning their craft in the first place. Stein, Bock, and Robbins had all spent time at Camp Tamiment, the leftist adult summer camp in the Catskills whose musical revues also nurtured Sid Caesar, Imogene Coca, and others, while Harnick had similar experiences turning out songs quickly at Green Mansions camp in the Adirondacks. All of them learned when they were young how to put together a new show every few days. It was a nice warm-up for *Fiddler*.

As the script got tighter and more focused, many songs were rewritten or replaced. Given all the book changes Robbins instigated, not to mention the considerable revamping of the second act while on the road, Harnick counted up fifty songs written for the show, which used sixteen.

Bock and Harnick both admit that they generally wrote a lot more songs than they needed. *Fiorello!* had about the same three-to-one ratio as *Fiddler*, and *She Loves Me* was maybe two to one. Harnick has quipped that he "never mastered the knack of getting the right idea the first time around," but he also has said each rewrite got him closer to a character and made that character more real to him.

Harnick was writing lyrics on hotel stationery, scraps of paper, and, sometimes dangerously, in his head. On an earlier musical, for instance, Harnick was walking around Manhattan, concentrating so hard on putting lyrics to a melody Jerry Bock had written that the lyricist stepped in front of a truck. "The driver slammed on the brakes and honked his horn," said Harnick. "I looked up, startled, and then kept right on walking, working on the song. Jerry told me to be more careful."

In Detroit, he put that same sort of concentration into a song he'd been thinking about for weeks. During their rehearsals in New York, said Harnick, it struck him "that it would be very funny if there were a song that started with Tevye saying to Golde, 'Do you love me?' and her looking at him as though he's out of his mind and saying, 'Do I what?' But I had no idea of where to go with it. When we got to Detroit, I started to take long walks, thinking about what they would actually say. At the end of a week, I was lucky if I had maybe sixteen lines.

"By the end of the second week, I had enough to give to Jerry Bock. I remember telling him, 'I tried to make this into a song, but it doesn't look like a song. It looks like a scene, but do what you can. If you find the right music and it needs changing, I'll revise, like I always do.' To my delight, Jerry set it exactly as I wrote it. So, it is as much like a scene as it is like a song.

"We put the song 'Do You Love Me?' into the show and it worked. Then, a few days later, I went to see the show and they sang the song. To my astonishment, I choked up. I thought, I'm going to disturb the audience. I'm about to start sobbing. So I raced out of the theater, asking myself what was going on. Then I thought, Oh, my God, I have written what I wished the relationship was between my own parents who fought so much."

Toward the middle of *Fiddler*'s five-week run, a new batch of reviews confirmed the wisdom of their many changes. Already *Fiddler* had solidified enough to make Richard Christiansen, of the *Chicago Daily News*, mark it as "an almost certain hit."

One day later, *The New York Times* reported "good response" to the show in a brief article headlined "Detroit Responding to *Fiddler on Roof.*" Despite both a newspaper strike and heat wave, the paper reported "generally favorable critical notices" and an audience of seventy-five percent of capacity. "The strike has cut into promotion efforts and has seriously affected attendance and box office sales," a theater official told the paper. But he also said that given those circumstances, they were "pleased" with ticket sales.

By the end of the three and a half subscription weeks, said Harnick, the show was selling at least ninety percent. By the end of the five weeks, they were selling out.

Although the show did not die in Detroit, it certainly changed. When *Fiddler* opened in Detroit, Charles Durning was in the show as a Russian priest, and by the time it closed, both Durning and the priest were gone. Nearly all of the ten songs in the first act stayed in the show, but the second act left Detroit almost entirely redone.

Sister Mary Immaculate, then executive secretary and treasurer of the National Catholic Theater Conference, had been one of the Fisher Theatre's satisfied customers during that period. She was so taken with it she ordered a "houseful of seats" for conference delegates who would be in New York the next summer, she later told *The New York Times*. When a startled box office salesperson asking if she really thought the show would run for a year, Sister Mary Immaculate replied that she thought "it'll run forever. It's the most catholic—small 'c'—show I ever saw."

Its creators still needed some convincing, however, perhaps because they were simply too close to it. "*Fiddler* for us was endless rewriting," Bock said. "There were no days off, no time to take much of a breath, and see the show and wander away. There was always something to do."

Between Detroit and Washington, Harnick went back home briefly to his New York apartment. He had just gotten to sleep when he was awakened by a crash in the other room. He jumped out of bed and ran out to find that a picture had fallen off the wall and was lying amid shards of glass on the carpet. It was a print he had bought from a Russian artist that depicted Tevye talking to Sholem Aleichem. "I thought, Oh, my God, that's a terrible omen," said Harnick. "But when I got to Washington, I told somebody what happened, and he laughed it off. 'Don't worry,' he told me. 'You know what that means? It's going to be a smash!'"

Fiddler closed in Detroit on Saturday, August 22nd, and opened at Washington, D.C.'s National Theatre on August 26th. The musical launched the National's 1964–65 season and stayed for two and a half weeks before continuing on to New York.

When asked if there was a moment he truly knew their show was a hit, Harnick said, "The hint of it was those lines in Washington. People in Detroit must have been calling their friends and relatives. We don't know if they were saying, 'You've got to see the show,' or as Zero Mostel believed, 'You've got to see Zero Mostel.' Probably a combination of the two. And when we went to New York, the same thing happened. It's never happened to me again."

Reviews in Washington were a little better than in Detroit. *The Washington Post*'s Leo Sullivan found the show "a beguiling folk tale set to music." Although he found the score "doesn't seem to possess a singable hit," Sullivan did praise many of the cast members and ended his review recommending the show to his readers.

Washington Star drama critic Harry MacArthur said *Fiddler* "is virtually certain to be established as another Harold Prince hit. This Tevye is the sort of perfect match of part and player that some actors go for a lifetime without ever finding."

Longtime *New York Times* theater critic Frank Rich had an eye on *Fiddler* since its earliest days, largely through his teenage friendship with librettist Stein's son Harry Stein. Harry Stein and Rich went to every performance and many rehearsals in Washington, said Stein, and so it happened that they were at the Wednesday matinee during the show's first week in Washington when things went awry.

As Rich recounts the afternoon in his memoir, *Ghost Light*, Mostel was singing "If I Were a Rich Man," when he suddenly stopped singing and asked them to bring down the curtain—he was about to be sick. Before rushing out, Joseph Stein whispered to the two teenagers that Mostel's understudy Paul Lipson had "only been rehearsed as far as this scene!"

"I remember the theater was absolutely packed," said Michael Hackett, today chair of UCLA's Department of Theater and a prominent director, but then a fourteen-year-old seeing his first pre-Broadway show. "The curtain came down and everyone waited outside for what seemed to me was maybe forty-five minutes."

Backstage, those forty-five minutes were loaded with activity. Lipson had been hired as Avram the bookseller with the understanding he would be understudying Mostel only until the producers found a more prominent actor to do it. When Mostel got sick, Lipson hadn't rehearsed the dances and didn't know many of Mostel's lines, but he agreed to go on anyway.

Everybody helped. Joanna Merlin, playing oldest daughter Tzeitel, remembered turning upstage and giving him lines. She called him "a very good sport," but concedes the situation was "very hairy." Or as Austin Pendleton put it: "I remember looking into Paul's eyes and seeing total fear."

Mostel was out six performances in Washington, with Lipson continuing to step in. His work in the role—which he would later play hundreds of times on tour and Broadway—also had a secondary effect. People could say: "Hey, this show in Washington that's already got such great word of mouth is not a one-man show," Lipson said later. "Other people can do it!"

Librettist Stein, who had been among those feeding lines to Lipson, was clearly relieved. "I remember we were scared to death to put him on," he said. "The astonishing thing was, as the audience was going out, I heard one woman say, 'Well, Zero couldn't be better than *that*!'"

While there was much less change in Washington than in Detroit, Robbins and company made some very smart last-minute additions to the show, including a new song for Motel and the finalization of a dance number that Robbins had been working on for a very long time.

In Detroit, tailor Motel sang the song "Now I Have Everything" in the first act and Perchik sang a variation of the same song in the second act. Although it *almost* sounded like a different song, because the lyrics and arrangement were different, "it was still obviously the same song," said actor Pendleton, "and you'd hear remarks from the audience like, 'Didn't they sing that in the first act?'"

Then the actor playing Perchik, Bert Convy, was sitting with Robbins's assistant Altman on the plane flight from Detroit to Washington and said that while he didn't really like the various songs Bock and Harnick kept writing for him, he really liked Motel's song, "Now I Have Everything." Since Motel was a religious man, said Convy, perhaps they could try something more biblical for Motel? Altman discussed the conversation with Robbins, and the director suggested the biblical idea to Bock and Harnick.

Just three days later, Bock and Harnick delivered "Miracle of Miracles," a joyous song Motel would sing when Tzeitel accepts his marriage proposal. The song traced God's many miracles—shaking down the wall in Jericho, parting the Red Sea, helping David slay Goliath—to conclude with: "But of all God's miracles, large and small/The most miraculous one of all/Is the one I thought could never be/God has given you to me."

Not long before they left Washington, Robbins was ready to stage the song and asked Pendleton to try singing it first so the director could see what the actor would do "instinctively." Then, after Pendleton gave it a try, Robbins sighed and said, "Well, I guess I'm going to have to stage it myself."

Ten minutes later, said Pendleton, the director came up with all the gestures for the song. After they rehearsed it, "the orchestra came in to play it, and the whole cast was in the house to hear it. Everyone came up to me afterwards and said, 'You son of a bitch, you have the best song in the show.'"

In Washington, Robbins also completed an elaborate dance number he had begun working on in Detroit. Among the many Hasidic weddings Robbins and Richard Altman had attended over the show's gestation period was one at the Ansonia Hotel on Manhattan's Upper West Side that had a little something special. Besides wedding rituals already incorporated in the show, said Altman, "a Jewish comedian did a funny dance while balancing an empty wine bottle on his head."

Altman said later that although Robbins didn't say anything, he had "almost hypnotic absorption" in the routine. Now, as the show neared Broadway, the director finally figured out how to turn the wedding's single comedian into a line of Hasidic dancers, all in black, dancing fervently with bottles on their heads.

There was just one problem. "By the time he called us all in for the bottle dance, everybody had gotten into the frame of mind that he was finished choreographing and there would be no more big dances for the men," remembered dance captain Bayes. "Some of the guys sort of stopped doing their workouts, and when he started doing the bottle dance, he lambasted them. Robbins said, 'Your body is your instrument. If I were conducting an orchestra and the violinist didn't take care of his violin, and he couldn't get the sound out of it that I wanted, I'd fire him. You could be fired for not keeping your instrument in shape for what *this* conductor wants to hear.'

"Then he brought out a bottle and said, 'This is what we're going to put on our heads.' After we learned the steps, we tried it using skullcaps under the bottles, but most of the dancers couldn't do it, so we put the wedding hats on. The dance is so simple but the audience thinks it is the most difficult feat they've ever seen. I directed and choreographed a production where I had a guy in his seventies doing it. It does not take a genius to do the bottle dance. It took a genius to create it."

How does it work? The dance itself is roughly three and a half minutes to five minutes, explained Rick Pessagno, a dancer who has performed the bottle dance on *Fiddler* tours. "The bottles are not secured in any way, shape, or form, and you have to balance them. Do they fall off? Absolutely. If you drop the bottle, you must step out of the line, and another dancer from the ensemble steps forward and completes it. It doesn't happen very often."

But it does happen enough to keep the edge on, observed choreographer/director Jerry Mitchell. Mitchell performed in *Fiddler* at age thirteen with Michigan's Paw Paw Village Players and did the bottle dance with a Velcro bottle on top of his hat. "I thought, This is so easy," he said. "Cut to learning the bottle dance from Jerry Robbins, and it's a real hat and a real bottle and there's no Velcro. There's danger. The bottle sometimes fell off. You had to rehearse it enough to maintain that balance, which is what makes it so thrilling. Jerry called the step that follows it 'ecstasy' because you *are* in ecstasy afterwards if you didn't drop the bottle."

When Robbins finished creating the bottle dance, he called the cast in to see it. Afterwards, recalled actor Charles Rule, everyone burst into applause. Robbins "was beaming ear to ear, he was just so happy. He had found the finale of the first act. We thought it was wonderful—none of us really hated Jerry, we just hated the way he treated us. . . . We gave him a big hand of applause and said it was sensational. He said, 'It goes in tonight!'"

That evening in Washington, Robbins and Altman were at the back of the house with set designer Boris Aronson. "The bottle dancers performed with absolute precision and grace," Altman later wrote, "and suddenly I felt Boris tugging at my arm. I turned to him and saw that tears were streaming down his cheeks. 'Any man who can do that,' he said, nodding toward Jerry, 'I forgive everything.'"

7

Opening on Broadway

There was hardly a break between *Fiddler*'s closing in Washington, D.C., on September 12th and the start of rehearsals again in New York on September 14th. Despite the work in both Detroit and Washington, there were still a few tune-ups to do before the Broadway opening.

The director was tinkering with the show until the very last moment. So while the scenery was loaded into the Imperial Theatre, the company was rehearsing a few blocks away. Robbins even scheduled extra rehearsals those few days, warning cast members that if they didn't want to wind up just performing in synagogues, they should use every second possible to make their show better.

That meant more work on the elusive second act production number that had plagued Robbins for months. "All through the eight weeks of rehearsals and the eight weeks on the road, the mantra of the show had been, 'We need a big number in the second act,'" said Pendleton. "He'd put numbers in and take them out, put them in, take them out. Eventually Harnick and Bock wrote a new song about a day in the life of the village, at the marketplace, which involved nearly everyone in the cast. We worked every day on that number, which was going to put the second act right over the top."

Robbins finally did a run-through in the rehearsal room just one week before opening night. "It was stunning," said Pendleton. "I remember thinking this is one of his greatest works. And then, when it was over, he said, 'We don't need a big number in the second act.' What had happened over all that time we were working on the show was that the second act had pulled together without the new number."

Meanwhile the buzz was building. People who had seen the show in Detroit and Washington got the word out to their friends. And, it turns out, to the city's freelance musician community. Much like actors earlier, the city's top instrumentalists also wanted to be in the show.

Erwin Price, a trombone player who wound up playing the entire Broadway run, had worked on other shows for Hal Hastings, the music contractor for Harold Prince's office, and when asked to play *Fiddler*, Price quickly agreed. "The advance word, which always filters back to New York, was that it looked like a big hit. It had a very prestigious group of people putting it together, and a lot of musicians tried to get hired for the orchestra. Hal was able to get some of the best players in town on harp, accordion, and clarinet to play klezmer music. Another trombone player was from the NBC Symphony Orchestra, which had disbanded, and the flute player was a quality studio player. It had that kind of caliber—really first-class musicians."

The day of the first preview on September 16th, there was an invited dress rehearsal in the afternoon. "They went nuts," remembered Pendleton. "One of my friends said, 'Will you tell me something—where's this second act trouble we've been hearing about for months?' People were moved and crying—it was the first time the show ever got that. By our last preview, the night before we opened, we got a standing ovation, which was very unusual then. Agnes de Mille was there and said this was Jerry's best work ever."

When it came time for the opening on September 22nd, producer Prince even invited Marc Chagall, who was visiting New York at the time. He wrote the artist that the show was titled *Fiddler on the Roof*, "which quite obviously is inspired by your painting."

Sholem Aleichem's daughter and granddaughter were there for the opening, an event that was occurring nearly fifty years after Aleichem had died in the Bronx. "My mother didn't know English too well and kept saying, 'That's not Papa,'" recalled Aleichem's granddaughter, the writer Bel Kaufman. "I said, 'Mama, that's not Papa but it's a beautiful American musical play, with beautiful music and marvelous lyrics.'"

The opening-night party was held at the Rainbow Room, the legendary Rockefeller Center restaurant and nightclub sixty-five stories above Midtown. According to "Frank Farrell's New York–Day by Day," on-time guests had to wait more than an hour outside the dining room for people still at the Imperial Theatre, lined up backstage "to congratulate the illustrious Zero Mostel for one of the greatest, most endearing portrayals in three decades of legit theater—and for giving Broadway its first resounding smash success musical of the new season."

When the formally dressed theater guests finally arrived, wrote Farrell, they danced the Hully-Gully, Watusi, and Twist to the music of Tony Cabot and his band. Edie Adams was there, and so was Senator Jacob Javits, who later joined Mostel for some dancing to Jewish folk music. But after performing onstage and backstage both, Mostel was beginning to wither and left the party fairly early.

Mostel had already gone by the time reviews started coming in late that night and, much as in Detroit, Prince again had to pass along bad news. He read aloud to his opening-night guests from Walter Kerr's less-than-inspiring review, which began like this: "*Fiddler on the Roof* takes place in Anatevka, a village in Russia, and I think it might be an altogether charming musical if only the people of Anatevka did not pause every now and again to give their regards to Broadway, with remembrances to Herald Square." Kerr's concluding line: "The result is a very-near-miss, and I very much miss what it might have been."

"When the reviews began to come in, the party emptied out fast," said Pendleton. "Even *The New York Times*, which was good, was cautiously good. Everybody was piling into the elevators. I was home in bed by a little after midnight."

Things looked a lot better the next morning. *Daily News* critic John Chapman called *Fiddler* "a work of art," noting he planned to see the show "a few more times—if I can get in." Chapman also called *Fiddler* "one of the great works of the American musical theatre. It is darling, touching, beautiful, warm, funny, and inspiring."

Nearly all the critics gave a tip of the hat to Chagall and to his stage interpreter, Boris Aronson, whom Chapman called "an Artist with a capital A." In most cases, Mostel couldn't have received greater praise if he'd written the reviews himself.

In general, however, reviews were mixed. The *New York Post*'s Richard Watts Jr. lauded Mostel but dispensed such dismissive phrases as "competent libretto," "pleasantly modest score," and "workmanlike lyrics." The *New York Journal-American*'s John McClain conceded the show "promises to be a sizeable success," but quibbled with what he saw as "arid areas" and "an over-abundance of self-pity" in Stein's book.

At *The New York Times*, critic Howard Taubman praised Mostel, saying, "If Sholem Aleichem had known Zero Mostel, he would have chosen him, one is sure, for Tevye. . . . In Mr. Mostel's Tevye, it has one of the most glowing creations in the history of the musical theater." While Taubman had some problems with the score—and later said he might have chosen another composer like, say, Leonard Bernstein—he did note that "criticism of a work of this caliber, it must be remembered, is relative."

For Emory Lewis in *Cue*, *Fiddler* was nothing short of a "spell-binding, glorious re-creation of the wonderful world of Sholom Aleichem. . . . *Fiddler on the Roof* has an ingredient most musicals ignore: content." Even tastemaker Ed Sullivan, the television host, weighed in to call *Fiddler* "one of the all-time great musicals of the American theatre."

This time, unlike Detroit, *Variety* came down on the positive side. "Add Zero Mostel to the tiny circle of great stars," wrote critic "Hobe." "He carries the song and dance version of Sholom Aleichem's stories to smash impact as the first blockbuster of the new season."

The day the reviews came out, actors and orchestra members coming in to play the matinee found there was a line around the block of people waiting at the box office to get tickets. "When that show opened and we saw the lines, we knew we'd be there a long time," remembered bassoon player Ron Jannelli, then twenty-four and playing his second Broadway show. "We had no idea it would run eight years, but we knew it would be a big hit."

By 1:00 p.m., there was a double line of about three hundred people. Producers served fifteen gallons of iced tea to people waiting in line during the afternoon, and all three of the Imperial Theatre's box office

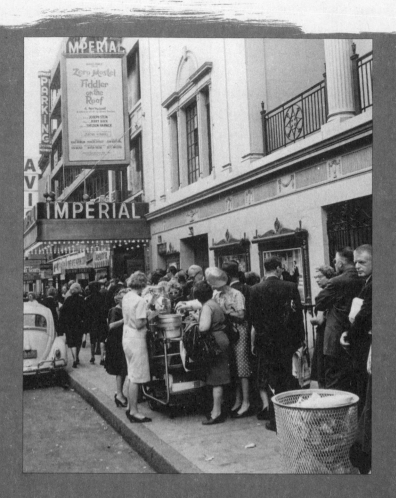

OPENING-DAY BOX OFFICE RUSH

According to *The New York Times*'s Sam Zolotow, there was a double line of about three hundred people by 1:00 p.m. the day after *Fiddler* opened on Broadway. Producers served fifteen gallons of iced tea to people waiting in line during the afternoon, and all three of the Imperial Theatre's box office windows were open. Producer Prince estimated that the advance sales from theater parties, mail orders, and box office purchases were $650,000,

while his general manager, Carl Fisher, said fifty-one theater parties had already made reservations for performances into 1965.

"Mail orders have been cascading upon the Imperial," reported the *Hackensack Record* in New Jersey. "More than two thousand pieces of mail were received in the first mail. Four additional mail order clerks and two extra treasurers were added."

windows were open. Producer Prince estimated that the advance sales from theater parties, mail orders, and box office purchases were $650,000, while his general manager, Carl Fisher, said fifty-one theater parties had already made reservations for performances into 1965.

Then there was the mail. "Mail orders have been cascading upon the Imperial," reported the *Hackensack Record* in New Jersey. "More than two thousand pieces of mail were received in the first mail. Four additional mail order clerks and two extra treasurers were added."

Before the show opened, composer Bock had called his friend and lawyer Richard Ticktin, worrying about his finances. Could he afford to buy a brand-new refrigerator? Ticktin told him to wait and see how *Fiddler* did. "I'd seen the wild enthusiasm at two previews," said Ticktin, "but did I know there would be three national companies following the Broadway company? Did I know it would become an international sensation with money flowing in all directions? I certainly did not. So I said, 'Let's hold off.'

"Then, the day after the opening, I walked down the street where it was playing and saw for the first time in my experience lines that curved around the block. I called Jerry and I said, 'You know that refrigerator? You can go buy it.'"

In early October, the *New York Times* critic Brooks Atkinson wrote a column praising the tales of Sholem Aleichem, observing along the way that enough of writer Aleichem's Yiddish prose came through in English to make *Fiddler* "intimate, funny, and touching and a major artistic achievement." Then, noting that Aleichem died in poverty, the critic ended his column saying that "now a lot of strangers are going to make huge sums of money out of his artful simplicity."

One of those strangers, the book writer Joseph Stein, responded immediately. In a letter to the critic on October 7, 1964, Stein noted that not only did none of its creators expect a big commercial hit, but that Aleichem's family shared financially in the show's success. Equally important, Stein added, "There was very little of the original Sholem Aleichem text that I could use literally. . . . I wrote five drafts of the book of *Fiddler* before arriving at the version now on the stage. I doubt that there is a total of a page of dialogue from the original stories now in the play. But I am enormously pleased at the constant references to the 'true Sholem Aleichem spirit' of the show."

RCA Victor recorded the cast album in an all-day session on September 27th, the Sunday after the opening, and soon came some very nice record reviews. *Variety* called it "a crackerjack original cast LP," with a score "loaded with lilting, flavorsome numbers." *Cashbox* expected heavy sales to send the album "soaring up the charts in short order."

Billboard writer Mike Gross wrote that the show should be a "hot box office ticket and a strong-selling original cast album property for RCA Victor." Noting several songs "could step out on their own," Gross found "Sunrise, Sunset" "especially noteworthy." His prediction: the album would fare well in the "original cast album sweepstakes this season."

For actor Harvey Fierstein, a future Tevye who first saw the show with his family from Bensonhurst, Brooklyn, "That music went directly into the zeitgeist of the community. You couldn't go anywhere then without hearing 'Sunrise, Sunset.' You'd turn on *Ed Sullivan* and there were Eydie Gormé and Steve Lawrence singing 'Sunrise, Sunset.' You'd hear Sammy Davis Jr. singing 'If I Were a Rich Man.' It was as if that score was *already* a beloved score, it went so quickly into popular culture."

Bock and Harnick's peers were also impressed. Composer and lyricist Harold Rome would frequently tell friends about his reaction to seeing an early performance of *Fiddler on the Roof.* When it ended, the man who wrote lyrics and music for *I Can Get It for You Wholesale* and other shows had tears running down his face. When someone asked him why he was crying, Rome replied, "I'm crying because I didn't write it."

8

Conquering Broadway

For the next few weeks, newspapers and magazines churned out a great many stories about both *Fiddler* and its star, Zero Mostel. *Newsweek*'s drama critic, Richard Gilman, writing the October 19th cover story, "Hail the Conquering Zero," noted that *Fiddler* "promises to be the biggest hit since *My Fair Lady* and is in fact doing better than that all-time favorite at a comparable stage." He reported that in just one day, the Imperial Theatre box office sold more than $67,000 worth of tickets, "a record for any Shubert theater, and the advance is well over $1.5 million."

Few actors or shows have received the sort of accolades that Mostel and *Fiddler* did from Gilman. Exiting the theater, wrote Gilman, Mostel was "a shaggy, corpulent, strangely charismatic figure whose presence brought the silence imposed by royalty." The actor's performance didn't just surpass the competition, wrote Gilman: "Indeed, it transcends and revolutionizes the uses of comedy for our time."

At the time he starred in *Fiddler*, Mostel lived on West Eighty-sixth Street in an apartment with room after room of art-filled walls that friend Ben Raeburn once described as Mostel's "personal museum." Besides the paintings by such artists as Picasso, Rembrandt, Renoir, Leger, and Klee, Raeburn reported bookcases full of art books, as well as books about theater. Kate Mostel once counted up stops at sixty-six museums on a month-long vacation in Europe.

Apartment walls also displayed many Mostel originals. Mostel long had a painting studio on West Twenty-eighth Street, and even during the *Fiddler* run, he tried to harness time and energy to work there. The phone in his studio was unlisted, but according to the play *Zero Hour*, actor/writer Jim Brochu's one-man homage to Mostel, that phone rang a fair amount. Brochu's play, which had successful runs in New York, Los Angeles, and elsewhere, was set in the studio as Mostel took a break from painting to do an interview.

To support himself as an artist, his chosen profession, the young Mostel had many odd jobs in the thirties and early forties. His first big job as an entertainer came in 1942 at Café Society Uptown—where he changed his name from Samuel Joel Mostel to Zero Mostel at the urging of Ivan Black, the Café Society's press agent—but he was also working then as an art lecturer, subsidized by the WPA. As he later told reporter Gilman: "I'm a painter who acts for a living."

The actor wrote and illustrated the 1965 book *Zero by Mostel*, and later exhibited his work in art galleries and museums. Press materials around that time noted that his paintings were in the collections of such museums as the Museum of Modern Art and Brooklyn Museum, while he later received the Albert Einstein Medal of Art from Middlebury College. There is a Mostel self-portrait near the front door of Harnick's New York home, and another hangs over the living room sofa at the Steins'.

His painting studio offered Mostel his only escape, said his nephew Raphael Mostel. "The experience of dealing with Zero offstage was remarkably similar to him onstage. He was always on. Performance was his default setting. He had the same personality with painting, where there was another side that was equally concentrated, but focused on the accomplishment of something quite different. He always saw himself as a painter who just did other things to support himself and his work. The greatest sadness of his life was that he didn't achieve the same recognition of his work as a painter."

While the only formal training he had was as a painter, he was clearly familiar with and passionate about other art forms, as well. "He was incredibly moved to create," observed his nephew. "He was completely untrained as an actor and had no formal music education, but he had a fantastic ear and he had sung cantorial music when he was a kid. He didn't read music, but he knew music well enough to perform opera; he did [Puccini's] *Gianni Schicchi* with the English National Opera."

He was apparently also an appreciative audience member. Ron Jannelli, a longtime bassoon player with the *Fiddler* orchestra, recalled how Mostel would come by to listen when orchestra members would play chamber music between shows. "He liked to hear it, and he was very knowledgeable," Jannelli said. "He knew every piece by every composer that we would play—'Oh,' he'd say, 'you're playing Haydn.' He would sit and listen, then talk to us after we played. Some people in the company balked; they wanted to rest and didn't want to hear any sounds going on between shows. We had to stop, but Zero got them to reverse the decision. He said, 'It's relaxing. I like it. I want to hear it.' So we got to continue. That was his doing."

It wasn't just the music, observed Erwin Price, who played trombone with the *Fiddler* orchestra during its long run on Broadway. "Zero loved music *and* musicians," said Price. "He felt comfortable with musicians. He was a down-to-earth guy, not a typical celebrity type. I loved Zee."

Mostel was in nearly every scene of the show, offstage only briefly, and the physical demands of the part took their toll on him. During the initial part of the Broadway run, he might stay in bed much of the day, getting up just a few hours before he had to leave for the theater. Because he grew his own beard and eschewed makeup, he didn't have to be at the theater as early as his colleagues.

Fiddler also affected him psychologically, said nephew Raphael Mostel. "This was a nightly psychodrama for Zero because it paralleled his own personal story. He was literally disowned by his parents for his second marriage, to Kate, who was Irish Catholic. His parents sat shivah, as if he were dead. The intermarriage scenes had to have been extremely painful for him, because that's basically his own story. He was acting the role his father played; eight times a week he was dredging up all sorts of personal memories and personal slights. He was embodying all the things he would have liked to have seen in his father in the character of Tevye."

Mostel was clearly very invested in the show—perhaps too much so.

TONY AWARDS

- 1965 Best Musical—Winner: book by Joseph Stein; music by Jerry Bock; lyrics by Sheldon Hamick; produced by Harold Prince.
- 1965 Best Composer and Lyricist—Winner: music by Jerry Bock; lyrics by Sheldon Hamick.
- 1965 Best Actor in a Musical—Winner: Zero Mostel
- 1965 Best Featured Actress in a Musical—Winner: Maria Karnilova
- 1965 Best Scenic Design—Nominee: Boris Aronson
- 1965 Best Costume Design—Winner: Patricia Zipprodt
- 1965 Best Choreography—Winner: Jerome Robbins
- 1965 Best Direction of a Musical—Winner: Jerome Robbins
- 1965 Best Producer of a Musical—Winner: Harold Prince
- 1965 Best Author (Musical)—Winner: book by Joseph Stein
- 1972 Special Award—Recipient: *Fiddler on the Roof* for becoming the longest-running musical in Broadway history.

Richard Altman recalled the time in the spring of 1965, when *Fiddler* was voted Best Musical by the New York Drama Critics' Circle. "The night after the announcement, Zero stormed into the Imperial Theatre, glowering and grumbling," said Altman. "'You don't give awards to the show,' Zero snarled. 'You give awards to *me*.'"

In late May, nominations for the 1965 Tony Awards were announced and *Fiddler* topped the list with nominations for ten of the twenty categories. Award presentations were set for June 13th at a dinner at the Astor Hotel.

Fiddler won nine Tony Awards: for Best Musical, for Jerome Robbins's direction, for Robbins' choreography, for performances by Mostel and Karnilova, for authors Stein, Harnick, and Bock, for costume designer Patricia Zipprodt, and for producer Harold Prince. Each winner thanked many colleagues in his or her acceptance speech, but none mentioned Mostel. When it later came time for Mostel to get his award as Best Actor in a Musical, he stood at the podium and said, "Since no one else has thanked me, *I* will thank me."

In August 1965, Mostel left the show, but despite worries to the contrary, ticket sales continued strong. For the show's second anniversary, September 22, 1966, producer Prince sent a huge cake—two and half feet wide and four feet long—to the theater, where it was consumed by cast members before that night's performance. "This is not a show anymore," said actor Herschel Bernardi, who was then playing Tevye. "People are coming to it as they would to a celebration—like a wedding or a bar mitzvah."

Prince expanded potential box office receipts just a few months later when, on February 28, 1967, *Fiddler* moved to the 1,650-seat Majestic Theatre from the 1,452-seat Imperial Theatre. The closing of *Breakfast at Tiffany's* made that change possible. (*Cabaret*, in turn, also moved to a larger house, settling in at the now available Imperial from its perch at the 1,287-seat Broadhurst.)

How did it do in the bigger theater? When Prince was asked to quantify the show's success later that year, he replied that so far the show hadn't an empty seat or empty place for standing room. Prince told the *New York Times* reporter Dan Sullivan that the producer and his investors had gotten back upwards of $3 million on their $375,000 investment, and RCA Victor had sold more original cast *Fiddler* albums than any original cast album before it. Besides playing the usual New York, Chicago, and London venues, said Prince, *Fiddler* was also playing three cities in Finland—Helsinki, Pori, and Tampere.

SOME FAMILIAR NAMES FROM *FIDDLER ON THE ROOF* ON BROADWAY

In 1966, Bette Midler made her Broadway debut in *Fiddler* as Rivka, a villager, and Joanna Merlin's understudy as Tzeitel. When Merlin left the show, Midler replaced her.

Adrienne Barbeau, who in 1968 made her own Broadway debut in *Fiddler*, also started in the chorus. First an understudy for second daughter, Hodel, Barbeau later assumed the role.

Tanya Everett originated the role of youngest featured daughter, Chava. She, Midler, and Barbeau shared a dressing room and a Broadway stage.

In the 2004 Broadway revival, Alfred Molina appeared as Tevye, Randy Graff as Golde, Nancy Opel as Yente, and David Wohl as Lazar Wolf, the butcher. Later, Harvey Fierstein succeeded Molina as Tevye, and replacing Graff as Golde were Andrea Martin, then Rosie O'Donnell.

Future *Glee* star Lea Michele was cast in the 2004 revival as young daughter, Shprintze, and as an understudy for daughter Chava. Also appearing as Tevye's daughters on Broadway over the years have been such prominent actresses as Liz Larsen, Sharon Lawrence, and Pia Zadora.

The *New York Times* critic Clive Barnes stopped by a few weeks later to assess *Fiddler*'s onstage success after three years. Not only was it doing great business, he reported, but the show held up. "All Broadway shows should be as fresh."

Sandra Kazan, a villager and understudy to Hodel, was the first to leave the show. Pregnant with daughter Francesca when the show was in Detroit, she had to keep asking the costume department to let out her skirts. A baby picture of her daughter fills an engraved picture frame that says "Love from the cast of *Fiddler on the Roof*, Nov 28, 64."

Pregnancy also led to the summer 1965 departure of Joanna Merlin, who similarly had wardrobe people letting out Tzeitel's wedding dress again and again. The actress found the wedding dance in which she and her groom were hoisted in the air by celebrants particularly frightening. "I was terrified every time they lifted me up in the chair," she recalled. "When I was four months pregnant, it was very scary."

Merlin returned to the show and Tzeitel for a while in 1966, the same year a talented newcomer named Bette Midler made her Broadway debut in *Fiddler* as Rivka, one of the villagers, and Merlin's understudy. "They were auditioning people to replace me," said Merlin, "and casting director Shirley Rich didn't want to bring in Bette. Shirley was very straight-laced and didn't like people to use four-letter words. But Bette was amazing. I called Hal Prince and said, 'You should see my under-study. I think she's wonderful.' He did, and she got the part. She played it for four years."

The book writer and lyricist Lynn Ahrens was in the audience for one of Midler's performances. Then a freshman at Syracuse University, Ahrens dragged her boyfriend to New York City to see *Fiddler*, her very first Broadway show. "I was mesmerized by the girl who played the el-dest daughter," said *Ragtime* lyricist Ahrens. "It turned out it was Bette Midler."

Actress Adrienne Barbeau, who in February 1968 made her own Broadway debut in *Fiddler*, was similarly impressed. Barbeau also started in the chorus, understudying middle daughter Hodel. She went on to play Hodel eight months later, but before she did, she sat in the balcony for two weeks just watching the show. Her strongest memory: "Watching Bette Midler play Tzeitel. She brought me to tears every night. There was never a performance when she wasn't giving her all."

Tevye's three daughters shared a dressing room, a Broadway stage, and even a sequence on the 1968 Tony Awards. As part of a tribute to past Tony Award–winning musicals, the three sisters sang "Matchmaker, Matchmaker" in front of a huge *Fiddler* poster. Barbeau's predecessor, Mimi Turque, and Tanya Everett, still inhabiting youngest featured daugh-ter Chava, swept the stage, with Midler between them, on the floor with her rag, just as she was at the theater each night. Midler soon tossed the rag over her shoulder and stood to join her sisters in song.

"We daughters thought 'Matchmaker' was the silliest thing we ever saw," Everett said candidly. "Throwing a mop onstage? All these other brilliant numbers, and we're throwing mops!"

While Mostel was succeeded by many a new Tevye during *Fiddler*'s lengthy Broadway run, Maria Karnilova long played Tevye's wife, Golde, with what one critic called "the rough tenderness of a warm blanket." She was still needling Tevye onstage as touring editions began to complement the Broadway run. In September 1968, a second road company opened in Dallas as the first stop in a thirty-three-week tour to 110 cities in thirty-four states and Canada.

In early 1969, when *Fiddler* had been running more than four years on

Broadway, the show's creative team agreed to set aside the rule about no amateur productions yet so that a production of *Fiddler* could take place at Harry A. Eiseman Junior High School 275 in low-income Brownsville, Brooklyn. There, despite reported anti-Semitism toward the school's many Jewish teachers, the show was performed by a cast of black and Puerto Rican kids that summer.

Their teacher, Richard Piro, even hosted rehearsals in his apartment during a teacher's strike. The show went on—documented by ABC-TV, *60 Minutes*, and, later, Piro's book *Black Fiddler*—amid both the strike and student riots. On opening night, there were thirty-five officers hidden upstairs, plus four downstairs and visible to the audience; during the first act, a group of black militants stoned the building with rocks and bricks. But when it was over, the cast sang "To Life" as they came down the aisle and onto the stage for curtain calls.

————

On Wednesday, July 21, 1971, just a few months before the *Fiddler* film's premiere, the show landed in first place as the longest-running musical on Broadway. It had finally passed *Hello, Dolly!* (not to mention *My Fair Lady, Man of La Mancha, Oklahoma!,* and *South Pacific*, its other close competitors) with 2,845 performances. Mostel's former understudy Paul Lipson, the current Tevye, had played the Russian patriarch 1,580 times, and had been in the show as Tevye, Avram the bookseller, and Lazar Wolf the butcher for three thousand performances.

Success by now was worldwide. *Fiddler* had played in sixteen languages and thirty-two countries from France and Spain to Rhodesia, Brazil, and New Zealand, reaching an audience of more than 35 million around the world. RCA Victor's record-breaking original cast album had sold about two million copies, and the show had now spawned another seventeen cast albums in various languages.

According to Carl Fisher, then general manager for producer Prince, more than two thousand performers had appeared in *Fiddler*'s three U.S. companies. A fact sheet prepared by press agents Sol Jacobson and Lewis

Harmon for *Fiddler*'s July 21st triumph reported total grosses of $50.6 million for the Broadway and national companies. *Fiddler* had returned total profits of $6.95 million on its original $375,000 capitalization, which represented a 927 percent profit for the show's initial investors and producer.

Festivities followed at the Broadway Theatre that night. At the end of the performance the city's charismatic mayor, John Lindsay, came out onstage, called the show a "landmark," and quipped that he was thinking about playing Tevye himself once his term expired in 1974.

Less than a year later, Mayor Lindsay was back for the "record-breaking celebration" on June 17, 1972, when *Fiddler* played its 3,225th performance, one more than *Life with Father*, to become the longest-running show on Broadway. Period. Six actors had followed Mostel as Tevye, and three theaters had hosted the show, each theater larger than the one before.

Every one of the Broadway Theatre's seats were filled, and five hundred people had been turned away. Crowds outside the theater stood below a marquee that noted, among other things, that *Fiddler* was now "Broadway's Long Run Champ." Audience members entered the Broadway Theatre to music from the All City High School Chorus, gathered on the sidewalk, and when the curtain came down, 3,225 balloons—one for each performance—rained down on the audience.

Onstage, the cast took its bow amid banners noting the number of performances of other contenders: *Life with Father* at 3,224, *Tobacco Road* with 3,182, *Hello, Dolly!* at 2,844, *Oklahoma!* at 2,212, *My Fair Lady* with 2,717, and *South Pacific* with 1,925. *Fiddler*'s creative team joined Mayor Lindsay onstage as a symbolic torch was moved along to producer Prince from Dorothy Stickney and Anna Erskine Crouse, widows of *Life with Father*'s creative team, Howard Lindsay and Russel Crouse. Next came four Tevyes—performers from Tel Aviv, Mexico City, and the Netherlands, plus the current Broadway Tevye, Paul Lipson—who sang "Tradition."

Prince also had his own performance that night. "I reprinted the New York and Detroit reviews, put them together in a nice, gold-lined commemorative program, and gave them to everyone in the audience so they could see how unwelcoming most of the reviews were," Prince said several years later. "Sometimes you do get the last laugh."

Fiddler finally folded its tent on Broadway on July 2, 1972, just two weeks after all the partying. The show was losing money, Sheldon Harnick said at the time. Advance sales were minimal, and Harnick figured that the last week alone they would lose about $30,000. They had been losing money for the prior two months, he told *The New York Times*.

Fiddler held its title of the longest-running show in Broadway history for more than seven years, until *Grease* surpassed it on December 8, 1979. It was in the sixth spot in *Variety*'s Top 10 in June 1994, then dropped to thirteen in 2008 in the listing of the Broadway League. However, while *Fiddler* was passed over the years by such shows as *The Phantom of the Opera, Cats, Les Misérables,* and *Mamma Mia!*, in 2013 the League still pegged it as the sixteenth-longest-running Broadway show.

As *Fiddler* productions flourished, Jerome Robbins promised one quarter of one percent of his share of *Fiddler* author earnings to the New York Public Library for the Performing Arts for the film and video archive at the Jerome Robbins Dance Division. As of June 2012, *Fiddler* royalties received by the library had reached more than $3.7 million.

In 1987, Robbins was on hand at the library to celebrate the formal naming of the dance film collection as the Jerome Robbins Archive of the Recorded Moving Image. The director and choreographer recounted that day his childhood trips with his parents to the New York Public Library's children's room and later, the research trips he made to the library when he was working on *Fiddler*. "That this archive is funded through *Fiddler* makes a nice circle," said Robbins.

9

London Calling

As performer after performer inhabited Tevye onstage, none would rival Mostel's celebrity but one: Chaim Topol. And that almost didn't happen. The first time the Israeli actor was offered the part, in a 1965 Tel Aviv production, he actually turned it down.

"I'd gone to see *Fiddler* when I was in New York," Topol explained, "and there was Zero Mostel making jokes onstage like, 'Mrs. Finkelstein, are you yawning because I'm boring you or did your husband keep you awake all night?' The audience was having a wonderful time, but I was brought up on Sholem Aleichem stories. I was quite angry about Zero making jokes, and I imagined everyone else in Israel knew the stories and would be angry, too. So I said, 'No, I don't think it will work in Israel.'"

But it did indeed work in Israel and, eventually, for Topol, as well. Actor Bomba Zur played Tevye in Tel Aviv for a year, succeeded by Shmuel Rodensky. When eight performances a week proved too much for Rodensky, said Topol, he was asked to share the week with Rodensky. By that time, Topol had seen Mostel deliver a more restrained performance in New York "and I understood how great he was. I said, 'I'd love to do it.'"

Topol's mixed emotions about Mostel's performance were not unusual. An incredibly talented but difficult actor, Mostel would not just add shtick when it pleased him, but also taunt other actors onstage with him, making faces at them or pulling at their false beards, sometimes tormenting the orchestra, as well. Called by the press everything from "former night club buffoon" and "nitery clown" to "incorrigible imp," Mostel was not one to restrain himself.

Offstage, too, he was a performer, entertaining whomever might cross his path. His nephew Raphael Mostel said that as a child he always looked forward to a visit from "Uncle Zee" "because he was an incredible person for a kid. He'd be sitting at the table, and all of a sudden the silverware would be animated into an incredible show. Or he would pretend to be a percolator. He would sit in a chair, explain that the water level is up to here, the coffee grounds are up to here, then perk. It's hard to imagine, but you could actually visualize all the bubbles coming up."

All he needed was an audience. Ron Jannelli, a bassoonist in the *Fiddler* orchestra, re-created a Mostel sighting one night at Sardi's: "A few of us had gone there for dinner between shows, and in comes Zero with a group of people. He sits down at the table right next to us with his group, including a woman interviewing—or trying to interview—him. There was bread and butter on the table, and he broke off a piece of bread and started to butter it. Then he started buttering his arm, and he kept moving the butter up his arm toward his shoulder. He put the last piece of butter on his forehead and called the waiter over to ask for more butter."

But his onstage behavior was less amusing. "He was an exhibitionist, and he could not take orders," said Maria Karnilova, who originated the role of Golde, Tevye's wife. "He was a brilliant performer when he was in his right mind, but when he got cut loose, he just didn't know what he was doing. He was not professional. He would suddenly stop and talk to the audience and ruin the show."

The Producers choreographer and director Susan Stroman vividly remembers Mostel's kibitzing onstage when she was still in school and her older brother took her to see *Fiddler.* "Although I was young, I knew I was watching a genius. But what I really remember is how Zero broke the fourth wall. Even then, it didn't seem right to me for Tevye to leave Anatevka and talk to a woman in the front row."

Many people have similar Mostel stories. Future Tevye Theodore Bikel also was dismayed at what he saw as Mostel's lack of discipline. In his autobiography, *Theo*, Bikel wrote of seeing Mostel just three months into the run, already inventing new material. "He committed excesses on stage that delighted the audience because they were funny. Everything Zero did was funny, but not necessarily right."

Bikel also saw *Fiddler* revivals later where Mostel "managed more outrageous behavior. While playing the show at a theatre-in-the-round, he actually sat on a patron's lap in the audience." Another time, writes Bikel, after Mostel and actress Thelma Lee, then playing Golde, finished the duet "Do You Love Me?", "Zero ran up the aisle in the dark and shouted from the back of the auditorium, 'And that night Tevye had Golde!'"

The orchestra pit was not off-limits, either. Mostel would "take liberties" with the tempo on "If I Were a Rich Man," said Jannelli. "Milton Greene, the conductor, would have a hard time following him. So Zero would often lean over and say, in a joking way, 'Follow me, Goddamnit.'"

"Zero was a clown," said Jannelli. "He quite often would do something funny, get a laugh, and keep going. He'd build on it and just milk it until he was almost out of character. At the end of "If I Were a Rich Man," for instance, he would stick his rag into the milk bucket, which was filled with water, and while people were applauding, he'd lean over the orchestra and wring out the rag. We'd cover our instruments, but the music would get wet."

The situation on "If I Were a Rich Man" got so out of hand that director Robbins had to step in. Robbins had staged the song, Harnick said, "so that Mostel would raise his arms to heaven and sigh. Then, when he dropped his arms, one arm would go into a pail. When it came out, the sleeve was covered with milk. It was nice, because it was one more awful thing that happened to this victim. He would wring out the sleeve and go on with the song. Within three days, it was no longer a song about 'if I had money.' It was a song about 'what does a man do when he gets his sleeve covered with milk?' He made about four minutes out of it—including, of course, putting some of the milk behind his ears, putting some on the hub of the wagon to make it run more smoothly.

"The song went right out the window. It was funny, because Zero was brilliant. Then, I think at the fifth performance, Zero sighed, dropped his arm, took his arm out of the pail, and there was no milk on it. The pail was empty. That was Robbins's way of coping."

During rehearsals, he behaved himself quite well, observed Joanna Merlin, who played daughter Tzeitel. "It was only when he got in front of an audience that he started doing this shtick, and there was no stopping him. He was a comic genius, but he had a compulsion to make the audience laugh at any cost. He was always embellishing his performance at the expense of character and relationships, but the audience ate it up. When we did an Actors Fund performance, though, he didn't use shtick. He played it straight. He knew the difference."

Harnick also recalled that Actors Fund performance. "It was the best performance Zero ever gave, when the auditorium was filled with actors, and he didn't ad lib. He gave a brilliant performance because he knew that his peers would not tolerate his fooling around."

Mostel's behavior also upset the creative team, said librettist Stein's son, Harry Stein. "It drove the creators crazy. Mostel maintained his performance for only a few weeks after the New York opening, then it deteriorated. When Golde tried to speak to him when he was washing up for dinner, he'd say, 'Quiet, I'm praying.' And he would start praying in Yiddish and davening. The audience would laugh, and he'd do five minutes. It was cheap shtick, vaudeville. My father, Jerry Bock, and Sheldon Harnick hated it. When he was still undisciplined several years later for opening night at a revival, he got a standing ovation from everyone except the authors. They just sat there."

Asked when Mostel began to act like that, Bock once said: "The night after we opened. Up until that point, he was a pussycat. . . . It was when he was justly celebrated in New York that it happened. Up until then he was fantastic. He added so much. . . . Zero's improvisations pre–New York were very constructive, very creative and often gave us new insights into the character. Post-opening, they became rather destructive as far as we were concerned."

How did Stein, whose script Mostel was augmenting, deal with it? Said his widow, Elisa Stein: "Joe would tell Zero that Leonard Bernstein was in the audience, so he'd give a good performance."

"Zero got bored very quickly," Stein once told a reporter from *The*

Times in London. "One of the greatest performances I've ever seen was him on opening night. But after a couple months it was very difficult for me to watch it. . . . Eight weeks into the run, a fifteen-second piece of business was taking two minutes."

For example, in his book, *The Making of a Musical: Fiddler on the Roof*, Richard Altman described Mostel's antics in the scene where Tevye is warned by the constable about a possible bit of "mischief" expected against the Jews. Mostel was to make a gesture as the constable left, a gesture that was also a music cue for the conductor. At one performance, before the gesture, Zero pretended to strangle himself as if he were strangling the constable. When he got a laugh, he kept up the strangling a while longer.

But Mostel didn't stop with strangling. "Eventually, the routine consisted of strangling the constable, throwing the body down and kicking it, picking up an imaginary shovel, digging an imaginary hole, picking up the body and tossing it into the hole and then covering the hole with dirt."

His collaborators had been warned. Harnick still remembers Robbins telling him, "I don't want to see Zee two months after the opening, because God knows what he'll be doing." The audiences adored him no matter what he did, said Harnick, "but on a number of occasions, we had to ask him to not do certain things."

Prince was not surprised, either. The producer knew from working with Mostel on *A Funny Thing Happened on the Way to the Forum* that the actor could be a problem; on *Forum*, he wouldn't take notes from the director or producer, often "pursuing laughs and ingenious bits of business, obliterating the story."

As early as April 1965, Prince sent a letter to the creative team regarding his concerns about Mostel's onstage behavior. Noting that he had received "many criticisms" of Mostel's performance, he recounted a public criticism printed in the Louisville, Kentucky, paper in which its drama critic "took Zero severely to task" and urged his readers to wait until *Fiddler*'s national company starring Luther Adler came to town "to see the show properly performed." Prince also wrote that he believed the show would win "all the awards" and would sell out "for at least another year with or without Zero and probably longer."

Mostel's contract was due to expire that August, and by July, Prince was pretty sure a new contract with Mostel would be "impossible." "I didn't like what he was doing on the stage, but still, I agreed to meet Zero, and we met in his lawyer's office. We beat out a new contract which was okay. Very rich but very fair because he was now Zero Mostel. When I started to leave the office, the lawyer said, 'By the way, I forgot something. Zero wants a car and chauffeur to and from the theater.' I said, 'Ladies and gentleman, I've withdrawn this total negotiation. I will find someone else.' And I walked out the door, and left them all with their mouths *agape*."

After Mostel's final performance, on August 14, 1965, the cast and orchestra came onstage for a farewell party. "The theater was empty, and there was food and drink onstage," recalled musician Erwin Price. "Zero went backstage, where he had soap and water, and he shaved off his beard. He came back, half in costume, half out of it, a civilian again."

Harnick recalled feeling very nostalgic that night. "I went up to Zero and said, 'Zee, I really am very sorry to see you go.' 'No, you're not,' he said, 'You're sorry to see the grosses fall.' He was heartbroken when the grosses didn't fall, because he then had to acknowledge that he wasn't the reason for the success of the show."

Prince, meanwhile, was worrying about the next step. "I thought, 'Who am I going to talk the authors into who will really take back our show so it isn't the Zero Mostel Show?' Luther Adler came to mind. There was nothing about Luther and Zero that was remotely the same. Luther made a classic performance out of it. Then we moved to Herschel Bernardi, and so on. We moved further back toward what Zero had been doing but never exactly. Luther Adler was a perfect antidote to thinking this is the Zero Mostel Show; he was a very elegant, important theatrical name and very good."

While the show continued on Broadway, Prince also hired Theodore Bikel in late 1967 to play Tevye at Caesars Palace in Las Vegas. The producer seemed amused at how "people would go through the gambling casino, past the high rollers and slot machines, to see Teyve and his poor family starving in old Russia."

Bikel, on the other hand, was concerned at first that in the resort showroom, people would be sitting at tables, not in theater seats. "I was horrified on New Year's Eve to see that there was a noisemaker on every table," Bikel recalled. "Are they going to make noise while we are acting our hearts out as Jews in the shtetl? To our credit, nobody used the noise-makers."

The creative team also turned its attention to a London production of the show. Several established stars were considered, Prince wrote his collaborators, also noting "considerable enthusiasm for Chaim Topol." If they couldn't find a star, he thought the London producers could be willing to accept "the notion of an unknown who has star equipment."

So it was that while he was playing the part in Tel Aviv, Topol got a telegram from London asking if he'd consider auditioning to play Tevye in London. Just a few years before, Topol had won a Golden Globe award for his 1964 portrayal of an elderly patriarch in the award-winning Israeli film *Sallah*, and Prince had heard about the performance. "I saw the film, and asked the authors and Jerry Robbins to see it," said Prince. "We all agreed he would be good."

Apprised of their interest, Topol sent back a cable based on Joseph Stein's first line in the musical: "*Fiddler on the Roof*? Sounds crazy, but I'll try." He didn't speak much English, but he learned the score from the show's Broadway cast album and studied the songs with an Englishwoman who taught him the words. Then he went off to London for the audition.

What nobody apparently knew was that Topol, who played an aged Jew in *Sallah*, was no aged Jew himself. Even the William Morris agent sent to bring him to the theater was thrown off when they first met. Just back from a month in the Israeli military, tanned and with short hair, the thirty-year-old actor hardly looked like a shtetl patriarch. But the two men went off to the Drury Lane Theatre where assorted producers and the *Fiddler* creators were gathered to meet him.

When it was announced that Topol had arrived, everyone turned their heads to find him, looking straight through the young man at the back of the theater. Topol pointed at his chest: "It's me." Then he walked up to the stage and sang, "If I Were a Rich Man," with all of its many stage gestures.

"I had seen Topol in an Israeli film, playing an old man, so when he came to audition, he startled us," Stein recalled. "He was extremely well prepared so that from the moment he started to audition, we felt we had our London Tevye."

They let him sing the entire song, a song that runs maybe five minutes, which is unusual for an audition. Then they asked if he could sing another song, "Sabbath Prayer." Topol sang "Sabbath Prayer," then three more songs before someone asked him how many times he had seen the show. "Four times," replied the actor. "Twice with Zero and twice in Israel."

The producers and writers were amazed and asked Topol: "Do you mean after four times you know exactly the movements and positions onstage?" "Yes," answered Topol. "I saw it only four times . . . but I probably played Tevye forty or fifty times."

When they asked him to do a scene, however, he got worried. He'd tried to learn a few scenes by heart in English, but his English was still pretty poor. He jockeyed for time, saying he was hungry. They went to lunch, and he apparently won them over.

Topol went to London six months early to work on his English and rehearse. He learned the part phonetically, studying with Cicely Berry, a voice coach with the Royal Shakespeare Company. By the time the show opened at Her Majesty's Theatre in February 1967, the actor felt his English wasn't too bad.

The actor also liked playing older characters. Early on, when he was at the Habima Theatre in Israel, he'd studied how to play an elderly man "when you're not so springy and your muscles are not so elastic."

Topol had learned "to tie up muscles," a technique he found could tame his body to be a certain age. "It's not that you start thinking that way, because you don't have the experience of years," the actor said. "But the physical behavior you project to the audience does quite an important job. You can easily break the illusion if you make one single mistake. Suddenly you're springy, the illusion is broken, and they don't trust you anymore."

Jerome Robbins was also there to hone his performance, something Topol clearly appreciated. "Jerry gave you instructions that were so clear, so to the point. You knew exactly what he wanted, and if you didn't know, he would demonstrate. He'd say, 'I want to see pride. No, I don't want you to come down. Go up.' It was so clear. It was a joy to work with him. He certainly got out of me what I could bring to the part."

Topol's friend Miriam Karlin, who played Golde in the London production, also praised Robbins's work with Topol. "What Jerry did with Chaim Topol was fantastic," she said. "Because Chaim Topol had already played this in Israel in Hebrew for a very short season, he had his own way of doing it . . . and it was way, way, way over the top. To watch Jerry working with Chaim, it was like you've got a great big onion, and he took away so many layers of skin until gradually there was this wonderful little core, this jewel in the center. . . . That's what I saw happen. . . . He [Topol] eventually gave it such dignity, it was just terrific. And that was Jerry."

Like Mostel, Topol received raves from the critics. "Once in a generation there suddenly arrives in our theatre a great star," wrote the *Evening News*. The *Sunday Citizen* called his "the performance of a lifetime." *News of the World* said, "A bearded man in patched pants becomes king of London's musical stage, a star overnight." Sixteen critics named the show "the best foreign musical of the season."

In June 1967, Topol left the London production briefly to return to Israel for the Six-Day War. He was too late for the fighting but entertained soldiers on the Golan Heights. "He was a huge smash very early in the run, the war came up and he went," said Prince. "Can you imagine the amount of publicity that generated?"

Ask Topol. "It was a celebration before the war but afterwards, you couldn't get a ticket," said the actor. "The praise I got from the black market people was incredible! They were so kind to me that when I needed tickets I couldn't get at the box office, they would get me the tickets."

Topol's description of his London audiences could work as well for the

As *Fiddler on the Roof* traveled the world, few countries were so welcoming as Japan. The first production of *Fiddler* in Japan opened in Tokyo on September 6, 1967, and starred the noted Japanese actor Hisaya Morishige. It has since been presented in Japan more than 1,300 times and become Toho Co., Ltd.'s most popular American musical.

Morishige went on to play Tevye onstage nine hundred times in his career. When he stopped playing Tevye after nearly twenty years, he told Tokyo's *The Daily Yomiuri,* "I felt as if I was saying good-bye to a good friend."

audiences that U.S. revivals and tours alike report again and again. He described "a torrent of families. Parents brought their children and children their parents, and we sometimes had four generations of family in one row." Talking about all the fund-raisers, all the sobbing in the theater and women repairing their makeup in the powder room, Topol spoke of *Fiddler* as "definitely more than a show." In fact, one of Topol's friends said to him: "I don't know what things will be like when the Messiah comes, but as far as the Jewish community is concerned, *Fiddler*'s the next best thing."

It was hardly the Jewish community alone. In London, as in New York and throughout America, *Fiddler* played to strong houses long after every Jewish person in town may have seen the show. The London production ran for 2,030 performances, with Topol starring in 430 of them. Besides doing a Broadway revival of *Fiddler* in 1990–91, Topol was back on London's West End in *Fiddler* revivals in 1983 and again in 1994.

While Topol did go on to play Tevye many, many times onstage, it was that first London run that was to change his life forever. In February 1968, the very last week he was in the show, Norman Jewison, future director of the film, was in the audience.

Part 3

THE MOVIE

10

Enter Hollywood

Film director Norman Jewison saw *Fiddler* its very first week, but it wasn't easy. He was in New York for only a few days, and there were no tickets. Eager to see it, he finally called producer Hal Prince for help. There wasn't a seat in the house, Prince told him, but he did offer a solution; Jewison saw the show from a cushion in the first balcony.

Also in *Fiddler*'s Broadway audience early on was film producer Walter Mirisch, who quickly shared his discovery with Arthur Krim, chairman of United Artists film studio. Krim had worked with Mirisch several times before but was skeptical. He thought it might do well in New York, given its large Jewish population, but an international audience seemed unlikely.

Jewison had no idea yet that he'd be asked to direct the screen version, but Mirisch was so impressed with what he saw onstage that he was determined to produce it for the screen. "I tried to convince United Artists to buy it right then, but though they liked it, they thought it was terribly ethnic," Mirisch said. "I was patient, though. Even though there was no film I'd ever wanted to do as much as *Fiddler*, I was willing to wait."

The deal took a while. For one thing, the stage show was still inordinately successful. By the time United Artists was in final negotiations for *Fiddler* film rights in early 1966, Broadway revenues since the show's September 1964 opening were already more than $6.3 million. An Israeli production had been playing in Tel Aviv for six months, and the show's first national company was due to start in a few months.

United Artists purchased the *Fiddler* film rights on February 1, 1966, for about $2 million plus a profit percentage. There was also an agreement that given the show's continuing good box office, the film would not be released to theaters for a while.

The next question was who would direct it. Mirisch and United Artists had worked with Jerome Robbins on *West Side Story*, but that didn't turn out well. After Robbins and codirector Robert Wise had shot about half the film, Robbins was pulled off the project. "It was clear to him as well as to everyone else that the picture was lagging and there was too much indecisiveness," Walter Mirisch said. He may have been in favor of having two directors originally, he said, but, "it doesn't work."

Most people who saw *West Side Story* felt it worked out just fine, of course, and even Mirisch conceded that the film's producers got the best of both Robbins and Wise. The film community apparently agreed; when *West Side Story* won its ten Academy Awards at the 1961 Oscars ceremony, Robbins and Wise shared the Oscar for directing.

Nearly a decade later came the chance to turn Robbins's production of *Fiddler on the Roof* into a movie. But according to then United Artists president David Picker, Robbins was not interested in directing the *Fiddler* film. UA was contractually obligated to ask if Robbins, who directed the stage version, wanted to direct the film version, as well, so Picker met with Robbins over lunch to talk about it. "I asked if he would like to direct it, he said 'no,' and that was the end of it," said Picker. "We fulfilled our obligation to Jerome Robbins, and after he said 'no,' we went to Norman Jewison."

The timing was good for Jewison, whose film career had taken a strong upward spin during the prior few years. He hadn't yet made *Moonstruck* or *Jesus Christ Superstar*, but he had already made nine other films. Among them were three with Mirisch and United Artists: *The Russians Are Coming, The Russians Are Coming* (1966), *In the Heat of the Night* (1967), and *The Thomas Crown Affair* (1968). *In the Heat of the Night*, a powerful study of Southern racism, had received the Oscar for Best Picture against such contenders as *The Graduate* and *Bonnie and Clyde*.

While *Fiddler* turned out to be his first film musical, Toronto-born Jewison had directed or produced many television musicals in both his native Canada and in the United States. He had directed *Your Hit Parade*, as well as specials for Judy Garland, Harry Belafonte, Danny Kaye, and Andy Williams. His other television credits included both *The Fabulous Fifties* and *The Broadway of Lerner and Loewe*.

The way Jewison remembered it, he received an unexpected call one day from UA chairman Arthur Krim's office, asking if the director could come to New York for a meeting. "I had no idea it was about *Fiddler*," said Jewison. "I was stunned when I got to New York for what became for me this historic meeting."

In Krim's office that day were Krim, Picker, and several other UA executives whom Jewison recognized. Said Krim: "What would you think if we asked you to produce and direct the film version of *Fiddler on the Roof*?"

Jewison was speechless. He thought about how much he loved the play. Then he looked around the room and realized everyone else there was Jewish. His heart was pounding furiously as he thought to himself, "My God. They think I'm Jewish. What am I going to tell them? I've done all these pictures with them, and it never occurred to them that I'd be a goy. Is it going to be a disappointment to them? Am I going to lose this opportunity?"

It took a while, but the director finally responded with, "What would you think if I told you I'm a goy?' The room was quiet at first. Then Arthur Krim leaned forward, put his hands together, and said, "Why would you think we asked you to direct this film? We don't want a piece of Yiddish kitsch." "Do you believe that line?" Jewison said later. "The man covered himself beautifully. No wonder he was an adviser to JFK."

Jewison said yes, of course. But during the very pause in which he was trying to figure out how to tell a room full of Jewish movie executives that a man named Jewison wasn't Jewish, he was also thinking about Jerome Robbins. "I'd worked in New York on a lot of music and television, and I was so aware of Jerry's influence. I really thought he was a genius. He had great ideas, and I loved what he did with certain scenes in *Fiddler*."

Jewison asked directly why they were choosing him instead of Robbins and was informed of assorted problems that had occurred with Robbins on *West Side Story*. Actor George Chakiris, who won a supporting actor Oscar for *West Side Story*, summarized those problems many years later, saying, "Jerry was a perfectionist. He could always find a better way to do something."

Directing films is considerably different than directing for the stage, however. "On films, you have to make decisions," Jewison said. "There's no such thing as perfection. If you can't say 'print,' it means you are a director who has no idea about the complexity of the medium. And poor Jerry was reshooting everything. When a lot of theater directors see the playback of what they did, they want to redo it. Film directors know that when you're doing a shot, you are not going to be on the shot for more than a moment. You are pre-editing in your head. and I don't think theater directors pre-edit in their heads like film directors do."

Jewison, in contrast, was already a seasoned director with a solid track record. "We wanted Norman to direct because he was a very good director," said United Artists executive Picker. "Norman made very successful movies for us, and we felt he could do a very good job with this. He was the perfect choice."

Once he had agreed to the assignment, Jewison called his agent, Larry Auerbach, at William Morris. When Auerbach asked Jewison what he told Krim, the director recounted his remark about being a goy, adding, "How can I do *Fiddler on the Roof*? I've never had a seder with my family." Replied Auerbach: "Norman, you weren't black, and you made *Heat of the Night*. Don't worry about it."

In truth, Jewison was more excited than worried: "The whole world thinks I'm Jewish. Son of a Jew—Jewison. So I've been called 'Jewboy' and 'Jewie' all my life. I always wanted to be a Jew, and I think that was part of my passion for making this film. Sholem Aleichem really is the soul of Yiddish culture in a way, isn't he?"

When Jewison left Krim's office, however, he did worry a little. All he'd been told about his assignment was that Krim didn't want a piece of Yiddish kitsch. And then, as he was walking toward the door, he saw he was being followed by UA's head of business affairs, William Bernstein.

Bernstein was full of ideas on where to shoot the film. There were wonderful locations in Manitoba, Canada, locations full of wheat fields that looked like the Ukraine. But Jewison was already thinking about Eastern Europe. He wanted to look first in Romania. There wasn't much filmmaking then in Romania, but the director thought Romania would look a lot more authentic than Manitoba.

He was trying to show Russia at the turn of the century, under the tsar, Jewison insisted, and where better to do that than in Eastern Europe. "I was sure he could see millions of dollars being spent and would run back and say, 'We got big problems with this kid.' They wouldn't like the idea of my looking at locations thousands of miles away from Midtown Manhattan."

But aside from that discussion, Jewison said, he didn't remember receiving any other directions. So he began to organize a team of collaborators, generally people he knew well and had worked with before. Among them were Patrick Palmer, head of production, production designer Robert Boyle, cinematographer Oswald Morris, casting director Lynn Stalmaster, and, almost immediately, the musician John Williams, "because I needed a brilliant conductor/composer."

Meanwhile, much as director Robbins had done several years earlier, Jewison tried to get everything rolling at once. He hired Joseph Stein, the stage musical's librettist, to write the screenplay, and he began scouting locations in Eastern Europe. Once word got out that he would be directing the *Fiddler* film, his phone started ringing with actors and agents eager to talk with him about casting. It was a very busy time.

For the first few months, he concentrated on learning as much as possible about Jews and Judaism, visiting Jewish museums and research libraries in Los Angeles and New York and, later, in Israel. He studied the photographs of Roman Vishniac, who had documented Jewish life in Eastern Europe in the thirties, calling Vishniac's photography a key source for the film's production design. And he immersed himself in

Sholem Aleichem and in Russian-Jewish history so he could, in turn, immerse his audience in the world he planned to portray onscreen.

As he did all that research, perhaps the most he'd ever done on a film, he became more and more convinced of his decision to shoot somewhere that already looked the way Anatevka might have looked in 1905. They weren't seeking just a cinematic setting, he felt, but rather a place that recreated Sholem Aleichem's stories "of people leading lives as they had lived them for generations, in an atmosphere where you can become used to the cruelties of your neighbors, the regular pogroms, and just carry on with raising your chickens and marrying off your children—those that survived."

Jewison and his production team traveled thousands of miles, looking at villages from Austria and Israel to Hungary and Romania. At one point, since his producers were pushing for places like Kansas and Saskatchewan because they looked like Russia, he even tried—unsuccessfully—to shoot in Russia itself. "Even though I had made *The Russians Are Coming*, and I was kind of wired in, it just was impossible because we couldn't get Lloyd's of London to insure the film."

The director found Romania close to perfect, but the village he most liked was just fifteen miles from the Russian border, and he couldn't get insurance there, either. Jewison ended up in Yugoslavia, in what is now called Croatia. Yugoslavia's President Tito "loved movies as much as he loved hard currency," Jewison wrote in his memoir, "and he maintained one of the largest standing armies in Europe. Lloyd's of London were happy to provide the necessary insurance." A bonus came later when Jewison learned that Tito would provide the film with a full cavalry regiment of trained soldiers and horses.

The army wasn't all that was appealing to Jewison about Yugoslavia. The movie's souvenir program also noted that the countryside near Zagreb was replete with "strong peasant types, unpaved streets filled with cows, chickens, and geese, and houses that could have been lifted out of a pre–World War I East European village. . . . The sets, constructed for the film, blended naturally with these surroundings, after a few electrical wires were removed."

Jewison, who also temporarily removed a few Yugoslavian telephone poles, was after authenticity, he said again and again. "In trying to re-create the world of Sholem Aleichem and bring it to life, it would have been doing him and the property a great injustice had we not searched all over Europe to find exactly the right settings, the right villages, the right atmosphere, and the Chagall-like quality that the film must have," Jewison told a reporter from *American Cinematographer* magazine.

Before they started building their sets and augmenting the village life they found near Zagreb, they drew on real villages they found in their travels. As they went through Yugoslavia and, later, Israel, the production team accumulated photographs and sketches they'd be able to use later to create an Anatevka thriving with peasants, marketplace, and synagogue.

They did extensive research in Israel, too, on Jewish life generally, said production designer Robert Boyle, "so we wouldn't go astray on any of the religious problems or anything else." But in visiting yeshivas, librar-ies, and universities, Jewison wanted more than just to acquaint Boyle and the others "with Orthodox Jewish traditions. I was trying to put everybody in the mood."

In Israel, Jewison consulted with Jerusalem Cinematheque founder and director Lia Van Leer, who screened archival films for the director "to help him with the period details." John Williams joined the director in Israel, too, using time at the University of Jerusalem to study tapes of shtetl bands. At a Jewish film museum in Haifa, they also spent two or three days looking at Jewish films from Russia and Poland.

As they traveled, Jewison and his team also met with Russian and other Jewish immigrants who might have stories to tell of their own ex-periences. The director wanted to capture not just the changing traditions that were at the core of the stage play, but something more: "I wanted audiences to really feel the racial hatred."

One of the strongest scenes in the film reflects Jewison's goal. It comes about midway through the film, when Tzeitel and Motel's wedding cele-bration is disrupted by a group of Russians who tear apart the party and with it pillows given as wedding gifts. That scene, with white feathers flying everywhere, was inspired by a story told at an Israeli kibbutz by an elderly couple recalling a pogrom from their childhoods in a Ukrainian village.

Putting scenes like that on paper was the job of screenwriter Stein. The director felt that since Stein wrote the stage musical, he would "know all the characters inside out." It would also not be "much of a stretch" for Stein to expand his script to include more of the village of Anatevka, not just Tevye's immediate surroundings.

"I asked him to open it up," said Jewison. "A movie is so different from a play. We're taking the story out into a real world and off the stage, and when you take it off the stage, you have real horses and real geese and pigs. It was difficult sometimes because Joe was of the theater and didn't visualize scenes in the same way as someone who was experienced with filmmaking. So I worked closely with him and did a lot of rewriting."

But while Stein's first draft was nearly identical to his play script, Jewison wasn't eager to make radical changes. "I didn't want to alter it too much," Jewison explained. "The play had been too successful to warrant changing any major plot points."

By the end of 1969, Stein had turned in his final opened-up screenplay, Jewison had found a home for his Anatevka in three Yugoslavian villages, and casting was well under way.

11

Casting the Movie

Norman Jewison didn't have Chaim Topol in mind when he started his *Fiddler* odyssey. About all he'd decided was that he wanted both to shoot his film in Eastern Europe and to find a Tevye who truly looked and sounded like he belonged there.

The director was also pretty sure he would not be hiring Zero Mostel. The very day Jewison met with United Artists executive Krim, his mind filled with excitement about the opportunity he'd just been handed, one of his first thoughts was that Mostel's performance was just "too big." "I thought he was too American and didn't sound like a Russian Jew," said Jewison. "Although I was moved by the play, I wasn't as moved as I wanted to be by his performance."

Besides seeing Mostel play Tevye onstage, Jewison also screened Mostel's films and even met with the actor. "I didn't like his take on the character of Tevye," the director said frankly. "I felt he wasn't real, and we wanted the film to be believable. The audience picks up on that immediately."

They had to consider Mostel, of course, and Jewison felt under great pressure. "I think the casting of it was the most agonizing thing I ever went through," he once told National Public Radio's Scott Simon. "Zero was brilliant on stage, but he was always a little outside the play. It was really 'his show,' whereas I felt I wanted to deal more with the Sholem Aleichem story, and the reality of Russia at the turn of the century."

Jewison's partners on the film felt similarly, including UA executive David Picker, who saw the Broadway production from a seat in the second row. "When you sit that close to Zero, you see it all," Picker recalled. "He was a larger-than-life performer, and it would never have worked with him on screen for that length of time in that role. There would have been too much Zero and not enough *Fiddler.*"

Meanwhile, Jewison was besieged by phone calls from actors and their agents eager to talk about the role of Tevye. Among the performers who expressed interest were Walter Matthau, Herschel Bernardi, Rod Steiger, Danny Thomas, Danny Kaye, and Richard Burton.

According to Jewison, the person who wanted the part most was Danny Kaye. Jewison had done a television special with Kaye, who was also a good friend, and said Kaye had long been interested in the part. "He had one passion—to play Tevye," Jewison said. "He said to me, 'I am a Russian Jew. I am perfect for this role. I sing. I do musicals.' I didn't know what to do. I didn't want to insult my friend, but I somehow just didn't see him in my mind's eye as Tevye. I felt he was too red-haired. Too light on his feet. Too *professional.*"

But Jewison wasn't sure either way. One morning he went over to Kaye's home where they discussed it at length over breakfast. Kaye talked about his father and how his real name was David Daniel Kaminsky. "He was telling me about his childhood and his *zayde* and how he could bring authenticity to it," said Jewison. "And I'm asking myself, Is that what I'm looking for? Danny Kaye is an established star. Do I want that?"

The director still wasn't sure when he got back to his office. Then, later the very same day, he had a call from his agent. Frank Sinatra had called, and *he* was interested in playing Tevye. Would Jewison go to Palm Springs? When Jewison said "no," his astonished agent replied, "You're turning down Sinatra?"

Jewison felt overwhelmed at that point, he said later. Lost. Then came Joseph Stein with a suggestion to consider Chaim Topol, born in Israel to a Polish mother and father. The creative team all knew Topol from his work on the London production of *Fiddler,* and they'd all looked at his work in the Israeli film *Sallah* when they were considering him for the London job. Not only had Topol convincingly played an old man in *Sallah,* but producer Mirisch had worked with Topol on the film *Cast a Giant Shadow*, in which he had again played an old man.

When the director learned that Topol was in his final weeks playing Tevye in London, he got on a plane for London. He saw Topol's performance, was very impressed, and went backstage afterwards to talk to him. Jewison didn't care that Topol was only in his thirties and would be playing a patriarch with marriageable daughters. After London, Jewison was convinced he'd found his Tevye. Topol had, among other things, "that don't-mess-with-me pride that the Tevye of my imagination had."

"Chaim Topol was made for this part," Jewison said at a Film Society of Lincoln Center screening of *Fiddler* in 2011. "Not only is he a fine actor, but there was a strain of dignity. It was the Israeli in him, the pride of being Jewish that really struck me. When he said, 'Get off my land,' you could see him stiffen up and stand as tall as he could. There was a strength that epitomized the hope that these people would somehow create a country of their own. I held off and I'm glad I did. Chaim Topol breathed life into Tevye."

Topol remembered well his own reactions to Jewison's visit. He didn't know too much about the director when he came backstage in London, so he was a little skeptical at first. When Jewison said he would be doing the film and was interested in having Topol play Tevye, the actor asked him when that would be. Jewison told him they'd be filming in 1970, said Topol, adding drolly, "It was 1968."

Jewison leveled with Topol, saying that while he wanted him very much, it wouldn't be easy because every good actor in the business wanted the part. Topol remembered thinking, "Who knows what will happen? Another Hollywood producer! He won't even remember my name in 1970. But to my surprise, he certainly did."

Topol had joked that nearly every well-known actor in Hollywood— "with the possible exception of Elvis Presley"—had been mentioned as a candidate. The actor said his money had been on Mostel, and he was "genuinely surprised" to get the part. He also said, "Zero was upset with me when he heard the news—who can blame him?"

Mostel was indeed distressed. His biographer, Jared Brown, quotes the actress Bettye Ackerman, widow of Mostel's friend, the actor Sam

Jaffe, as saying Mostel not getting the part was "Zero's greatest trauma and most painful experience." Thelma Lee, who performed with Mostel in the *Fiddler* production at the Westbury Music Fair on Long Island in October 1971, just before the film was released, told Brown that "you could not mention the movie to him. He was very upset, and rightly so, but he would not talk about it."

He would, however, do shtick about it. Mostel's son, the actor Josh Mostel, got a call a while later about playing King Herod in Jewison's 1973 film version of *Jesus Christ Superstar.* The younger Mostel reportedly said of the call: "From another room, I heard my father yell, 'Tell him to give it to Topol's son!'"

Topol's casting as Tevye was announced in the press in early 1969, but it appears most of Jewison's other casting wasn't done until many months later. Jewison and his casting team visited nine cities, including New York and London, as well as Los Angeles. When they had completed their casting, ten nationalities were represented and cast members ranged in age from two preteen actresses playing Tevye's youngest daughters to Molly Picon, then seventy-two.

Most important after Tevye was the role of Golde, Tevye's long-suffering wife. Jewison and Mirisch both wanted Anne Bancroft, but Jewison said he just couldn't convince her to do it. "I was really struggling with the casting of Golde," he said. "I didn't want to cast her until I cast Tevye, because I had to get two people who were comfortable together. And I loved Anne Bancroft—I felt she was the right actress."

Jewison had also been very interested in the Israeli actress Hanna Maron for Golde. Topol had suggested Maron, as well as another Israeli, Assaf Dayan, son of Israel's defense minister Moshe Dayan, for Perchik, so the director invited both Israelis to London for auditions. But tragedy struck when their plane stopped in Munich en route to London from Israel on February 10, 1970, where they were victims of a terrorist attack at the airport. Both were injured, Maron seriously, and wound up in the hospital. Topol was "totally distraught," neither could do the audition, much less the film, and, said Jewison, "I was devastated."

Maria Karnilova, who had originated the Golde part on Broadway, was also considered, entering a field of possible Goldes that included Colleen Dewhurst, Zoe Caldwell, Dorothy Loudon, Marian Seldes, and Beverly Sills. The competition eventually came down to the actresses Lee Grant, whom Mirisch worried had such "finely chiseled features" she might not be believable as a peasant, and Norma Crane, who eventually got the part.

Norma Crane, born Norma Zuckerman in Brooklyn, had performed on Broadway, been in such TV series as *The F.B.I.*, *The Defenders*, and *Gunsmoke* and, most recently, in the Mirisch Company's 1970 feature *They Call Me Mister Tibbs!* "There was something about Norma Crane," Jewison said. "There was a feistiness and a darkness about her. Tevye and Golde have a difficult relationship. Golde has a very strong ego herself as a character, and I got that from Norma."

In addition to his frequent casting director, Lynn Stalmaster, Jewison also brought in Richard Altman, Jerome Robbins's assistant on the Broadway *Fiddler*, to help with casting in New York. Altman knew the Broadway scene, said Los Angeles–based Stalmaster, and the casting director had worked with enough stage actors to know how important that was. "Most theater actors can make the adjustment to film quickly," said Stalmaster. "The idea that they'll come off too theatrical and sound like John Gielgud isn't true. Most of the great actors came out of the theater."

Jewison had hired Molly Picon, the Yiddish theater and film star, as Yente the matchmaker, "because of her reputation," he said. "She was a natural." So, he added, was the actor and acting teacher Paul Mann, who was cast as the butcher, Lazar Wolf. Mann, an early member of the Group Theatre, founded the Paul Mann Actors Workshop in 1952, trained many prominent actors and directors, and seemed perfectly cast as daughter Tzeitel's kindly but rejected suitor. Zvee Scooler, an elderly man with hollowed-out cheeks and expressive eyes who played a small part in *Fiddler* on Broadway, was cast as Anatevka's wise and adaptable rabbi in the film.

It was also in New York that venerable stage actor Louis Zorich was selected to play the Russian constable, a part Stalmaster noted "was a delicate character to handle." Zorich had worked with Jewison before, so

Jewison already knew his acting ability. But the director had another big concern. "He asked me, 'Louis, can you ride a horse?'" Zorich recalled, "and when I said 'yes,' he asked, 'Can you *really* ride a horse?' I said, 'Oh, sure.' Then, the third time he asked, I said, 'No, but there's a stable where I can go because we have a lot of time before the shoot.'" When he got the role, Zurich signed up for ten horseback-riding lessons.

Fiddler would be Zorich's first major film role, and although his parents were originally from Yugoslavia, where the film would be shot, he had some concerns. The evening he got the call from his agent that he had the role, he and his wife, the actress Olympia Dukakis, went off to a workshop they led for theater people. When Zorich started questioning, half-jokingly, the idea of going all the way to Yugoslavia for a film, someone in the workshop said, "Go, you should go. We'll all go with you."

In fact, six couples from the group did indeed go with them to Yugoslavia. On the days Zorich wasn't filming, he and Dukakis, then pregnant with their son Stefan, would work with the group in a little hall in Zagreb.

For the casting of Tevye's three older daughters, said Stalmaster, he hoped to find three young women who didn't necessarily look alike but who complemented each other. Many of *Fiddler*'s Broadway performers were just too old for the film, he observed. They could play the roles onstage, but in a film, they would look "too mature."

Rosalind Harris was performing on Broadway in the *Fiddler* ensemble and as understudy to Bette Midler when she heard about auditions for the film. "Bette said, 'Get your tush down there,'" Harris said, "and I went to Nola Studios where they were holding auditions. My agent couldn't get me in, so I waited there for four hours. At the end of the day, Richard Altman came out, and I said, 'I'm understudying Bette. I *am* Tzeitel.'"

Altman explained to her that they were booking actors through agents and only by appointment. But when she began to leave, Altman took another look at her and "suddenly realized that her tallish figure, dark hair, and oddly appealing face gave her a very Tzeitel-like quality."

Altman told her to come back the following morning and read for the casting team, which she did. "Then someone said, 'Get Jewison on the phone,'" Harris said. "They told me to go have tea, and I had about ten cups. Norman Jewison was there when I came back and he asked me to sing 'Matchmaker,' which I did. He walked around me with his fingers formed like a camera loop to imagine what I would look like through the lens of the camera."

Jewison apparently liked what he saw and sent her on to Stalmaster. Then she waited. "I didn't hear for weeks," Harris said. "I was on Broadway, playing Tzeitel, when one day, in between shows, Lynn Stalmaster called me. He asked me, 'How would you like to play Tzeitel in the film?' After I hung up, I started jumping up and down and screaming for joy, and when I went to do the show that night, I was hoarse."

Also auditioned in New York was Neva Small, later cast as Chava, the youngest daughter. Brought up in a musical family, the seventeen-year-old actress had been performing for years. By the time she auditioned for *Fiddler*, she had appeared in NBC's *The World of Sholom Aleichem* and on Broadway.

In the running for both Chava and Hodel, she had five auditions in New York and California before she was cast. She hadn't finished high school yet and had to appear before a judge and promise to come back after the film. And because she wasn't yet eighteen, she had to go with a guardian; her sister went with her, and the rest of her family joined them in Yugoslavia later to celebrate her eighteenth birthday.

Michele Marsh, the actress who was cast as middle daughter Hodel, had played the part of one of Tevye's younger daughters, Bielke, in *Tevya and his Daughters* when she was in high school. The Los Angeles–based performer was working in a show in San Francisco when a family friend learned that auditions were under way and even called Norman Jewison's secretary for her. In March 1970, Marsh auditioned first with Stalmaster, then with Jewison, and had several screen tests with potential Perchiks.

Then came a call that the director wanted to hear her sing again before a final decision was made. Marsh was sent off to work with conductor/composer John Williams, after which she sang for Jewison. Recalled Marsh: "Norman was a little concerned about the breathiness in my voice, but Johnny said, 'We can work with that.' Norman told me, 'You feel the song. That's what's important.'"

Fiddler may have been Jewison's first musical film, but his prior work in television musicals had showed him the difficulty of finding singers who could also act and move. "Some can sing like a bird but have a problem moving," said Jewison. "It's not relaxed or real. Actors express emotions in a musical form, which is very different than what they do in a straight play."

There were also three male suitors to cast, and applicants were numerous. Stalmaster started in Los Angeles, then moved on to New York and Europe searching for his Motel, Perchik, and Fyedka. On January 8, 1970, alone, six actors each had twenty-minute appointments in Los Angeles for Motel or Perchik, and the list of actors scheduled that day included John Rubinstein, Bob Balaban, and Richard Dreyfuss. In New York, said Stalmaster, he also read Robert De Niro for Perchik, "and, in retrospect, I should have sold him more. Those were the days when he still had to read for a part."

They found their Motel close to home. Leonard Frey, who began in *Fiddler* onstage in the smaller role of Mendel, the rabbi's son, went on to play Motel in the film, as well as onstage. He also had a breakthrough film role as Harold, the birthday boy in the 1970 film *The Boys in the Band*.

The part of Perchik went to Paul Michael Glaser (then known as Michael Glaser), who made his film debut in *Fiddler*, and would, a few years later, achieve stardom as Starsky in the hit ABC-TV cop show *Starsky and Hutch*. Glaser was on Broadway in *Butterflies Are Free* and also performing in the soap opera *Love Is a Many Splendored Thing* when one day he got a call from his agent that Stalmaster had suggested him for *Fiddler*.

Before his audition, the actor received script "sides," or scenes, to prepare, and Glaser couldn't believe what he was reading. He was way too old for the role. "I was twenty-seven at the time, and this was a seventeen-year-old kid in Russia," Glaser said with amusement. "But it was already set up for me to meet Norman Jewison at the Sherry-Netherland Hotel, so I said I'd go meet him. When he opened the door, and asked who I was, I told him my name, and he said, 'You're too old for the role.' I said, 'Yes, that's what I think, too.' Then he said, 'Well, I have forty-five minutes to kill. Come in anyway.'"

Glaser went in, read for Jewison, and apparently impressed him. A few days later, Jewison flew him out to California for a screen test, his first, and Glaser was soon offered the role.

That left the part of Fyedka, the Russian peasant who would win Chava's heart—and break Tevye's. Stalmaster traversed the globe, searching first in Stockholm, later in Rome. "I had a feeling about going to Rome," the casting director said. "The actors were coming to my hotel, and in comes a young man named Raymond Lovelock. He read for me, and I thought, My God, my instinct was right."

Lovelock was, in fact, already well known internationally. According to the film's souvenir program, the handsome young man was at twenty-one voted one of the three most popular young stars in Japan. Neither Japanese nor Russian like his character Fyedka, Lovelock was born in Rome to an Italian mother and English father.

Jewison and company wound up with quite an eclectic group of performers, and actor Glaser speculated it might have to do with his not being Jewish. "You might have had more homogeneity if you had a Jewish director," offered Glaser. "I looked at the daughters, and I thought, Those are sisters? Yet each one brought to it her own bit of charm. Norman, bless his heart, was always trying to do more than what Hollywood had done with musicals in the past."

Next stop, London, to rehearse their movie and record its score.

12

Making Music

n April 1970, cast members flew to London, where Jewison had already established his *Fiddler* base. The director was nicely ensconced at Pinewood Studios, about an hour outside central London, where his office looked out on formal gardens set amid the legendary studio's twenty acres of sound stages, studios, and more.

Jewison, born and raised in Canada, was more than ready to set up house in London for a while. He had been despairing of life in America since the assassinations of President John F. Kennedy, Martin Luther King Jr., and Robert Kennedy, not to mention his being beaten by the police during an anti–Vietnam War demonstration in Los Angeles. Even in its darkest moments, he wrote in his memoir, *Fiddler on the Roof* offered "joy in the music and hope in the exodus."

Jewison and his family lived first in a furnished flat in Kensington, then purchased Sean Connery's old house on Putney Heath. At Pinewood, meanwhile, the director worked with a creative team that included such prominent British craftspeople as film editor Antony Gibbs, cinematographer Oswald Morris, art directors Peter Lamont and Singapore-born Michael Stringer, costume designers Elizabeth Haffenden and Joan Bridge, sound mixer David Hildyard, and others.

It was at Pinewood, too, that everyone met to rehearse dance numbers and songs prior to recording them. Much as Jewison brought in Joseph

Stein for the screenplay, he similarly brought in *Fiddler* stage veteran and Robbins associate Tom Abbott to adapt the original choreography and add new steps where the movie demanded them. "I was a big Jerry Robbins fan," Jewison said. "I got two of his dancers [Abbott and Sammy Dallas Bayes] as choreographers on the film. So we preserved Jerry's choreography in the musical numbers."

Abbott, who had worked with Jerome Robbins on the *Fiddler* stage production as well as on the *West Side Story* film, adapted Robbins's original stage work and added new dance steps for the film. "I was given more dancers to work with than we'd ever had on the stage and much more space," choreographer Abbott said. "It was really like starting fresh."

Aside from one new song written for the film but later cut, the film's songs were those of Bock and Harnick's stage score. But just as *Fiddler*'s new life on film required some new dance sequences and newly written scenes and dialogue, so did it require additional music. Adapting the *Fiddler* score was the job of John Williams, a task which would later win him the first of his five Oscars.

When Jewison contacted Williams about adapting the *Fiddler* score, the composer hadn't seen the stage production but knew the principal songs. He felt those songs had already become part of the culture and was "thrilled, gratified, flattered even, at the idea of being able to contribute to the creation of a film of one of our greatest pieces of American theater."

Williams did piano accompaniment for some of the rehearsals, and noted that Jewison would perform all the parts as he prepared the cast. "Norman moved well," said Williams, "and he really demonstrated attitudes vocally and in lyric readings that the actors willingly adopted. And he could actually sing the parts."

The two men hadn't worked together much before, Williams said, although the composer had done some arrangements for the Judy Garland television show Jewison had directed. Even then, he said, the director "was absolutely fabulous with music and the singers and performers. I thought whoever made the choice of Norman Jewison for this film made a good one."

Jewison felt similarly about having Williams onboard, impressed by not just the composer's talent but also his dedication to the project. Since Jewison had moved his own family to London—where they all stayed for several years afterwards—he clearly appreciated the fact that Williams also brought his family with him and essentially moved to London for a while. He remembered Williams sitting in the front room of his London house, at the grand piano, writing and scoring music for the film.

There was already the well-received score from the stage production, of course, but Jewison needed more music. "I was asking for all kinds of extensions," the director said. "I was asking John to extend the score here, extend the score there."

The film also added a few new scenes that were not in the stage version. For example, there was now a scene where a Russian commander urges the constable to take more action against the Jews. Another is set in Kiev, although shot in Zagreb, where Perchik is giving a revolutionary talk when Russian soldiers come storming in on horseback, sabers aloft.

With the additional scenes, Williams had to come up with a fair amount of music to address situations the play hadn't had to address. The composer had done research in Israel with Jewison earlier, but felt he already had a strong sense of the musical requirements going into the project. "Most musicians with a literate music education will know well the idiom and modalities of Jewish music," the composer said. "It was familiar to me, particularly being an American and having had so many Jewish teachers."

He also was building on composer Jerry Bock's score, which he respected. "Jerry Bock's creation, the blood of all of this, was almost enough," said Williams. "The score was very rich, and with both its influence and my research, I was comfortable working with the material."

Perhaps Williams's greatest creative challenge was writing a long violin cadenza Jewison needed for the required six or seven minutes of film credits. And when that chunk of new music was completed, Jewison needed to hire a very good violinist to play the cadenza and other important violin parts in the film. Jewison turned to Williams one day and asked, point blank: "Who is the best fiddler in the world?" When Williams said "Isaac Stern," the director asked, "How do we get him to play the Fiddler?" Replied Williams: "You ask him."

Jewison, whose producers were still smarting from the idea of costly film shoots in Eastern Europe, made his hiring of Stern similarly non-negotiable. "All the Mirisch brothers saw was money going out the window," said Jewison. "I was going to spend a fortune on somebody to play *background* music. But I became totally committed to Isaac Stern. I even offered to pay for him myself, have the money taken out of my fee for the film. They said, 'No, we couldn't do that,' but that's how strongly I felt about it."

Convincing the incredibly busy Stern was another matter. Jewison decided it had to be done in person and got on a plane to Chicago where Stern was preparing to do a Beethoven concerto with the Chicago Symphony. The director had been told where Stern was staying, so he went straight there, then stood out in the hall listening to Stern rehearse. At the first pause, Jewison knocked on the door. When Stern started playing again, the music got louder and louder until the violinist opened the door, still playing the fiddle.

Stern told him to come in and pour himself a drink, which he did, and then they had a chat. Jewison explained that no, Stern didn't have to actually stand on the roof and play. A dancer would do that. John Williams would teach the dancer all the fingering, and the director would make sure it looked perfect. Stern reminded Jewison that the Fiddler's playing had to be a half tone flat because Chagall's uncle, who would occasionally take to the roof when he had too much to drink, never played the violin very well. No problem. Then Jewison sweetened the offer by explaining that not only was Williams writing a new cadenza for the overture but that Stern would be backed by the London Symphony.

Both earnest and charming, Jewison is not an easy man to turn down, and he could see Stern's eyes light up. When the director told Stern he came all that way "because I wanted to look in your eyes and tell you there's only one fiddle player in the world who should play this, and it's you," Stern replied that he wanted to do it, but he was very booked. The musician brought out his datebook and flipped through pages full of concert dates, including commitments for the three days Jewison needed him in London. It took a while, said Jewison, "but we did finally get him for three days with the London Symphony, and it was wonderful."

Not long after his meeting with Stern, Jewison acquired an unusual souvenir of his time on *Fiddler*. It happened because a friend saw a Chagall watercolor was coming up for auction at Sotheby's, tore the relevant page out of the Sotheby's catalogue, then took a grease pen and wrote on it, "You should have this." The date of the auction coincided with when Jewison would be in London rehearsing the film, and although he'd never before been to an auction, Jewison decided he would attend that one.

When the day for the auction came, Jewison was in rehearsal with Topol and excused himself for a while. That said, he got in the car with his chauffeur, Bert Lister, who had once worked for Noël Coward and had been at several auctions in the past. When they announced the Chagall watercolor, Lister gave him advice on what to do and when to do it. "It was a very hot day, and there I was in my jeans, T-shirt, and tennis shoes with all these international bidders and valuable paintings, and I was bidding on this little Chagall," Jewison said, amused. "When I started bidding, I could see all the heads turn and sensed the auctioneer was trying to make up his mind if he should accept my bid because of the way I was dressed. But I was standing back there with my chauffeur in full uniform, and I decided he probably thought I was a crazy rock star. And I got the watercolor, which is one of my most prized possessions."

When Stern arrived in London, Williams was ready for him. He'd written the cadenza, the variations for solo violin, and the reduced orchestra score for piano and went over to Claridge's Hotel to see Stern. The violinist had a piano in his suite, and the two men rehearsed together. Then, just a day or two later, Stern went out to the recording studio in Buckinghamshire, maybe half an hour from central London, to perform it with the London Symphony.

There were more than a hundred musicians on hand the day they recorded the sound track. In addition to the standard orchestra of about eighty-five members, said Williams, he added other musicians, as well. At one point, that included a mini-orchestra of balalaikas, Russian string instruments, that Williams and Jewison found at the Pushkin Club in London where they had a resident balalaika band. The band was hired

Sholem Aleichem, author of the Tevye stories, with his one-and-a-half-year-old granddaughter, Bel Kaufman, in 1912. Kaufman, author of the 1965 bestseller *Up the Down Staircase,* celebrated her one hundredth birthday on May 10, 2011. *Photo courtesy of Bel Kaufman*

Maurice Schwartz stars in the 1939 Yiddish film *Tevya. Photofest*

Harold Prince produced *Fiddler on the Roof*. Later the most honored producer/director in Broadway history, Prince had won twenty-one Tony Awards by 2013. *Photofest*

The creators: composer Jerry Bock (at piano), *(left to right)* lyricist Sheldon Harnick, librettist Joseph Stein, and director/choreographer Jerome Robbins. *Photofest*

Ticket buyers at Imperial Theater after *Fiddler*'s opening. The producers served fifteen gallons of iced tea to people waiting in line during the afternoon. *Photofest*

Zero Mostel, who created the role of dairyman Tevye, won a Tony Award for his show-stopping portrayal in the 1964 Broadway production of *Fiddler on the Roof. Photofest*

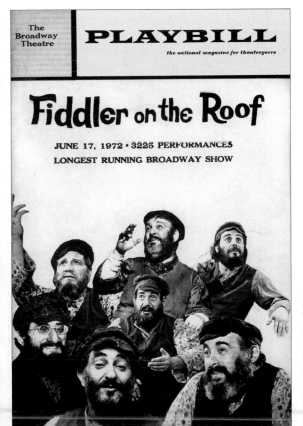

During the show's original, record-breaking Broadway run from 1964 to 1972, seven actors took on the role of Tevye: *(bottom row, left to right)* Jerry Jarrett, Paul Lipson; *(second row)* Jan Peerce, Herschel Bernardi; *(top row)* Luther Adler, Zero Mostel, Harry Goz. *Photofest*

Original Broadway cast of *Fiddler on the Roof* included *(right to left)* Austin Pendleton (Motel), Bert Convy (Perchik), Zero Mostel (Tevye), Maria Karnilova (Golde), Joanna Merlin (Tzeitel), Julia Migenes (Hodel), Tanya Everett (Chava), Marilyn Rogers (Shprintze), and Linda Ross (Bielke). *Photofest*

Villagers in black hats and coats perform Jerome Robbins's fabled "bottle dance" at the wedding party of Tzeitel and Motel in the musical *Fiddler on the Roof. Photofest*

Many actresses had their Broadway debuts in *Fiddler on the Roof,* including *(left to right)* three of the women playing Tevye's daughters: Adrienne Barbeau (Hodel), Bette Midler (Tzeitel), and Tanya Everett (Chava). Everett originated the role of Chava. *Photofest*

Director Norman Jewison and Chaim Topol, portraying dairyman Tevye, talk on the set of the film *Fiddler on the Roof. Photofest*

Chaim Topol is the dairyman Tevye in the film *Fiddler on the Roof*, here leading his lame horse through the countryside and back to his village. *Photofest*

Michele Marsh (Hodel) and Paul Michael Glaser (Perchik) defy tradition in a "modern" dance in the film *Fiddler on the Roof. Photofest*

Neva Small (Chava), Michele Marsh (Hodel), and Rosalind Harris (Tzeitel) dance in a scene from the film *Fiddler on the Roof. Photofest*

Austrian-born Theodore Bikel felt that playing Tevye was like playing his grandfather. *Photofest*

Harvey Fierstein plays Tevye in *Fiddler on the Roof.* Playing his five daughters are *(left to right)* Betsy Hogg, Sally Murphy, Alison Walla, Laura Shoop, and Tricia Pauluccio. *Photo © by Carol Rosegg*

Actor Henry Goodman appears as Tevye in *Fiddler on the Roof,* which opened on May 19, 2007, at the Savoy Theatre, London, produced by Kim Poster for Stanhope Productions. *Photo © 2007 by Catherine Ashmore*

Hisaya Morishige performed the role of *Fiddler on the Roof*'s Tevye nine hundred times in Japan. *Photo courtesy of Toho Co., Ltd.*

Lin-Manuel Miranda *(center)*, creator and star of the Tony-winning musical *In the Heights*, adapted *Fiddler*'s song "To Life" in a special wedding song for his bride, Vanessa Nadal. The wedding video had nearly three million hits on YouTube by early 2013. *Photo by JDZ Photography LLC*

and brought to the recording studio, where its musicians sat in front of the eighty-five-piece orchestra.

Also recorded were more than sixty singers in the film's chorus. Getting a chorus that large to come up with perfect diction was a challenge, Williams said: "You need to hear every word. The British choruses singing in the English language are the best in the world because they sing final consonants, and their articulation is very good. We sometimes had big ensembles, sometimes small, and it was a complicated sound track to put together."

When Isaac Stern arrived at the recording studio, Jewison had his new Chagall watercolor with him and ready. Inside the studio was a huge window of soundproof glass, and Jewison started tapping on the glass. Then he put the artwork up against the glass, and Stern came over to look at it. "I heard him then, on the speakers," recalled Jewison. "He said, 'Chagall is with us.'"

At the time *Fiddler* was made in 1970, singers in musical films prerecorded their songs in the studio, something they usually still do, despite the success of live singing in director Tom Hooper's smash 2012 hit *Les Misérables*. "Everything is prerecorded so everyone has to look like they're singing," Jewison said. "Singing to a recording of one's own voice is an art in itself."

Since the cast would have a few weeks off between London rehearsals and shooting in Yugoslavia, the director wanted them to use their time off fruitfully. Singers received small cassettes of their songs to listen to and play again and again so that when they got to Yugoslavia, the songs would be very familiar. Once they were actually filming, the previously recorded songs were played over loudspeakers as the actors lip-synched their own voices.

When the miming began, few performers worked as hard as Tutte Lemkow, the Norwegian actor and dancer Jewison had chosen to play the movie's rooftop fiddler. "I remember John Williams rehearsing this guy for *hours* with his fingering," Jewison said. "When I said, 'John, he's going to be up on a *roof*,' he told me, 'I know you. You'll end up with a close-up, and his fingers will be on the wrong goddamn keys. All the musicians will know it's a fake.'"

Jewison laughed. "A fake? The guy's not even a fiddle player. He's a dancer. I cast him because of his look and the fact that he could dance. But John even assigned a fiddle player to rehearse with him until the man was totally exhausted. When they hit the playback, he had to follow exactly what Issac Stern had played, and it was very precise. If the bow came off the fiddle an instant too soon, somebody would yell at him about it."

The miming, lip-synching, and more would begin in Yugoslavia on August 10th.

13

Shooting the Movie

By the time everyone arrived in Yugoslavia in early August 1970, the sets were built and ready for them. There, in three tiny villages south of Zagreb, the cast and crew were expected to spend more than three months on location.

The fictional town of Anatevka was emerging in the Yugoslavian countryside courtesy of production designer Robert Boyle. Boyle had already worked with Norman Jewison on several films, including *The Russians Are Coming, the Russians Are Coming,* and *The Thomas Crown Affair,* two of Jewison's biggest hits.

The Yugoslavian village of Martinska Ves stood in for the Russian part of Anatevka. Lekenik, with its wood structures, was the site of Anatevka, where new construction would hopefully look very similar to existing buildings. In Mala Gorica they built the marketplace—apparently so real-looking that during filming a local resident actually tried to buy a horse—and the synagogue.

Boyle worried at first that he and his team were "starting from scratch." While Yugoslavia did have those wonderful little villages, they were somewhat different from the Russian shtetls of *Fiddler*'s story. Boyle and his crew would need to create a marketplace and town square, build Tevye a farm and farmyard, construct a proper synagogue, and, they would soon learn, pray for snow.

Fortunately, many of the area's wooden houses closely resembled houses in some areas in Poland, the production designer said, and he found the peasant cultures "generally similar. A milkman in a small village in Yugoslavia had the same methods of working and living that a peasant would have in the Ukraine or in Poland."

Boyle also found that the Yugoslav workers doing carpentry and masonry were good-natured and very hard workers. He recalled that they not only would sing and dance, but they "worked their tails off." He was also impressed that when they finished a building on the set, they would put a little cut tree on top. "It's a sign of life," he observed.

The production bought up old barns made of aged oak timber, and "extraordinary" local workers used some material from the old barns to build the shtetl synagogue, Boyle said. While wooden synagogues in Europe had been burned down by the Nazis, Boyle was able to find drawings of those synagogues and create a composite for the one they would build in Anatevka.

When writer Herb Lightman, longtime editor of *American Cinematographer*, arrived on the set, he found something "straight out of a painting by Marc Chagall and looking as though it had been there slowly falling down for centuries." He observed that buildings from the nineteenth century were left untouched, while others had false fronts added.

One Yugoslav cottage was used as both exterior set and the location's production office, Lightman reported. Some of the other cottages still had the actual inhabitants living inside, Lightman said, noting they "gathered in fascinated groups each night to watch the shooting."

The actors, too, were impressed by the set. Louis Zorich, playing the Russian constable, recalled that "everything about it was incredible. I'm not Jewish, but it felt like a shtetl. Every detail. When I went on the set, I felt I was right there at that time."

Putting the newly built Anatevka on film was the job of cinematographer Oswald Morris, a man who would later win an Oscar for his effort. Morris had "swotted up the script" during an Italian holiday and felt "more than ready" for what he called "one of the biggest tests of my career. Thereafter, when we were actually filming, I felt I knew the script better than Norman himself."

Morris's first challenge was to come up with a way to best capture the earthen colors he saw everywhere—in clothes, houses, even faces. So while Boyle and company were finishing up their sets, Morris did some color testing. When he wasn't able to find colored gauzes to get the sepia brown effect he wanted, he used women's silk stockings, a technique that worked well when he did the film *Goodbye, Mr. Chips*. The cinematographer sent an associate to Zagreb to get ladies' stockings in the largest sizes available, so they could use the tops of the stockings and not have the seams interfere with the shot.

Morris tested his makeshift gauze by shooting the three daughters, in costume, as well as some interior and exterior shots. He then rushed the film to London and back. Morris liked what he saw and felt confident of his decision when he showed the footage to Jewison. After half an hour of looking at the color tests, wrote Morris in his memoir, Jewison said, "Ossie, that's it! That's the way our *Fiddler* should look!"

At the end of some very long days, cast and crew would head back to Zagreb, today the largest city and capital of the Republic of Croatia. Then the second-largest city in Yugoslavia, Zagreb offered far more amenities than the villages less than an hour away.

Topol, Jewison, and a few others stayed elsewhere, but most of the actors settled in at the Hotel Esplanade Inter-Continental, which billed itself as the "jewel of Zagreb." According to the hotel's brochure at the time, Zagreb was a city "at the crossroads of highways leading to Italy and Austria, Greece and the romantic Adriatic Coast," and the hotel was nothing less than "the hub of the city's social life and home of international travelers." Waiters in native costume served native dishes, the casino hosted games of chance, and everything was close at hand, from news to currency exchange.

Actress Molly Picon made the most of those international amenities. When the actress wasn't needed on the set, she wrote a friend, she and her husband, the actor Jacob (Yonkel) Kalich, were "hanging around the hotel reading the *Herald Tribune*, London *Times*, and *Manchester Guardian*."

PERFORMERS IN BOTH FILM AND STAGE PRODUCTION

Zvee Scooler was cast as Mordcha, the innkeeper, in the show and, later, as the rabbi in the film, *Fiddler on the Roof.*

Leonard Frey, who began in *Fiddler* onstage in the smaller role of Mendel, the rabbi's son, went on to play Motel in the film, as well as onstage.

Sometimes they would go see foreign films with Yugoslavian subtitles, she wrote, or even "take long walks into town, up the hills and through the parks."

The actresses playing the three daughters would visit together and spend evenings in one another's rooms. Before filming, they agreed among themselves that, since they were playing European women, they shouldn't shave their underarms or legs. But when they leaned back on a bed in one scene, Jewison saw what they hadn't done and stopped the shot. According to Rosalind Harris (Tzeitel) the director yelled, "'Stop! Cut! . . . Take them off the set! Shave their pits!'"

The three young women and Paul Michael Glaser would ride from the hotel to the set with a driver who Glaser swore was a dead ringer for Nikita Khrushchev. Transportation was generally in Mercedes driven by retired police officers, although according to Morris, Topol didn't use them, saying that on principle he declined German cars. A large Volvo was reportedly shipped to Yugoslavia just for him.

Topol also brought religious rituals with him to Yugoslavia. His family was on location with him, and on Friday nights, Jewison would attend their Sabbath dinner. "I never work on Yom Kippur and pray Rosh Hashanah won't fall on a working day," Topol said. "The Jewish tradition was part of the atmosphere of the film."

What was missing from the film atmosphere, however, was snow. Asked what was his greatest challenge on the film, Jewison would always reply that it was the weather. The year before they were shooting, there were huge snow drifts on the ground and cloudy skies above, and they were not worried about creating Russian winters for their film. But when they were scheduled to shoot the cold, snowy scenes, there was nothing but sunshine.

"I stood in snow up to my knees the year before at the same location on the same date," Jewison said. "When I came back a year later to shoot the picture, the bloody flowers were blooming. When that happens, it's a nightmare, because nature is not cooperating. It was really heartbreaking for me, and a big disappointment of the location."

Even if snow did fall every so often, it wasn't enough to make any impact. They needed to have at least the illusion of snow, however, so they imported polystyrene granules to simulate snow. But the government nixed the idea, said Morris, saying that polystyrene "in any form would pollute the soil on which the peasants' livelihood depended."

Then the production team learned that nearby marble quarries created marble dust during cutting. Unlike the polystyrene, said Morris, the dust did not pollute the environment. When the production team asked local authorities if they could use various sizes of marble powder and granules for hedges, ditches, and roads, they got all the permissions they needed.

All the snow in the movie is marble dust, and sometimes it even worked psychologically for the cast. (Glaser recalled that when they added the marble dust to look like snow, "the temperature immediately felt like it dropped.") And when the weather wasn't cold enough for the actors' breath to be visible, Morris would ask them to suck ice cubes until the clapperboard went down, then spit out the cubes and act as it was very, very cold outside.

This was a particularly inventive group of people. Consider, for instance, the many scenes where Topol was shot talking to God. Jewison and company needed to come up with a way that Topol would always look at the exact same spot, and their solution was pretty unusual.

"The first time we do the shot and he talks to God, we establish where he would look," Jewison explained. "I remember getting a stick and putting a piece of white cardboard on it, then moving it up and down and watching his eyes through the camera. When he does a take, it has to be the same spot, or it wouldn't look right. Finally, someone drew a star of David on the cardboard so Topol would always be able to see his country's flag; he would look there and feel he was talking to God."

Zagreb stood in for the film's scene in Kiev, and members of the Yugoslavian army on horseback, sabers drawn, assumed the roles of soldiers disrupting a rebellion. Jewison wanted to have a horse ride up the steps to the raised platform where revolutionary Perchik was rallying townspeople. "He was going to use a stuntman, but I said, 'It's okay, Norman, I worked with horses. I can do that," recalled Glaser, who was playing Perchik. 'So I go to play the scene, and this guy comes galloping up on the horse, and by the time the horse reached me, I realized it was a *big* horse. It proceeded to knock me down."

Glaser had a similar experience when they were filming the Russian "mischief" at Tzeitel and Motel's wedding. Once again Jewison offered a stuntman as stand-in when Perchik got hit over the head with a candlestick, and once again Glaser declined. He'd be fine. "So they gave me a little padding in my hat," said Glaser. "Then the guy came up and smacked me, and it was really intense. I don't think it knocked me out, but it came close."

Topol, in turn, had a terrible toothache when they were filming "If I Were a Rich Man." If the audience caught "a touch of angst" to the song, he said, "it comes from my teeth, not from my heart."

Topol also appreciated how Jewison, too, threw himself into the work. "There's a big difference between theater and filmmaking," the actor said. "In theater, when you play a scene, you have the reaction of an audience— you know you will get a laugh or applause or whatever. When you do it in front of a camera, it is a very different atmosphere. There's no audience.

"But with Norman, it was incredible. *He* played the audience. When it was a serious scene, you would hear his voice full of tears. When it was a comic scene, you would hear him laughing. He was absolutely *replacing* the audience. And there could be fifteen or twenty takes. With an audience, you can't tell the same joke twenty times and expect them to react. Norman would react *twenty times*. It is unique for a director to really be with you as an actor that way."

While many villagers were played by Jewish actors that Jewison cast in London, the director said most of the extras were Yugoslavian. "Look at these faces," he said at one point. Morris, too, raved about the authenticity of the people who populated their set. "On a film of this scale the crowds do play an important part," he told a reporter who visited the set. "It would be very difficult to find faces like these anywhere else."

They also had to age several of the actors, including not just Topol, but also Golde (Norma Crane) and Lazar Wolfe (Paul Mann). Aging their Tevye was a bit more complex given Topol's relative youth. Every morning, said Jewison, makeup people would stop by his trailer to clip white hairs from his beard and apply them to Topol's eyebrows.

That wasn't the only cosmetic change on the set. Jewison thought Michele Marsh would look more Jewish if she had brown eyes rather than blue and had her fitted with brown contact lenses. But the actress couldn't tolerate them and was squinting badly, she said. So once they discovered Rosalind Harris, playing Tzeitel, had similar blue eyes, they let it be. Actor Glaser had more success with the contact lenses that turned his blue eyes brown and which he wore in the film.

Yugoslavian residents employed as extras were paid additional money to let their beards grow out. One American extra even received a letter from the film's assistant director, Terry Nelson, encouraging him to develop "the rugged look of the man from the shtetl in the Ukraine: tanned, full-bearded, long-haired. Don't be afraid of too much hair—whatever we can't use, we can chop off. The suntan on the face and hands will aid us greatly."

Apparently so. "Our experience in Yugoslavia suggested that anyone with a sufficient growth of beard need only don a black hat or even a kippah, not to speak of a beaver hat, to look Jewish," Topol wrote in his autobiography. The actor credited Jewison with being able "to coax such a performance even out of his extras that by the time they were finished they began to look Jewish."

All three of Jewison's children appeared in the film at one point or another, and so did Topol's children. His youngest daughter, the future stage actress Adi Topol Margalith, said she liked that when the match-maker showed up with two young boys in one scene, "one was my brother." Then a toddler, she also later recalled her affection for, among other things, a goat that roamed the set.

Indeed, Jewison had a lot of nonhumans to deal with on the set. Glaser was sure that Jewison brought in a butterfly wrangler to manage all the butterflies in the dance scene by the river with Hodel and Perchik (actors Marsh and Glaser), while the director takes pride in knowing his direct intervention saved a Yugoslavian horse from the glue factory.

Then there were the geese and pigs. Just *herding* the geese was an enormous problem, Jewison said, rolling his eyes. "Geese all move together and you have to get a goose boy, somebody in the village who knows how to handle the geese. All the geese came out of the houses early in the morning, and I could never figure out how they'd know where to go back to the evening. I asked, 'The geese come back to the house like dogs?' And the farmers said, 'Yes.' 'How about the pigs?' I asked. 'Same thing,' said the farmers. All the animals knew where they belonged."

Louis Zorich had augmented riding lessons he took earlier with more training in Yugoslavia from the film's horse wrangler, so by the time they shot his scenes on horseback, he felt competent about his riding. But when it came time for the constable to oversee havoc at Tzeitel and Motel's wedding, there were some problems. The shot was a close-up of man and horse, and the horse wouldn't stay still. So Jewison got several crew members to quickly build a fence around the horse so it couldn't move. "Here I was, this Cossack, and I couldn't control the horse," Zorich recalled with some embarrassment. "But the fence worked."

As Jewison was about to shoot the scene where the Russian constable tells Tevye the Jews must leave Anatevka, Jewison approached Zorich to chat. "He said, 'You and Tevye grew up together in this town; you went to school together and you played together. So when it came time for you to chase the Jews out of Anatevka, it wasn't easy.' That made a world of difference for me. When I said I had my orders, it was a very emotional statement for me to make. People told me that as I was on my horse watching them get ready to leave, Norman did a close-up so you could see in my eyes the pain I felt chasing the kid I grew up with out of town."

Neva Small, the teenager playing Chava, was also overwhelmed with emotion on the set. When Tevye spurns her for wanting to marry the Russian Fyedka, "It was a heavy scene," she said. "And when we were done, I went behind a tree and wept. It was release and relief."

Indeed Jewison, too, was sometimes caught up in the power of Joseph Stein's screenplay. A documentary that accompanied *Fiddler*'s Collector's Edition in 2006 shows the director not only mouthing the words to songs along with his actors, but also feeling their characters' losses. When he was shooting the final exodus from Anatevka, one of the most moving scenes in the film, he was wiping away tears.

The set was several miles outside Zagreb, in fairly untouched countryside. Hardly anyone spoke English, said actress Marsh, and many nearby homes lacked electricity. Glaser, in turn, wondered aloud if all the Yugoslavian extras in the film were wearing costumes or their own clothes, which looked a great deal like the costumes.

"I remember going through the town of Mala Gorica where they built Anatevka, and you really couldn't tell where you left one town to go to the other," recalled Glaser. "In Yugoslavia at that time, they had just started driving cars, and most of the transportation was by horse-drawn wagons with rubber tires. There was just one main street and if you walked through the town, you would come into where Anatevka was built."

But there was one big reason you knew you were on a movie set, Glaser added, and that was a big inflatable hangar the production team had handy for use as a cover for the set in case of bad weather. The hangar, however, was loaded with problems. While it worked well when there was electricity, the electricity was unreliable, said cinematographer Morris. They could return in the morning to see the hangar had collapsed with everything inside, and they'd have to pump it all up again.

An emergency generator helped, but there were more challenges. Even if it wasn't hot outside, "the hangar was a red-hot oven," said Morris. "With no ventilation whatsoever, we soon had sweat pouring from every part of our bodies. It was even worse for the actors, whose faces were glistening within thirty seconds, and we had to stop frequently to make running repairs to their makeup."

To cool things down, they tried spraying the outside of the hangar with water, courtesy of a local fire brigade. But the water hitting the rubber outside not only made a lot of noise but it also raised the hangar's humidity inside.

Within the huge inflated tent, they had built the interior of Tevye's farmhouse, a replica of the barn, and some other little sets, and production designer Boyle felt it didn't work too well for that, either. The rain made it sound like "being on the inside of a drum," said Boyle—Glaser analogized it "to being inside a tin can"—and many interiors they'd hoped to do in Yugoslavia wound up being done later on a soundstage at Pinewood Studios back in London.

They were fortunately able to film in Yugoslavia the evocative scene of villagers marching at sundown in a wedding procession lit by candles. According to Morris, it had to occur during what he called "the magic hour . . . about twenty minutes in the Mediterranean when you can catch the glowing sun as it starts to bury itself in the horizon." Using three cameras—one manned by Jewison—Morris and colleagues had just that tiny block of time "to light sixty candles at the start of the procession, film the procession coming towards the camera . . . blow out the candles and then, having relit the candles, reshoot the scene before the sun disappeared behind the hills."

Morris added a little of his own magic, as well, Jewison told Scott Simon on NPR's *Weekend Edition*. The cinematographer "put a small hole with a battery and a tiny light on the inside of the candle that they could hide with their hand, which would reflect up into their faces."

By fall, when they shot the scene, the nights were getting colder, affecting the bottle dance that followed the wedding. "Dew settling on the pressed clay surface of Tevye's yard made it very treacherous underfoot," said Morris. They also didn't have enough "fuller's earth to throw on the damp ground to give the impression of dust flying as the dancers leapt and twirled." So they rebuilt the set at Pinewood and did the bottle dance there.

Writing to a friend from the set, actress Picon joked about what she called "the glamour of movie-making on location." At that time, she wrote, she'd been doing a night scene from 2:00 p.m. to 2:00 a.m. "in mud and rain and biting cold, and I bought me long johns and sweaters and carry a little flask of whiskey."

Later, in London, the actress told *New York Times* reporter Bernard Weinraub, "This is like a document of historical significance. It's part of a world that's gone. What began with *Fiddler* and the life in the nineteen hundreds ended, finally, with Hitler. . . . The world that we're portraying has been destroyed."

Jewison and team returned to London in early December, jetting in from Zagreb by charter, with shooting expected just two days later. Back at Pinewood, they shot the bottle dance and other interior sequences that they were unable to do in Yugoslavia, as well as the complicated Tevye dream sequence.

When he finally got done with the shoot and a later minishoot to try again, unsuccessfully, for snow in Yugoslavia, Jewison wrote a friend about the experience. "I finished shooting in Yugoslavia two weeks ago. After all the delays in forcing the extension of time and the return to Yugoslavia, I still missed the fucking snow. It had melted five days before we returned. We got nothing but bright sunshine so I had to scramble around and wait for clouds and so on, trying to get as bleak a feeling as possible. I must say, I'm glad it's over. After seven continuing months, I was beginning to feel my age. It really has been a brute of a film to shoot.

"I have just spent two weeks in Switzerland skiing out all my hostilities and fatigue and depression and feel almost whole again," wrote the director. "Had great snow. . . ."

14

Opening the Movie

The world premiere of *Fiddler on the Roof* was on November 3, 1971, at New York's Rivoli Theatre. The evening began with a cocktail party at UA chairman Arthur Krim's home, which producer Mirisch described as being peopled with "a glittering assemblage of press, film, artistic, and political personalities." It concluded with a "gala champagne supper dance" at the Americana Hotel, where the event's honorary committee included Governor and Mrs. Nelson Rockefeller, Senator and Mrs. Jacob Javits, and Mayor and Mrs. John Lindsay.

"What an opening it was," actress Michele Marsh wrote her mother. "Red carpet, crowds of people, cameras flashing right and left, TV and radio interviews. Absolutely incredible. We were surrounded by celebrities. Helen Hayes, Maureen Stapleton, Carol Channing—so many. And the big party dinner after was so posh, you couldn't believe it."

Opening night was a benefit for the Will Rogers Memorial Hospital in Saranac Lake, New York. Television cameras were on hand to chronicle the evening, which also drew a group outside the theater called Student Struggle for Soviet Jewry, which waved banners for the TV cameras that said "Let Tevye's Children Go." They mingled with people hoping to catch a look at the celebrities.

After the movie, about one thousand of the evening's fourteen hundred theatergoers moved on to the Americana Hotel for a $150-a-person (or $200 for center aisle seats) champagne dinner dance. At the party were such people as Abe Fortas, the former Supreme Court justice, and Diane von Furstenberg. Dinner included petite marmite Henry IV (consommé with vegetables), and poussin en casserole royale (boned and stuffed squab). There was also a fashion show by Swakara, a fur company that reportedly had underwritten part of the cost of the supper, which included such "models" as Barbara Walters. Overheard at the opening-night benefit: "Everybody's Jewish these days."

Less pricey charity benefits followed for the next several nights. On the second night, the evening benefited the Stanley M. Isaacs Neighborhood Center, which included dinner before the film not at a grand hotel, but rather at the Horn & Hardart automat near the theater. The movie was twenty-five dollars for adults and ten dollars for children, with a buffet dinner of roast beef and more for seven dollars. Scheduled the third night was a benefit for the Greek Orthodox Charities, with a hundred-dollar tab for the film and supper.

Then came the reviews. The major critics lined up eight favorable, six negative, and two mixed, according to *filmfacts,* a publication of the American Film Institute. Some people liked Topol, some didn't; one critic said Isaac Stern's playing "practically lifts you out of your seat" while another scorned the use of "such a high-culture hero." Molly Picon's Yente got raves from some critics, brickbats from others. One critic noted it was "hard to resist the film's invitation to a nice cry," while another simply pegged it a "nine-handkerchief" film.

The *Los Angeles Times'* critic Charles Champlin lauded its artistry, entertainment value, and "inspired craftsmanship." *Saturday Review*'s Hollis Alpert praised both Jewison and Topol, calling the film probably "the most satisfying musical film ever."

Writing in *The New Yorker*, Pauline Kael also complimented Jewison and Topol, but she didn't stop there. Although she did have some problems with the film, commenting on unrealized characters and camera-heavy work on the dancing—complaints other critics also had—she found "the movie has an overall ongoing vitality that is overwhelming." It was for Kael "the most *powerful* movie musical ever made."

New York Times critic Vincent Canby, however, had many problems with the film. Canby did like the score, saying it was a "mixed marriage—between Tin Pan Alley and Jewish folk music—that really works," but that was about it for praise. He objected to what he called "visual and aural grandeur" too rich for the film's characters and criticized bringing in not just Isaac Stern but the London Symphony. Canby found the show too literal and too epic, overwhelming not just Aleichem but the Jerome Robbins choreography. With the addition of real houses, animals, and villages, he wrote, "they've not just opened up the play, they've let most of the life out of it."

Newsweek's Paul D. Zimmerman spared almost no one, concluding that "it is with a sizable thud that *Fiddler on the Roof* reaches the screen." And Molly Haskell, writing in *The Village Voice*, complained the film was too long and too literal, not going much beyond "a reverent re-creation of the stage production."

The trades, however, emphasized the film's box office potential. *Variety* critic "Land." noted it was still running on Broadway and came "with the impetus of preordained want-to-see. In short, *Fiddler on the Roof* is a powerhouse attraction." His conclusion: "Essentially the verdict is one of boffo box office."

Fiddler opened in Los Angeles on November 5th at the Fox Wilshire Theater, in Boston on November 10th, and around the world by year's end. Argentina came first in late November, followed by Sweden, the UK, Italy, Denmark, West Germany, Finland, and Japan in December. Moviegoers saw *El violinista en el tejado* in Spanish-speaking countries, *Un violon sur le toit* in France, *Il violinista sul tetto* in Italy, and *Viulunsoittaja katolla* in Finland.

The actresses playing Tevye's three older daughters attended many of these openings. In December, the three daughters left New York's festivities to visit nearly one foreign city a day, jetting off first to Tokyo and London, then scheduled for Stockholm, Paris, Hamburg, Munich, Zurich, Geneva, Barcelona, and Madrid.

Neva Small, who played Chava in the film, recalled the fascination with *Fiddler* in Japan. The Japanese were particularly taken with Ray-

ACADEMY AWARD NOMINATIONS AND WINS, 1972

Won:
- Best Cinematography—Oswald Morris
- Best Sound—Gordon K. McCallum, David Hildyard
- Best Music (Scoring: Adaptation and Original Song Score)—John Williams

Nominated:
- Best Picture—Norman Jewison
- Best Actor in a Leading Role—Topol
- Best Actor in a Supporting Role—Leonard Frey
- Best Director—Norman Jewison
- Best Art Direction–Set Decoration—Robert F. Boyle, Michael Stringer, Peter Lamont

mond Lovelock, who played her Russian beau Fyedka in the film and was already a big star in Japan. "If you look at the marketing then in Japan, it looked like *Gone With the Wind*, with Raymond Lovelock holding me in his arms," the actress said several years later. "Tevye is pictured in a corner. It was Raymond Lovelock in the Fyedka story."

In Israel, Jewison was seated next to Golda Meir, then prime minister of Israel, at the film's premiere there. The director said that during one point in the film, he saw the prime minister wipe away a tear.

Fiddler on the Roof received eight Oscar nominations. It was up for Best Picture against *A Clockwork Orange*, *The French Connection*, *The Last Picture Show*, and *Nicholas and Alexandra*. Topol was nominated as Best Actor, along with Peter Finch, Gene Hackman, Walter Matthau, and George C. Scott. Other nominations included Best Directing, Best Actor in a Supporting Role (Leonard Frey as Motel), Art Direction, Cinematography, Best Music (Scoring: Adaptation and Original Song Score), and Best Sound.

The 44th Academy Awards ceremony, honoring 1971 films, was held April 10, 1972, at Los Angeles' Dorothy Chandler Pavilion. The evening's big winner was not *Fiddler* but instead *The French Connection*, which took home Oscars for Best Picture, Best Directing for William Friedkin, and Best Actor for its star, Gene Hackman. Screenwriter Ernest Tidyman received his award from Tennessee Williams, and Jerry Greenberg received the Film Editing award from Jill St. John and Red Buttons.

Fiddler won three of its eight nominations: Best Cinematography (Oswald Morris), Best Music (Scoring: Adaptation and Original Song Score) (John Williams), and Best Sound (Gordon K. McCallum and David Hildyard). McCallum, who received his award from Sandy Duncan and Michael York, called *Fiddler* "a film of which I shall always be proud."

John Williams received his Oscar from Betty Grable and Dick Haymes. In his acceptance speech, he thanked "for all of us" Harnick and Bock for their score, which "has enriched all of our lives"; he further thanked Jewison, violinist Stern, and his colleague Alexander "Sandy" Courage.

"It was an opportunity and challenge to get a classic piece of American theater transposed to film in a way that did honor to the material itself," Williams said many years and Oscars later. "It's a fabulous show with a great score. To put it on film is to be given the opportunity to immortalize it, and we all felt it had to be made as well as human hands could make it. That was the fun and the challenge and responsibility of it, musically and dramatically. It has given me joy to this day. It was a great life experience and one I wouldn't trade for anything."

Cinematographer Oswald Morris was working on the film *Sleuth* in England and couldn't attend. Instead it was director Jewison who received the Oscar from presenters Ann-Margret and John Gavin. As he praised Morris and thanked the Academy, Jewison confirmed that yes, it was true that the cinematographer shot the picture through a lady's silk stocking.

"It was entirely appropriate that Norman should collect the Oscar on my behalf," wrote Morris in his memoir. "He was the inspiration of one of my most rewarding creative experiences."

The creative team won other awards as well that year, including the Golden Globe for Best Motion Picture (Musical or Comedy). Morris also won for Best Cinematography from the British Society of Cinematographers, and Stein won a Writers Guild Award for his screenplay. Topol won a Golden Globe (Best Motion Picture Actor—Musical/Comedy) as well as a David di Donatello Award at the Taormina Film Fest in Sicily in 1972, which he noted is not just the Italian Oscar but also "it is made of solid gold."

A disappointed Norman Jewison, who had the customary acceptance speech written and in his pocket, fared much better at the 71st Oscars. On March 21, 1999, he received the prestigious Irving G. Thalberg Memorial Award, presented to him on the same Dorothy Chandler Pavilion stage by Nicolas Cage, which was given for a body of work that included not just such earlier work as *In the Heat of the Night*, *The Russians Are Coming*, and *Fiddler*, but also the films that came later—*Jesus Christ Superstar*, *Moonstruck*, . . . *And Justice for All*, and others.

By 1999, Jewison's films collectively had won ten Academy Awards and received forty-five nominations. He personally had been nominated three times for Oscars.

Jewison considered *Fiddler* his most popular film, and the film's appeal mirrored that of the stage production. While the film cost more than $9 million to produce, it was the most profitable film in the history of United Artists at that point, according to producer Mirisch, and earned $50 million in film rentals in its initial release.

In his 2008 memoir, Mirisch wrote that the film is an "evergreen"; it doesn't age and continues to be "exceedingly popular" in the home video market. Among his conclusions for its success: "The love of a father for his daughters, his caring for every nuance of their lives, and their respect and caring for their parents said much to a great many people, particularly in the aftermath of the Vietnam War and the hippie movement."

Fiddler also launched a Jewison family tradition. The director sang "Sunrise, Sunset" at his daughter's wedding, and when he remarried in 2010, he played it again at his own wedding. Neither he nor his wife, the writer Lynne St. David-Jewison, are Jewish, but they were married under a chuppah by a rabbi Jewison met when her synagogue screened the film.

"I had asked the rabbi, 'Can you marry a goy?'" said Jewison. "She said she could marry anybody, but it's got to be a Jewish wedding. And it was just that."

Around the time of the film's fortieth anniversary, it was included in a Jewison retrospective held by the Film Society of Lincoln Center. Introducing Jewison and lyricist Sheldon Harnick for a Q&A following the film, moderator Josh Strauss said to Jewison, "For a guy who isn't Jewish, you made the best Jewish movie ever made." Harnick added his own compliment, saying he'd heard "that the cast in Yugoslavia was so happy with your work they made you an honorary Jew and changed your name to Norman Christianson."

Part 4

THE PHENOMENON

15

All Those Tevyes

By the time the film was released in the fall of 1971, another prominent actor had taken a place among the notable Tevyes onstage.

Leonard Nimoy's turn playing Tevye came about almost accidentally. In 1971, he had grown a beard for a part he had coming up in a western, and while in New York, he decided to stop by and talk with his new theatrical agent. "After we talked for a few minutes, he looked at me and asked, 'How would you like to play Tevye in *Fiddler on the Roof*?' I was immediately attracted to the idea, so he made a call to a producer doing a summer production, and I went directly to an audition. Since I'd never seen the show, I did a very mediocre audition. I went to see the show that night, auditioned again, and they hired me."

Nimoy toured with *Fiddler* for eight weeks to cities in Ohio, Massachusetts, and upstate New York (and, later, did another production for a week in Atlanta). The actor, who had performed in Yiddish theater as a young man, said it was "an enormously emotional experience. My folks came from a shtetl in Russia and when I broke out in *Star Trek*, they were interested but it was a world they didn't understand. When I appeared in *Fiddler*, they got it. It was a homecoming for me.

"I've done a lot of work I've forgotten, but *Fiddler* is very much in my brain. I can remember the theater, the audiences. The cast, when we were closing, gave me a pair of candlesticks engraved with a blessing. I said if I never acted again, it would be okay—that's how powerful the experience was for me. Everything I had invested in the art form and everything I was as a person came together in that production."

It was also a personal experience for Vienna-born Theodore Bikel. Bikel's father would read aloud Sholem Aleichem stories and plays after dinner, in Yiddish. His father's father came from that era and that area of Eastern Europe, and Bikel had gone there summers as a boy. When he later wound up playing Tevye, said Bikel, "I felt I was playing my own grandfather. It was like taking an old garment out of the closet that I hadn't worn for a long time."

Neither Bikel nor Topol played Tevye in the first Broadway incarnation of the show, but seven other men did. One after another came Zero Mostel, Luther Adler, Herschel Bernardi, Harry Goz, Jerry Jarrett, Paul Lipson, and Jan Peerce, several of them doubling back over the years to play again a part that was too good to pass up.

Luther Adler was Mostel's first successor, having taken the stage a few times for him earlier. Adler, who made his acting debut in Yiddish theater as a child, was the son of Yiddish actor Jacob Adler and brother of actress and acting teacher Stella Adler. An early member of the fabled Group Theatre, the actor made his musical debut in the show, but he didn't stay long on Broadway.

Herschel Bernardi, who also got his start in Yiddish theater with his family, took over from Adler in November 1965, and played the part hundreds of times on Broadway and on tour over the next several years. By the time he reprised the part at Lincoln Center in 1981, he guessed he had played Tevye "maybe one thousand times."

Over the course of those performances, Bernardi won the heart of lyricist Harnick. "Zero was unquestionably the funniest Tevye, but the best for me was always Herschel Bernardi. Herschel could sing, was disciplined, and had a wonderful sense of comedy. He was a fine actor. He had everything."

Bernardi was succeeded first by his understudy, Harry Goz, then by Jerry Jarrett, then by Paul Lipson, Mostel's original understudy. The seventh Tevye, Metropolitan Opera tenor Jan Peerce, stayed just a few months in the show.

Paul Lipson returned, becoming the last Tevye in *Fiddler*'s original

Broadway run, and he did so saying, "between me and Tevye there was still some unfinished business." The actor, who also subbed as Tevye for several of his predecessors, had played Tevye more than two thousand times by his death in 1996.

Musician Ron Jannelli, who stayed with *Fiddler*'s original Broadway orchestra for six years, played for them all. "Each one had his own style," remembered Jannelli. "Zero was always my favorite, but it was such a great part that they all could do it well."

Audience members, too, came back again and again, watching the parade of Tevyes. Rev. Joshua Ellis, formerly a Broadway press agent, first saw the show on March 3, 1965, his sixteenth birthday, with the original cast. He also saw it with Adler, Bernardi, Goz, Lipson, and Bikel. "Who doesn't see *Fiddler on the Roof* over and over again?" asked Ellis. "It's one of the great musicals. The Tevyes I saw were reasonably alike, but to my thinking, they have never been able to hit the places that Zero Mostel could hit. His arms were short and his body round—the part was custom-fitted to a very unusual little body. Jerome Robbins created a suit for him that fit perfectly."

That's the way it works, explained Harvey Fierstein, the actor/playwright who would later play Tevye himself on Broadway. "As an author of musicals, I know what happens when you're in rehearsals," said the Tony-winning librettist of *La Cage aux Folles*, *Kinky Boots*, and other shows. "The reason there is only one original is that as you're rehearsing, if the actor playing the role doesn't get a laugh, the line is cut. It might have been a great line for Topol or for Herschel Bernardi, but if it didn't work for Zero, it got cut. So the show got molded to Zero."

Actually, long before Mostel came along, there was a real milkman named Tevye who had no daughters at all but happened to deliver milk, cheese, and sour cream to Sholem Aleichem. According to Aleichem's granddaughter, Bel Kaufman, her grandfather liked to sit and talk with him. When Aleichem started writing in the Jewish press a series of stories about Tevye the milkman, said Kaufman, "Tevye became a celebrity in the town. When he'd bring the milk and cheese, people would say, 'Come in, Rebe Tevye, have a glass of tea, Rebe Tevye.' Of course, Harnick, Bock, and Stein wrote a totally different Tevye."

The Broadway Theatre

PLAYBILL

the national magazine for theatregoers

Fiddler on the Roof

JUNE 17, 1972 • 3225 PERFORMANCES
LONGEST RUNNING BROADWAY SHOW

Seven actors played Tevye in *Fiddler*'s original long-running Broadway production. One after another came:

- Zero Mostel
- Luther Adler
- Herschel Bernardi
- Harry Goz
- Jerry Jarrett
- Paul Lipson
- Jan Peerce

How does one describe the Tevye of Harnick, Bock, and Stein? The English actor Henry Goodman, who played Tevye on London's West End in 2007, called him "a teddy bear and a tyrant. He's Moses and a mouse. He wants his daughters to have a future, like any father anywhere, but his is a life of grinding poverty. Tevye knows snow and ice and cold and vast spaces and soil that won't crack so you can't plant anything in it, cows that freeze in the winter. He knows harsh times, and in that context, the warmth and joy of this small community, and the Torah and religion and storytelling and his family, are the absolute solace of his life."

It's actually exhausting to play Tevye, added the Olivier Award–winning actor. "The rehearsal process is so grueling, you have to get fit in order to do it. Then, you're doing it eight times a week. You need a big, hungry heart to play the role well again and again, and when you give that much, you're spent emotionally."

When Luther Adler toured California in *Fiddler* for twenty-five weeks in 1966, the actor told the press it was too strenuous for him to do it any longer. "I have eleven singing numbers, five dance routines, thirty-four entrances and exits, plus assorted costume changes. In a show that runs a little short of three hours, I'm offstage only eighteen clocked minutes. Anyone who thinks he can do such a stint for several years should have his head examined."

Consider John Preece, the Tevye known to thousands of people around the country who have seen him in countless touring productions. The actor had mixed feelings about his achievement, quipping, "I'm not entirely sure if it's something one should be proud of, or if it's time for someone to take you aside and have a really long talk with you." On the other hand, he also considered Tevye "the best-written role for a male actor in the history of musical theater. Any actor who is physically capable of doing the show would love to be performing this part."

By late 2011, Preece had appeared in *Fiddler* more than 3,400 times, mostly as Tevye. "I'm on stage eighty percent of the time and it's pretty physically demanding," Preece said at sixty-three. He doesn't play tourist. "When you're on tour, you rest as much as you possibly can. . . . If the hotel has a restaurant, that makes me happy. We rest. That's what we do."

Unless, of course, you're Theodore Bikel, still performing as Tevye well into his eighties. One week in Canada, he wasn't feeling well, certain he had some kind of flu, but he didn't miss a performance. "Kids a third my age get a sniffle, and already they can't play," he said. "I don't do that. On one of the long tours, in the mid-nineties, I was the oldest member of the cast, and I was the only one who never missed a performance."

As for how many times *he's* played Tevye, Chaim Topol said he stopped counting after three thousand and guesses the number totaled close to 3,600 times by 2012. He played it in Tel Aviv and London, Tokyo and Osaka, Australia, Canada, and the United States, including several tours. He even performed with his youngest daughter, Adi Topol Margalith, first in London, then in Edinburgh in 1994. "It was really nice to have a taste of the past with my own dad," said the actress, who later played daughter Tzeitel with him in Israel as well. "Usually you have to learn to know the actor, but here it was so much easier."

Playing the Edinburgh Playhouse that year, Topol told an interviewer it felt "just wonderful." He told her the first time around, he'd spent half his energy and concentration just portraying someone of Tevye's age. "Now the age comes naturally, and I can concentrate on the part!"

Zero Mostel came back, too, of course. While Mostel was only on Broadway initially for less than a year, he went on to do several summer tours of *Fiddler* for the Guber and Gross music fairs. Producer Bill Ross told Mostel biographer Jared Brown that the tours were "one of the most horrendous times of my life, because of Zero."

In contrast, a summer *Fiddler* tour with Mostel was one of the best times of his life for Jerry Zaks, who would later become a Tony Award–winning director. It was on one of those summer tours that Zaks, then a young actor, learned a lot about acting and directing both.

Zaks was hired to replace an ailing actor set to tour as Motel the tailor, and went into rehearsal with Zero Mostel in New York. "I was in awe—everyone was slightly in awe," he said years later. "Herschel Bernardi and Paul Lipson were also pretty damn good, but anyone who has ever played that role after Zero—and you can quote me—has been an absolute and utter pretender. Everyone. You can talk about talent, but that's so subjective. For me, it was the utter fearlessness that he had.

"Here's a fearless moment. We were all in our dressing rooms one night, and we could hear the show over the squawk box. In the scene where Tevye and the butcher are toasting the butcher's impending marriage to Tevye's daughter, they were starting to do the song, 'To Life,' and the orchestra came in double time for some reason. Next thing we hear is 'stop'—and I mean, *loud*. We all ran out to see what was happening, and we saw Zero stand up and cross slowly to the orchestra pit. The audience was rapt; they didn't know what was going to happen. Zero looked into the orchestra pit and said, 'Like this, to life, to life,' and the orchestra welled up underneath him. The music director was gone the next day."

Then came Zaks's own trial by fire. "So I'm playing Motel the tailor, who is usually played like a simpering nervous schmuck, and I don't know how to do that. I came in feeling fully entitled and as much a mensch as possible; I wasn't directing at the time, but that's how I would have directed me. So we do this bit where he's pacing back and forth, and in rehearsal, he says, 'Just follow me and keep trying to get my attention.' Then he would look around for me, and say, 'What is it?' and I would do my line.

"At the first performance, in front a thousand people, I'm following him, saying, 'Rebe Tevye.' He whirled on me and yelled, 'What is it?' There was a spontaneous rage aimed at me, which I didn't expect, causing me to recoil backwards. As I was about to say the next line, he said, under his breath, 'Don't move,' because the audience was roaring. And I didn't. If I had spoken, not only would it have killed the laugh, but my line would be lost. If I held that position and didn't act, and he held his position and didn't act, the laugh would build. That's when he voiced 'the notes' because that's when he thought them. He didn't edit himself too much."

It wasn't the only time Mostel told Zaks what to do right in the middle of a scene onstage. In the show, Motel has to tell Tevye, "even a poor tailor is entitled to some happiness." It's one of *Fiddler*'s classic lines, and Zaks recalled that Mostel would say his own line, then add, under his breath, "Now give it to me!" At that point, said Zaks, "you can dwell on how inappropriate that is or you can ask, 'Is he right?' And he was right. Then, one night he did it again, and I was so furious I got up into his big fat face. I stood on my toes and said, 'That's right, Reb Tevye, that's right,' and I can remember seeing my spit going into his face. Then, in the silence just before the audience roared, I heard him whisper, 'That's it. That's it.'"

As his confidence grew, Zaks tried a little shtick himself, pretending he was crushed and physically incapacitated when Mostel appeared to sit on him in the same scene, and he got some very good laughs. Then, one intermission, he heard over the loudspeaker, "Jerry, would you go to Zero's dressing room, please." Zaks was scared, thinking he was going to get fired—"I'd heard stories about stars firing people who were getting big laughs."

That isn't what happened, however. Zaks walked into Mostel's dressing room. The star was sitting at his mirror, wearing his blue bandanna soaked in Sea Breeze. "This little thing you're doing?" said Mostel. "I watched today. It's very good, but listen to me. At the end, where you shake your leg, you don't need it. It's cheap, and believe me, I know from cheap."

Producers of the 1971 Tony Awards invited Mostel back for an encore of "If I Were a Rich Man." Mostel may have left *Fiddler* half a decade before, but the show apparently hadn't yet left him. Slipping easily back to Anatevka, he was a peasant bon vivant in a blue jacket, buttons popping, with a yellow cap on his head. He talked to God, did some praying, screamed at servants the way his wife Golde might scream at servants if she had any. He crossed his eyes as he sang of problems that "would cross a rabbi's eyes," and singing about geese and chickens, mimicked their sounds. There he was again, alternating shtick with a belly-shaking strut, hands clutching the air as he shimmied across the stage.

Mostel got to do the entire show on Broadway again as well a few years later. In 1976, the actor spent six months touring with *Fiddler* to Los Angeles, Denver, St. Louis, Washington, D.C., New Orleans, Detroit, Chicago, Boston, and elsewhere. The tour ended on Broadway, with Mostel and *Fiddler* nestled at the Winter Garden Theatre from December 1976 until June 1977.

Mostel brought with him an Exercycle and worked out each day to stay in shape. He also relied heavily on his dresser, Howard Rodney, who had worked with him on the original *Fiddler*; Mostel's needs were so great, for companionship as well as chores, that he eventually made sure that Rodney stayed next door to him in the hotel and paid for it.

The tour did very well, with good crowds and good notices across America. His scrapbook from the tour includes clippings that boast sell-outs and very nice reviews. *Chicago Tribune* critic Linda Winer reviewed the revival there in mid-September, saying the actor "pads around the stage like an ancient Talmudic pachyderm." Jay Carr in the *Detroit News* wrote: "If I were a rich man, one of the things I'd do is pay Zero Mostel whatever he wants to revive *Fiddler on the Roof* every few seasons."

In Los Angeles, where *Fiddler* was booked at the city's Shubert Theatre, the publicist Judi Davidson had set up a visit for Mostel to Johnny Carson's *The Tonight Show*. When the actor went out onstage, he sang a few choruses of his celebrated "If I Were a Rich Man," and stopped. To see the rest, Mostel told Carson's audience, people would have to call the Shubert Theatre to get tickets. Within minutes, said Davidson, "Phone lines lit up at Shubert theaters all across the country."

Variety reported sellouts for the Los Angeles engagement, and the *Los Angeles Times* drama critic Dan Sullivan called *Fiddler* "a show that ripens instead of withering as the seasons pass." The *Los Angeles Herald-Examiner* called Mostel "a national treasure."

By the time Mostel got to Washington, D.C., perhaps one hundred million theatergoers had seen *Fiddler* somewhere in the world. On opening night at the Kennedy Center, the audience gave Mostel a standing ovation, then kept applauding so long that the curtain went up and down ten times. Critic David Richards called Mostel both "a sort of Father Courage," and "a hero of wonderfully robust humanity." For Richards, "the show bears up just beautifully."

Jerome Robbins showed up for the tour in Boston. According to Mel Gussow's report in *The New York Times*, Robbins was "exercising his option as the musical's original director," and stopped by to restage the revival prior to its Broadway opening. The following week, during rehearsals, Mostel and Robbins "seemed to circle each other warily, as if they were testing to see who was in charge," wrote Gussow. The director made several requests of Mostel, who replied, many times, "We'll talk about it later."

Mostel was a hit in New York just as he'd been on the road. Critic Gussow, writing in *The New York Times,* came up with lines like "the king returns to his throne" before the show even opened. His colleague Walter Kerr wrote later, "God knows he is one of the four or five funniest men left alive."

After the opening-night performance, people wedged into Mostel's dressing room where he greeted and teased guests while he reclined in a bathrobe. For the ensuing party at Tavern on the Green, the actor arrived in an outfit that looked to Gussow like "a cross between a tuxedo and a prayer shawl."

The press also congratulated director Robbins. "*Fiddler on the Roof* is a terrific piece of work, as the current revival reminds us," wrote *Newsweek*'s Jack Kroll. "In its power to move audiences *Fiddler* has very few rivals among American musicals."

Fiddler played 167 performances at the Winter Garden in 1976 and 1977. But this time around, as in 1964–65, Zero gave one performance at first, then started embellishing it. When the show first opened in 1976, the *New York Post*'s Martin Gottfried said Mostel "owns the part of Tevye. . . . His stagemanship is tremendous." But in February 1977, just a few months later, Gottfried commented on "ad-libs, shtick, and his various other self-indulgences" as "unprofessional . . . disdainful of theatre; inconsiderate of the company; contemptuous of the audience."

When Mostel ad-libbed at the expense of Thelma Lee, his Golde for the revival, she said, "It didn't bother me because I was a stand-up comic, and I could deal with anything that Zero did. I actually liked it; it was interesting. In the dream sequence one night, he ripped my nightgown off. But I just finished the number in a blanket. And the audience just screamed. Then afterwards they built me another nightgown underneath the nightgown, so that if he pulled one off, the other one stayed."

The actor definitely had his fans. Rose Tillotson Price, a violist who played much of the time for that revival, first saw the show in 1963 as a teenager and was very impressed. Mostly, though, she never forgot Mostel, and in 1976, she had the chance to observe him close up. "Zero was unbelievable," she remembered. "He *was* Tevye. You could see him transform into that character. A lot of people who played Tevye did great jobs, but Zero was a ghost of Sholem Aleichem's pen."

That revival marked Mostel's last performances as Tevye. Not long after *Fiddler* closed, the actor taped what would become his final television appearance, guest starring as a fearful, wonderfully over-the-top poet on *The Muppet Show*. He then spent much of the summer preparing to perform in Arnold Wesker's new play *The Merchant*, an adaptation of Shakespeare's *The Merchant of Venice*.

In early September, Mostel was in Philadelphia, where the play would begin its pre-Broadway run. There, just before the the Saturday matinee of *The Merchant* on September 2nd, the actor began to feel sick. He was seen by a doctor, then sent to a hospital near the theater and released. Unfortunately, Mostel later returned to the hospital, where he died the evening of September 8, 1977, of a burst aorta. He was sixty-two years of age.

Mostel "made audiences roar with laughter and cry with a sense of human frailties," wrote Robert D. McFadden in Mostel's obituary for *The New York Times*. "Mr. Mostel was the actor's actor, the critic's actor and, perhaps most important, the theatergoer's actor."

Robbins got involved again with a *Fiddler* revival in 1981 at Lincoln Center's New York State Theater. Herschel Bernardi and Maria Karnilova were back in their prior roles as Tevye and Golde. At that point, Bernardi had played Tevye "maybe one thousand times" and said, "When they asked me to do it again, I said, 'Naaah,' but then they said that Jerry Robbins would come back and direct."

Karnilova had also played Golde many times, creating the role in the show's Detroit tryout and then taking it on to Washington, D.C., and Broadway, where she stayed for many years. How did she do it? "It's a good enough script so that you can escape into the words no matter how many times you've said them," she said in September of 1967, as the show was about to enter its fourth year. "Even when you can't, there's still the realization that the audience is being moved. You always get a charge out of that."

Fiddler hadn't changed all that much over the years, Karnilova said in 1981. "It's a masterpiece. Why fool around with a masterpiece?"

Aside from *Jerome Robbins' Broadway* in 1976, Robbins did not direct another musical. "I saw this *Fiddler* in Boston, and I was very proud," Robbins said at the time. "It has a subject that's very strong, that's—what's the word?—universal. . . . The other shows that come along and are offered to me just aren't that good."

Fiddler, however, kept going. It was back on Broadway again in 1990 for 245 performances, this time staring Topol as Tevye. "More than the Rodgers and Hammerstein musicals, beloved as they are, more than *My Fair Lady*, dazzling as it is, *Fiddler* seems to transcend its theatrical status," wrote David Richards in *The Washington Post* of that 1990 performance. "In the twenty-six years since it opened on Broadway, the show itself has become a tradition, passed on lovingly from parents to children."

Yet critic Richards also encountered a "certain mustiness" about *Fiddler on the Roof*, suggesting it might be time to experiment a little with the show's "respectful replications." It took a while, but fourteen years later, someone did just that.

16

Something Different

irector David Leveaux was in rehearsal for his revival of the Broadway musical *Nine* in 2003, when he got a call from producer Susan
Bristow. She wanted to know if he had any interest in taking on a
new production of *Fiddler on the Roof*, a question that both surprised and
intrigued him. "I didn't expect anyone to approach *me* about a show like
Fiddler," said the British director. "I assumed they would approach an
American director and would want a fairly conservative revival of the
show."

Leveaux was not the first person you'd think of to direct *Fiddler*.
While he would later receive a Tony Award nomination for his direc-
tion of *Nine,* he was usually associated with plays, not musicals. Work-
ing on both London's West End and Broadway, Leveaux had been very
successful directing revivals by such playwrights as Tom Stoppard and
Eugene O'Neill, receiving earlier Tony nominations for Stoppard's *The
Real Thing*, as well as for O'Neill's *Anna Christie* and *A Moon for the
Misbegotten*.

But Leveaux much admired *Fiddler*. "I had always thought it was the
most perfect musical. The book, to begin there, is a structural masterpiece, quite aside from the phenomenal compression of character and
narrative Joe Stein achieved. And who doesn't have a response to that
music? When she asked if I would talk to the writers, I thought, Who

wouldn't want to sit in a room and talk to Joseph Stein, Sheldon Harnick, and Jerry Bock?"

When Leveaux then talked with the writers, he said, they made it clear to him that at their ages, they knew they wouldn't have many more chances to see the show on Broadway and didn't want just a copy of the well-known version. While the director felt that version had essentially "become a kind of steadily filtered version of the original," he also knew changes would need to keep "a delicate balance. My sense was they weren't asking for some massive, conceptual directorial idea imposed on the show, but rather *Fiddler on the Roof* for a new audience, as well as the audience that loves the show. And they said, 'Yes, that's exactly what we want.'"

Leveaux sought to craft the world of 1905 Anatevka as an innocent village before the fall, and to do so true to its time. "The real emotional dynamic exists between our postlapsarian knowledge of what happened when all that was destroyed and what happened when they got to Poland," said the director. "But that was our knowledge, not theirs. It's very important you don't create a drama that is itself creating that issue of prescience. These are not people overshadowed by the Holocaust. *We* bring the Holocaust to that event."

Rather, for Leveaux, *Fidder* was a folk drama. Birch trees would give a sense of the idyllic. The roof would be not just symbolic but "magical" and float over the stage, above the birch trees and lanterns. "That's the fundamental truth about musicals. You're asking the audience to gather around a specific campfire, and if you don't identify what campfire it is, that fundamental aspect of ritual is lost."

Boris Aronson's famous Chagall-inspired set was eschewed for a contemporary one by British designer Tom Pye, who got rid of the turntables of the 1960s and much of the scenery. Leveaux, who knew he was going into the 1,700-seat Minskoff Theatre, also put the band onstage, saying, "As a director, you always want to get the audience as close as possible to that world."

Producer Susan Bristow had suggested English actor Alfred Molina as Tevye, said Leveaux, who had known Molina for years and loved that idea. Not only did Molina have great range as an actor, but he was "somebody you instantly want to be in a room with. That seemed very important for Tevye, because that's the person who takes you by the hand and leads you through the story."

Molina didn't seem fettered by memories of Zero Mostel, Chaim Topol, and the rest of the Tevyes who'd come before. "The fact that others have played a part doesn't take away anything for me," he said. "For the time I occupy this little space in the theatrical universe, I am Tevye and Tevye is me."

The producers didn't ask Molina to audition, nor were they worried about his not having done much singing onstage, he told the New York *Daily News*. Ditto for his not being Jewish. "I don't think it bothers anyone," he said. "If it does, that's their problem. No one complained when Liev Schreiber played Henry V. I think it's irrelevant."

With Molina in place, Leveaux began to put together the rest of his forty-member cast. Broadway musical veteran Randy Graff came in as Golde, Nancy Opel as Yente the matchmaker, and David Wohl as Lazar Wolf the butcher. Future *Glee* star Lea Michele was cast as the young daughter Shprintze, and as an understudy for daughter Chava, the youngest of the daughters with a major role.

Actor David Wohl, who had been hearing buzz about the show for months, was called back after his first audition and asked to perform a song that showed more of his singing range. The actor chose "Sunrise, Sunset," a song he knew well. But this time his audience included the people who wrote the song, and Wohl was a little nervous.

When he finished "Sunrise, Sunset," Wohl looked at Bock, Harnick, and Stein, then said, "I can't believe I just sang this song for you guys." Stein's reply: "Don't worry about it. We're probably going to cut that number anyway."

At the start of 2004, Broadway audiences could look ahead to a great many revivals in the coming months. Seven of the thirteen musicals and plays scheduled for the first half of 2004 were revivals. And perhaps the most anticipated, judging by its seven-million-dollar advance sales, was the revival of *Fiddler on the Roof*. It was the first Broadway revival of *Fiddler* in fourteen years and the fourth since the original production.

Given that expectation, Leveaux made it clear in press interviews he wasn't planning drastic changes to something that worked so well. "There's already a vast audience that loves the piece, people who will be bringing their children to the theater, perhaps for the first time," he told the *New York Times* writer Matthew Gurewitsch. "It's very important not to disappoint."

The director also made it clear, however, that he didn't plan "to re-create *Fiddler* for pure nostalgic value." So Bock and Harnick wrote a new song for the show, Stein trimmed several passages, and there were even some changes to the choreography. "I said from the beginning that we would absolutely honor Robbins," said Leveaux. "At the same time I absolutely reserved the right to rethink the musical staging." The director didn't touch the bottle dance—who would?—but he did toss out the brooms in "Matchmaker."

Along the way, the director decided to get rid of the musical number "The Rumor," a song sequence that had previously both marked a passage of time and provided extra minutes for a scene change. Norman Jewison had dropped it from the film, and Leveaux didn't think it was particularly strong, either. Instead, he thought, What about if the matchmaker had a song, since her tradition was also changing? So Leveaux asked Bock and Harnick to write a new song, and, he said, "I was astonished they said they'd give it a go. One of them said, 'Oh, my God, it's back to that hotel room in Detroit!'"

Writing the song "felt like yesterday," said Bock. "Exactly the way it felt when we were out of town. The same excitement. The same pressure."

Yet Bock conceded "there was a quiet but discernable shock at the assignment." Bock felt they hadn't expected it and weren't sure it was a good idea. Harnick saw both sides, agreeing with Leveaux that the changing tradition of the matchmaker hadn't really been explored but worrying that there just might be nothing new to say at that point in the show. Timing was also a consideration as the assignment came when the show was already two weeks into rehearsal.

What wasn't a problem, both men have said many times, was that working together on the new song, "Topsy-Turvy," would be their first collaboration in thirty-four years. "We were both a little ill at ease when we started," Harnick said, "but very soon the years fell away, and it was like we never stopped working together."

Bock and Harnick had been one of the top songwriting teams on Broadway, particularly during their strong decade of the 1960s. They wrote scores for seven Broadway shows together, starting with *The Body Beautiful* in 1958 and continuing through *Fiorello!* in 1959, *Tenderloin* in 1960, *She Loves Me* in 1963, *Fiddler on the Roof* in 1964, *The Apple Tree* in 1966, and *The Rothschilds* in 1970.

The two men chose to go their separate ways after *The Rothschilds*, a painful decision they didn't talk about for years. The way Harnick explained it, Bock was close friends with Derek Goldby, the show's director, and the producers, Harnick, and others wanted to bring in Michael Kidd to direct, which they did. "Jerry never forgave me," said the lyricist, "but through the years, we had business together, and when we did a revival of *Fiorello!* at the Goodspeed Opera House, it revived memories of the original. So did revivals of *She Loves Me* and *The Apple Tree*. Little by little, we became friends again but never friends to the point where we wanted to collaborate again."

Given their continuing joint appearances for revivals and seminars, Harnick pointed out that they really had to maintain a relationship, "and as it happens, it's been an amiable one." Interviewed with Harnick about the situation by Terry Gross on NPR's *Fresh Air*, an exasperated Bock finally told Gross, "Terry, we weren't divorced. We were romantically separated."

Much as they had done forty years earlier on *Fiddler*'s out-of-town tryouts, the songwriters worked quickly. Just a few days after they got the assignment, they dropped by the rehearsal room on Forty-second Street with their wives and performed the song for Leveaux at the piano. When they got to the end and Leveaux was pleased with it, the director said, "They were visibly relieved."

Leveaux then asked them to play it for the whole company, they agreed, and the group moved to the larger rehearsal room down the hall.

Bock went to the piano, Harnick stood nearby, and cast members sat around them on the floor. Many were weeping, recalled Leveaux, "at the pleasure of watching these guys, creators of one of the most famous musicals ever written, show them it is never over. It was a huge inspiration to the company."

Leveaux's 12.5-million-dollar production opened on February 26, 2004, but it did so twenty minutes late for tragic reasons. As the opening-night audience waited for the Minskoff Theatre curtain to rise, Sonia Rabinowitz Cullinen, older sister of Jerome Robbins, had a fatal heart attack in her seat. (Cullinen, ninety-one, was instrumental in Robbins's early career, inspiring him by example as a dancer and encouraging him to study dance.) Paramedics unsuccessfully tried to revive her, then took her to Bellevue Hospital Center where she was declared dead.

"I know people were very upset," said the director. "They had to take her through the backstage area, and it was a very somber thing. When a company is about to go on for opening night, and you hold the curtain, it's really tricky because their energy is all over the shop. Then this terrible thing happens and there's a great shadow. You have to find a way of playing the play despite the collective sense of shock in the audience and the company."

The show went on. But at the evening's conclusion came an opening-night fracas that had the New York theater world buzzing. At its center was *New York Post* theater columnist Michael Riedel, who had referred to the production in print as both "ethnically cleansed" and "de-Jewed," and had heard, he said, "that my columns were driving Leveaux absolutely bonkers."

Then, after the opening-night party, Leveaux dropped by Angus McIndoe's restaurant nearby for a drink. There was Riedel, who couldn't resist telling Leveaux that "intellectual Brits" like the director didn't have either the passion or the soul "to understand the American musical."

"I was beginning to understand what this whole thing is really about," said Leveaux. "And I've got a horrible feeling it's about a Brit doing an American classical musical. When he leaned over, I picked him up and put him facedown on the floor. That's the true story. I didn't slug him or break his watch."

Various reporters ran different accounts of the incident, with *The New York Times*' Jason Zinoman noting that "Mr. Riedel admits he was tipsy and had just finished insulting English directors who, he said, ruin classic American musicals. . . . Almost as soon as Mr. Riedel hit the floor, exaggerated accounts of the incident started to circulate. A fairly popular spin was that Mr. Leveaux landed a punch that sent Mr. Riedel to the emergency room. . . . Mr. Riedel was not injured."

Riedel wasn't the only writer critical of Leveaux's interpretation. The critic said, for instance, that his comments picked up on an earlier essay by the novelist and law professor Thane Rosenbaum about such things as the production's "absence of Jewish soul," which truly "opened the floodgates for me." Later, cultural critic Ruth Franklin wrote an essay for *The New York Times* titled "Shtetl Shtick," that questioned not just this production, but librettist Stein's "drastically oversimplified" adaptation of Sholem Aleichem's stories, which she found cartoonish, condescending, and "pure Broadway."

Franklin's criticisms were not new to the show's authors. Writer Philip Roth had famously referred to *Fiddler* as "shtetl kitsch" in *The New Yorker*, the same magazine in which Cynthia Ozick had earlier come down hard on the changes she saw foisted upon Aleichem's prose. For Ozick, *Fiddler's* book and lyrics were an "emptied-out, prettified romantic vulgarization . . . whatever its success as a celebrated musical, the chief nontheatrical accomplishment of *Fiddler on the Roof* has been to reduce the reputation of a literary master to the very thing he repudiated."

Such observations were rarely made by theater critics, however. Even reviewers critical of the Leveaux production generally leavened their comments with praise for the original production. In a review titled "A Cozy Little McShtetl," the *New York Times* critic Ben Brantley, "a goy myself," didn't much like this production but wrote that watching it, "it is still possible to understand why *Fiddler* became the mammoth hit that it did."

Reviews as a whole were all over the place, alternately praising and damning the director, actor Molina, other cast members, and the set designer. Even the satirical revue "Forbidden Broadway" threw in a parody—"*Fiddler* with no Jews/sounds crazy, no?" *Washington Post* critic Peter Marks, who grew up in a home where *Fiddler* was "spiritual sustenance," was outraged at Leveaux's production, calling it "perversely antiseptic" and saying it was as if the director "had the village emptied of thick, filling borscht and replaced it with a pallid consommé." Marks's new title for the production: "Violinist on the Verandah."

More positive was *New York* magazine's John Simon, who wrote "that the production is more ecumenical than previous versions is to be applauded; accusations that the show has been goyified are baseless." And at *The New Yorker*, critic John Lahr was taken with "this elegant revival" from its very start or, as he put it, "first ravishing moment," finding that the English director, star, and designers brought "a certain cultural detachment, which imposes a powerful lucidity on the story and allows its moral debate to gather proper poetic momentum."

Time's Richard Zoglin thought Leveaux's update might not please Hadassah theater groups, "but that's no reason to dismiss a striking Broadway revival that manages to shake off the cobwebs and relocate the emotional core of a show too often typecast as your grandmother's favorite musical. This is a *Fiddler* for everybody." Concluded *Variety*'s Christopher Isherwood: "It takes courage to tinker with a musical as beloved as *Fiddler on the Roof*."

Leveaux's "courage" was rewarded with six Tony nominations, including nods for actor Molina and Best Revival, and the show went on to play nearly two years on Broadway. Alfred Molina, however, was there for only one of those two years.

In early November, a few months before Molina left the show, word got out that Harvey Fierstein was being considered for the part. To many people, the blatantly gay performer was still in their minds as the oversized, reclusive Baltimore hausfrau Edna Turnblad in *Hairspray*. But he was also a much-lauded actor and playwright. His Tony Award for *Hairspray* arrived after he'd already won 1983 Tony Awards as both playwright and actor for his first major play, *Torch Song Trilogy*, and a 1984 Tony for the libretto of the musical *La Cage aux Folles*.

Few people knew *Fiddler* the way Fierstein knew *Fiddler*. At his childhood home in Bensonhurst, Brooklyn, *Fiddler* was among the many Broadway shows for which his mother got theater tickets as soon as she could, always trying for the three-dollar tickets in the first row of the mezzanine. And like Jewish mothers in many homes in the 1950s and 1960s, she always bought the cast album and played it for the family so they'd know the music first.

"My world exploded open when I saw *Fiddler on the Roof*," Fierstein wrote in *The New York Times* blog many years later. "I was a pre–bar mitzvah Brooklyn kid who thought the world existed in two parts: my neighborhood and then everything else. When the curtain at the Imperial Theatre rose on a man with covered head and tsitsis exposed from beneath his vest, I thought I was hallucinating . . . I fought not to stand up in my seat and yell, 'I'm Jewish, too!'"

In 2003, Fierstein ran into producer Susan Bristow, whom he'd heard was involved in the 2004 *Fiddler* revival. "I said, 'You know who should be in it?,' said Fierstein. "And she said, 'Who, you? Who are you going to play, Golde?' It wasn't such a weird thing to say since I was playing Edna in *Hairspray* at the moment. But I think she saw my face, and she got immediately embarrassed. She said, 'Alfred Molina is doing it.' And I said, 'Good luck.'"

But a year later, the situation had changed. Fierstein had done *Hairspray* for two years and had promised himself a year off to do some writing when Bristow gave him a call with an attractive alternative. As Fierstein told it: "She said, 'So, Mr. Big Mouth, how would you like to play Tevye?' Then she said, 'Just promise me one thing—think about it, and don't shave until you make up your mind. Just in case.'"

Fierstein did think about it. "Obviously right after *Hairspray*, I was really hot, and it was a big thing to see what I would do next. Most people would say you need to do something else original, don't do a revival, and especially not a revival that's already been open for ten months. But Jack O'Brien, the director of *Hairspray*, said to me, 'You either do it or you spend the rest of your life telling the story of how they asked you to do it, and people sort of nod and say, 'Yeah, right.'"

It took Fierstein about a week to make up his mind. He went to see the show, then told Bristow he wanted to sing the score for the creative team. The way the gravelly-voiced performer figured it, he had "a very specific voice" and they should hear him sing it. And he didn't want to just sing one song; he wanted them to listen to him sing the entire score.

So Fierstein rehearsed with the show's music director, then went into a rehearsal room with Stein, Bock, and Harnick. When he finished singing "Tradition" and "If I Were a Rich Man," the three men stood up and told him to do the show with their blessing. That, however, was not what he wanted. "I said, 'Sit the fuck back down.' 'If I Were a Rich Man' certainly is not an easy thing to pull off, but you can pull it off, and you have to also get the emotional life out of 'Sunrise, Sunset' and the dream and other songs. So they heard me sing the whole score. And when I sang 'Chavala,' I looked up and Jerry Bock was weeping. I sang it like a Kaddish, the prayer for the dead."

When it was announced that Fierstein would be starring in *Fiddler*, "there were a lot of heads that shook," said the actor. "As an artist, I found that very insulting. Tevye is Jewish. I'm Jewish. I was the right age to play it. Culturally, I am very close to Tevye. To me, the stretch is playing the Baltimore housewife. I'm not a five-hundred-pound woman who takes in laundry."

As with Molina, reviews were mixed for Fierstein. In a *New York Times* review titled "An Exotic Tevye in Old Anatevka," Ben Brantley wrote that "it would seem that this *Fiddler* has gone from having too little of a personality at its center to having too much of one." Countered Clive Barnes in the *New York Post*: "Harvey Fierstein is a splendid Tevye . . . and his dancing is the best I have seen from any Tevye—Jerome Robbins himself would have been enchanted."

Then came the casting of Rosie O'Donnell, the actress, comedian, and talk show host, as Golde. The *New York Times* writer Jesse McKinley called it "one of the boldest bits of replacement casting in Broadway history." Harnick told the reporter, "Harvey I had grave doubts about and he's marvelous. So hopefully lightning will strike twice."

If critics were harsh on Molina and Fierstein, they were savage about Rosie O'Donnell. Brantley, writing in *The New York Times*, criticized her posture ("plant yourself on the floor as if you were an oak"), her accent (which "trots the globe, through countries real and imagined"), and her acting style ("she can be relied upon to react with italicized gestures and facial expressions to what everyone else is saying").

As for Fierstein, who played opposite O'Donnell as surely the most unusual couple in Anatevka, Leveaux said the actor and playwright "came onboard in a very, very creative way. He wasn't going to play any old Tevye. He wanted to find out what *his* Tevye would be in this version. I remember one detail that absolutely catches him. We were working on the scene where Hodel is off to Siberia to join her husband and is saying good-bye to Tevye at the railroad station. Harvey said, 'I want to give her my gloves,' and the detail was brilliant, like a punctuation mark. He naturally, deeply understood it."

Summarized Leveaux: "I think he's a formidable Tevye—and I hope he plays it many times."

17

Traveling America

Harvey Fierstein did not stay away long from Anatevka. As for Zero Mostel, Chaim Topol, and Theodore Bikel, the lure of Tevye was too strong. In a world where *Fiddler* revivals were a constant, it was only a matter of time until another chance came along.

Revivals and touring productions never stop. "If you are running a theater, and you want to make money, *Fiddler* is a shoe-in," said Paul Blake, former executive producer of The Municipal Theatre Association of St. Louis (The Muny), arguably the largest theater in the country. "It's a show people always want to see."

It doesn't even matter how often a tour plays a city, said Blake, who learned the hard way during his stint at The Muny. Although a production he did in St. Louis with Theodore Bikel was successful, he was reluctant to tour it. "I thought Topol had just done it, and nobody would want to see it again two years later," Blake explained. "Then another producer took *Fiddler* to secondary markets, and it sold out everywhere. It was so successful that after a year and a half, it was time to go back and play the major markets again."

Besides productions of *Fiddler* originated by individual theaters like The Muny, *Fiddler* and other shows have also long played the country's schools, community centers, and regional theaters. Many of those productions have been licensed through New York–based Music Theatre International (MTI).

According to Music Theatre International CEO Freddie Gershon, MTI licensed about 2,500 community theaters and about 4,300 high schools mounted productions of *Fiddler* between 2001 and 2011. He estimated that since the 2004–05 season, MTI's licensees had reached three million people in professional venues in the U.S.

In 1994, Music Theatre International launched "Broadway Junior," including among its offerings *Fiddler on the Roof* Junior, a shorter version of the show. Since Broadway Junior started, said Gershon, more than fourteen thousand *Fiddler* Junior performances have been done in schools, parks, community theaters, religious centers, and military bases.

MTI's big cardboard box marked "WARNING! Wonderful memories inside!!" arrives full of instructional guides and manuals for its *Fiddler* Junior productions. Inside are, among other things, a brochure for parents called "Family Matters! A Parents' Guide to the Magic of Theatre"; tips include how to help their children memorize dialogue as well as how to deal with what happens when the show concludes and children have "post-show blues." Young actors are cautioned to "mark your music with large commas to remind yourself where to take breaths while singing."

Gershon likes to tell about visiting a multicultural New York City public school early on in Broadway Junior's existence and bringing songwriters Bock and Harnick along with him. "They'd seen professional children's groups do the show," said Gershon, "but they had never seen 'real' children do it. There were people in the audience in strange but interesting attire from Africa and the Middle East, the boy playing Tevye was a Bangladeshi and his Golde was played by a Japanese-American girl probably fourteen inches taller than he was.

"Here was an audience of newcomers to America who wanted their children to go to public school and assimilate but not lose the culture of where they came from. These parents were strict with their own daughters; they all know about matchmakers. They cried, they screamed, their camcorders were on, their flash cameras went off. Every rule in the theater was broken, and while it was going on, I turned and looked at Jerry and Sheldon. Oh, the sobbing of those two men.

"Afterwards Jerry Bock said, 'I never saw anyone clear his throat or get up to go to the bathroom.' I didn't see a parent or sibling shift in his seat in this curtainless, unamplified, overly hot, without air-conditioning public school cafeteria. When the show began, they were transported to another world. There were no turntables. No fabulous lighting. Tevye's milk wagon was made of cardboard, with a little sign that said 'milk' written with a Magic Marker. But none of that made any difference."

The reason, observed Sammy Bayes, was that "every family can associate with the breaking of traditions and the rebelliousness of the young. Persecution is as old as the Bible. So everybody who sees the show can relate to it. It stuck to what needed to be told, and that was the human story."

Besides the many productions licensed by MTI, other amateur and professional tours also cross the United States again and again. Maryland-based Troika Entertainment, for instance, toured upwards of one thousand performances of *Fiddler* in dozens of cities and towns between 2004 and 2012. Troika chief executive officer Randall A. Buck explained that while one of their productions might stay in a big city like Chicago or Dallas for a week or more, it can also stop in smaller markets for five-performance weekends or even single-night performances. In one week, for instance, one of Troika's *Fiddler* tours played York, Pennsylvania, one night, Williamsport, Pennsylvania, the next, then Akron, Ohio, for two nights. It stopped next in Van Wert, Ohio, and finished out the week in Danville, Kentucky.

"If *Fiddler* is not the number one, most beloved musical, it would be in the top five," said Buck. "It is a show that will simply sell itself on just a title. That's despite the fact that the first act is over an hour and a half long, and the whole show is every minute of three hours. In today's world where you can barely keep anyone's attention for thirty seconds, it is stunning people will sit through that entire show."

In fact, they're often hooked from the very first line. Rick Pessagno, a dancer and choreographer who toured with *Fiddler* in Topol's 2009 farewell tour, recalled vividly the audience reaction when Topol first appeared onstage. "When he came out and said, 'A fiddler on the roof. Sounds crazy, no?' the audience response was unbelievable," said Pessagno. "It was like a rock concert. People screamed and applauded."

Fiddler audiences like to take something home with them, as well. Among Troika's "featured products" are not only the usual key chains, lapel pins, magnets, and caps, but also thirty-dollar "If You Were a Rich Man" T-shirts and forty-dollar shot glasses that say "To Life!" in many different languages. At Creative Goods Merchandise, which stocks *Fiddler* items in theaters for Troika, director of operations Kyle McGinley said CDs also sell very well. "A lot of the time, when people see *Fiddler*, they're shocked at how many familiar songs there are. They pick up the CD because they enjoy the songs so much."

As *The New York Times*' Ben Brantley said reviewing David Leveaux's 2004 Broadway production: "Jerry Bock's score still registers as a tasty, sticky pudding of corn syrup, Eastern European inflections, and Broadway razzmatazz, with homespun, clunky lyrics by Sheldon Harnick." Added Brantley: "Anyone who hears 'If I Were a Rich Man' or 'Sunrise, Sunset' is fated to live with these songs in his head until he dies."

David Andrews Rogers, who has conducted the orchestra for Troika's *Fiddler* tours, is well aware of the popularity of those songs. "How many contemporary shows have as many recognizable songs?" asked Andrews Rogers. "With other musicals, you may remember one song, maybe two. With *Fiddler*, you've got five, six, seven certified hits in the show. I hear people humming along, and there's a self-satisfied sigh from audience members in anticipation of songs they know.

"I frequently look out over the pit wall and see grandparents with children, people who grew up with the show or performed in it and are eagerly waiting to watch the story unfold all over again. Their high school or synagogue did it, and they feel a sense of ownership over the stories."

Given the many productions of *Fiddler* every year, everywhere, school and other productions have also spawned lifelong fascination with the show. Wilmington, Delaware–based Gerri Smith Weagraff, for instance, might have trouble recalling when she *wasn't* doing *Fiddler*. In 1973, in the tenth grade, *Fiddler* was her first musical and, she said, "It's what made me fall in love with musical theater. My friends were auditioning for a community theater production of *Fiddler* and said I should come along. I did and got cast as Hodel. My parents said I was a shy, quiet child before and, in that spotlight, I became a different person."

Her 1986 run in *Fiddler* changed her life even more, when she was cast as oldest daughter Tzeitel in a community theater production, and a young man named Paul Weagraff was cast as Motel the tailor. "We started dating during rehearsals, got married thirteen times onstage, and then did it for real."

When she did *Fiddler* again in 2004, her children both joined her. The family has done so many productions of *Fiddler* and other shows—almost twenty productions before their children went off to college—that in their community they've been nicknamed "the von Weagraffs."

In recent years, with her children grown, Weagraff has also toured with *Fiddler* professionally throughout North America, playing older characters and, eventually, Golde. Between 2010 and 2012, she appeared in about four hundred productions in almost every state, plus six Canadian provinces. As she put it: "My parents saw me in Florida, cousins saw me in California, one niece was in Albuquerque, and another in Texas. I am Jewish, and I feel a real connection to the story, knowing my grandparents and great-grandparents lived that sort of life."

With time and technology, a few things have changed in the world of Anatevka. For one thing, not many shows today have painted backdrops, noted Ken Billington, a prominent Broadway lighting designer whose credits include lighting *Fiddler*'s 1976, 1981, and 1990 Broadway appearances. "I remember in the last revival, it played Los Angeles and one of the reviews talked about 'the cut-down touring scenery,'" said Billington. "Although we had the original set onstage, a lot had changed between 1964 and 1990. Everyone thought this was the cheap way to tour the show, but no, that's the way the show was created. It's that people expect different things now."

Expectations about sound have changed even more, Billington added. "When it was done originally on Broadway, there were six-foot microphones along the edge of the stage, which were run from backstage. There were no wireless microphones, but we played very large theaters and everybody heard everything. By the 1990s, we had a full forty-five-foot sound truck, the size of a semitrailer, with thirty wireless microphones, a microphone for every instrument in the orchestra pit, and a stack of speakers, and we were doing the exact same show in the same auditoriums."

Bassoonist Ron Jannelli, who played with the original *Fiddler* orchestra on Broadway, has seen similar changes in the orchestra pit. "The pit is deeper now because of electronics," he said. "Everything is heavily miked, and there is no live sound really anymore. It all comes from speakers. It used to be that my bassoon would stick up above the railing of the orchestra pit. I could see the people in the first row and they could see me. The pit wasn't that deep, so there was a certain amount of live sound that went out into the house. We had to play softly to not drown out the actors."

The choreography, however, hasn't changed much and probably won't, so long as Sammy Bayes continues his lifetime vigil. When the show was running on Broadway in the 1960s, Bayes would watch a scene or dance, then jot it down and set it in stone in a book of choreography and staging that still travels with licensed productions of the show. "Every director and every company has its own version, and that's their prerogative," said Bayes. "My job is to insert Jerome Robbins's choreography without disturbing the vision of the director."

While traveling the world as Robbins's emissary and frequently directing *Fiddler* abroad, Bayes has been planning ahead. In his seventies, he has now trained two younger choreographers to take over for him when he can't do it anymore. "One fellow is in his fifties, and the other in his twenties," Bayes said. "I figure when I'm gone, the guy in his fifties will take over, and when he's gone, the guy in his twenties will take over. Then, hopefully, he will train somebody."

But meanwhile, there are shows to assist all over the globe. Among them: a production in England in 2007 starring that country's celebrated actor Henry Goodman.

18

Fiddler Goes Abroad

After English actor Henry Goodman's Olivier Award–winning performance in 2000 as Shylock in Shakespeare's *The Merchant of Venice*, his director, Trevor Nunn, asked if Goodman would be interested in playing Tevye in *Fiddler on the Roof*. The answer was "no." "I didn't want to be a professional Jew," Goodman said several years later. "Like all principal actors, I really value the range of work that I do. I'm very proud of my roots, but I don't want to be ghettoized as a Jewish actor."

The prospect came up again in 2006 when Goodman and the director Lindsay Posner were looking for a new project to do together. This time, however, the actor was more receptive. He was a few years older, had tackled more classic roles, and was ready to draw on his heritage. He had, after all, grown up in London's East End, a place his grandparents landed when they got off the boat from a shtetl themselves. He'd read Sholem Aleichem and Jewish history so, he said, "it was not the first time I put my foot in that soil."

Enter Samuel West, then artistic director of South Yorkshire's Sheffield Theatres, the largest producing-theater complex outside London. West had recently taken over Sheffield, which had a distinguished musical theater pedigree under its former leader, Michael Grandage, and he liked the idea of producing *Fiddler* in Sheffield's Crucible Theatre. The Crucible's 980-seat house had a smaller budget than London's West End theaters, which meant fewer musicians, dancers, and sets. But with the audience surrounding the stage, said Goodman, "we achieved the intimacy and sense of a village coming to life."

Neither Sheffield nor northeast England is known for a large Jewish population, but it does have a strong theatergoing tradition. *Fiddler* opened in early December 2006, and broke local box office records over its eight-week run. "It went through the roof," said Goodman. "It was *fantastically* well received. Then, of course, London producers got interested and descended on Sheffield."

Getting to London's West End was not easy, however. For one thing, they had to convince Robbins's longtime attorney, *Fiddler*'s "doorkeeper" Floria Lasky, to grant them the rights. Other prominent British directors had reportedly tried to adapt it and were refused the rights. Lasky asked to see a tape of their show, which they sent, and what Goodman calls their "sweet little production with six dancers instead of twenty and all sorts of compromises to the show's 'bible'" didn't impress her in the least.

What nobody planned on was the tenacity of Kim Poster, an American-born, London-based producer who had earlier produced *Amadeus* on the West End. "The acting was superb, and the scenic design was just gorgeous," Poster said. "What the Sheffield production lacked was an understanding of integrating dance and music in the storytelling process. I expressed my reservations to Sam West, saying I couldn't help but admire how sturdy the production itself was, and he said, 'If you feel so strongly, why don't you change the orchestrations and the choreography and bring it into town?' That was not what I went there to do, but he threw the gauntlet down. I said, 'I'm going to do it.'"

The producer set up a phone call with Lasky for Goodman and director Posner, who argued the case for their production. Sensing some give from Lasky, the British team eventually agreed to redo the show under the tutelage of Sammy Bayes, the man Robbins had personally trained to preserve his choreography, and to add actors, musicians, and budget to bring the show more in line with other professional *Fiddler* productions.

To rework the Sheffield orchestration for the West End, Poster and Bayes brought in Larry Blank, a Los Angeles–based orchestrator/conductor who knew *Fiddler* well. Blank reduced the original Broadway orchestration for twenty-five musicians to a more klezmer-sounding ten musicians. "It had every bit of rhythm and timing that was in the original production," said Poster. "He did that brilliant thing of making ten pieces sound like twenty-five."

Fiddler on the Roof transferred from Sheffield to London's Savoy Theatre on May 19, 2007, for what *Variety* called "the uncommonly reasonable cost" of $932,000, and recouped twenty-five percent of its costs in four weeks. The *Daily Express* called the show "thrilling . . . as good as musical theatre gets," while *The Times* called the production "poignant, witty, and spectacular." *The Daily Telegraph* called it "a sensational revival . . . *Fiddler on the Roof* will raise the roof in the West End."

Both actor Goodman and director Posner were also given praise. The *Evening Standard*'s Nicholas de Jongh said Posner's "mature, heartfelt, impeccably executed revival, receiving a deserved transfer from Sheffield, is a perfect reminder of why this tune-stuffed show has been fiddling its way to box-office gold since 1964." Critic Tim Walker at *The Sunday Telegraph* declared himself ready to take what he called "the Topol part" and make it "now unquestionably Henry Goodman's."

Producer Poster's personal highlight came the night that Robbins's lawyer Floria Lasky, then quite ill, nevertheless flew to London to see the show. When Poster went over to sit with her at intermission, she saw tears in Lasky's eyes. Then Lasky told the producer she had prepared for two different scenarios that evening. "She told me, 'I was either going to give you *this*,' and she took out a little bar of chocolate, 'or *this*,' and she handed me a little jewelry box. I opened it, and on my grandmother's grave, I am telling you the truth—she gave me an emerald and diamond ring."

The London production was extended twice and went on to play until February 16, 2008. It was *Fiddler*'s fourth West End production, and by that time scores of theaters throughout Europe, Asia, and elsewhere had also re-created Anatevka onstage.

"We were surprised when we saw it in Helsinki," Harnick said candidly. "They cut some things, and when we asked why, they said, 'It had no relevance to us. There are no Jews in Finland. Where the stories hit us is the changing of tradition. We are also a small country living next to this giant bear, and what you have written is extremely meaningful to us.'"

The New York Times gave the show's many overseas lives extensive coverage. A reporter was in the audience for the West German debut February 1, 1968, at Hamburg's Operetta House, for example. Playing Tevye was Israeli actor Shmuel Rodensky, who had played the role three hundred and fifty times in Israel. The actor said in an interview before the performance that some of his Israeli friends were against his taking the job. "I thought to myself, There are good artists in Germany, but Tevye should be played by a Jew. I know this Jew, Tevye, and I should play him."

A production in Prague opened a few weeks later, and by the time *Un Violon sur le toit* opened in Paris on November 15, 1969, at the Théâtre Marigny, *Fiddler* had also played Melbourne, Vienna, and Rio de Janeiro. The German-Russian singer Ivan Rebroff, who learned the French part in four months, got excellent reviews. The critic at *Le Monde* also noted that "the French barriers against Anglo-American musical comedy were broken down with this show at the Marigny last night."

Nearly two decades after its Broadway opening, *Fiddler* finally opened in Moscow in December 1983, performed by the Soviet Union's only professional Jewish theater group. The impresario Yuri Sherling, a former Bolshoi dancer, told Associated Press reporter Andrew Rosenthal that *Tevieh from Anatovka* included "the first lines in Hebrew ever spoken on a stage in the Soviet Union."

Fiddler played Warsaw for the first time less than two years later, after earlier playing in Lodz, Poznan, and Gdynia, Poland. The Associated

Press said Polish cultural figures "heralded" the premiere as "symbolic of a change in official attitudes toward Jewish culture in Poland, the heart of European Jewry before it was eradicated by the Nazis." Just six thousand Jews remained in Warsaw when the show opened there, and Antoni Marianowicz, who had translated the musical into Polish, noted, "It is a much more important event than simply a theatrical play."

Fiddler's arrival in Poland, where composer Bock's family came from, was particularly meaningful to the show's authors. In 1985, the three men donated their royalties from the estimated 120 performances staged in Poland at that point to preserving the country's Jewish monuments. An Associated Press report, printed in Canada's *The Globe and Mail*, said, "Most of the money has gone toward the restoration of Jewish cemeteries desecrated during the war and left abandoned in some four hundred Polish cities and towns."

Fiddler has been back in Poland several times since then, much as it has been produced in hundreds of amateur and professional theaters every year internationally, observed Richard Salfas, vice president of International Licensing, at Music Theatre International. "*Fiddler* is done everywhere, all the time," summarized Salfas. "It is consistently in the top ten licensed shows from our catalogue year after year, and at any given time, there are close to ten professional productions throughout Europe."

"I get reports every three months from MTI," said Richard Ticktin, composer Jerry Bock's friend and lawyer. "The other day, I noted it was done in Senegal, which was the first time I'd seen that country on any report. Poland, Austria, Hungary, they're frequently on the list, but Senegal was a first for me. *Fiddler* has been done in probably one hundred thirty countries all over the world."

Are they alike, the audiences in Senegal, Poland, and Austria? Librettist Stein thought so. "I get a lot of joy from hearing the reaction of the audience," Stein said. "I never saw an audience that didn't stand up and applaud. I've seen it in ten countries and the audience is alike each time."

Bock and Harnick, too, often attended performances abroad and found it immensely gratifying. "When I'd go to see productions in Amsterdam or Budapest, the actors would tell me how much they felt for the material in terms of their own experience," Bock said. "Perhaps more than letters was actually being there and hearing them respond to the material and tell me tales."

Few countries seem to have embraced *Fiddler* more than Japan, where Bock called it "a phenomenal success." The first production of *Fiddler* in Japan, which opened on September 6, 1967, at Tokyo's Imperial Theatre, launched a continuing relationship, with hundreds of performances traversing the decades. Hisaya Morishige, who would go on to play the show nine hundred times, "had studied [Zero] Mostel's interpretation of the role," wrote *The New York Times*, and had received coaching from Herschel Bernardi, a Mostel successor who was vacationing in Tokyo at the time. The show was directed and choreographed by Robbins interpreter Sammy Bayes.

Violinist Isaac Stern was in Tokyo soon after the first Japanese production opened and was very moved, he wrote later. He had seen the show in New York starring Zero Mostel on opening night, then twice more, weeping every time. Invited to the Japanese production soon after it opened, he found he wasn't alone. "I looked around at the audience," he wrote in his memoir, "and saw half the women in the traditional kimono and half in Western dress, and practically everyone there was crying, too, including not a few men."

It took several years for the show to be done again in Japan, however. Norio Miyazaki, today executive producer of Japan's Toho Co., Ltd., explained that it took a while for Japanese versions of imported musicals generally to catch on in Japan. Although Toho had cast stars Hisaya Morishige as Tevye and Fubuki Koshiji as Golde, said Miyazaki, "it had been only four years since the dawn of Broadway musicals in Japan, and both staff and audience members seemed to be still in the trial and error stage."

Toho was back in 1975 with a *Fiddler* revival that fared better at the box office. For one thing, Morishige "came to realize that Tevye matched the essence of his art as an actor and this role would be his lifework," said Miyazaki, then directly involved with the show. Instead of the Imperial Theatre, Toho presented the show at the slightly smaller Nissay Theatre, which proved to be "just the right size." Equally important, noted the producer, "Mr. Morishige played the role as a family man, seeing his daughters becoming independent, and as a story of human love regardless of the Jewish characteristics."

The changes worked, the producer said. The new emphasis on family "reached to the audience and thus it became a beloved show," said Miyazaki. When *Fiddler* was presented again at the Imperial Theatre in 1976 after a regional tour, he noted, the curtain call lasted twenty minutes after each performance.

Morishige was fifty-four when he began playing Tevye in Japan, and the actor continued playing the patriarch for nearly twenty years. When he stopped playing Tevye, he told Tokyo's *The Daily Yomiuri*, "I felt as if I was saying good-bye to a good friend."

The first time librettist Joseph Stein was in Japan to see *Fiddler*, he remembered "being enormously concerned and enormously skeptical about how it would be received, since the culture seemed so distant. Then the Japanese producer asked me, 'Do they understand this show in America?' When I responded, 'Why do you ask?' he said, 'Because it's so Japanese.'"

It was when he saw the show in Japan, Stein said several years later, "that I realized we had unwittingly written something very special and apparently universal. The themes of the show are as true to the Japanese experience and Japanese culture as they are to the American or English: the breakdown of tradition, the differences between generations, the eagerness to hang on to a religious background. These things are very much a part of the human experience. I think if anything, *Fiddler on the Roof* is even more relevant today, because it talks about a world in turbulence."

Fiddler on the Roof became Toho's most popular American musical (followed closely by *Man of La Mancha* and *My Fair Lady*). By 2009,

Fiddler on the Roof had been presented 1,337 times, and it was scheduled for forty more performances in 2013. Said producer Miyazaki: "It has always been a very popular, often sold-out production."

MTI executive Freddie Gershon calls Japan a "very, very valuable market" and overseeing care of that market is Koji Aoshika, an MTI veteran who worked first in Japan and today occupies a Japanese-inspired office near Gershon's. Asked what *Fiddler* is about, Aoshika said, "It's about the story of family. Traditionally in Japan, whatever the father ordered, you had to do. Because *Fiddler* is about a father losing power and a daughter acquiring more freedom, it became like a Japanese family drama and more acceptable to Japanese audiences. The Jewish setting is not the theme of the show."

In 1987, composer Raphael Mostel was invited to compose music and perform it at the atom bomb commemorations in Hiroshima and Nagasaki in Japan and consulted various people in New York for advice. Among them was Eido Shimano, then abbot of New York's Zen Studies Society. When Mostel was ushered in for a formal audience, he said, "It slowly dawned on me that the reason why was less about Hiroshima and more because of my Uncle Zero. The abbot told me that when he first came to New York, one of the things he did as he was trying to learn English was to go see *Fiddler on the Roof.* He said he was so impressed by the way my uncle spoke directly to God, he saw the show nine times."

With its timeless themes, *Fiddler* has become a sort of tabula rasa for terrorism, repression, and prejudice that seems eternally pertinent. Warnings that "horrible things are happening all over the land" could apply to Nazi Germany, Vietnam, or Iraq as much as to pre-revolutionary Russia. So could Tevye's rejoinder to hearing "an eye for an eye, a tooth for a tooth": "And that way, the whole world will be blind and toothless."

"I related to the show because my grandparents went through the same thing when they suffered persecution at the hands of the Turks," said the actress Adrienne Barbeau, who first performed as Hodel on Broadway in the 1960s. Later cast as Golde at the Music Circus in Sacramento in the summer of 2012, Barbeau watched her director Glenn Casale remind his young cast to look at what was going on in Syria. "We are still going through this," she said. "It's just as timely today as when it was written."

Lynn Stalmaster, the film's casting director, had visited many countries, often watching *Fiddler* onstage with local residents. "In Munich, I was sitting there, and I looked around at all these Aryans, and very few Jews, and they were mesmerized and attentive," said Stalmaster. "It appealed to all ethnic backgrounds."

The better the play or film, the better it connects with audiences, observed the actor Theodore Bikel. "Audiences are bright and don't go just for what they are intimately acquainted with," said Bikel. "Non-blacks connect to plays by August Wilson. If it's a good play, it's a good play. I don't have to be Danish to like *Hamlet*."

On tour in the show, actor Bikel often saw audience members draw parallels with their own lives. He'd be in Hawaii, for instance, and come out to a sea of Japanese, Chinese, and Hawaiians, some of them crying, he said. "I'd ask them, 'What does this play mean to you? 1905? Jews? Pogroms? Russia?' and they'd say, 'Tradition.' They knew what it was like for children not to follow traditions."

Nearly everyone involved with *Fiddler* seems to have similar stories. Harnick recalled being at an Actors Fund benefit when the actress Florence Henderson came over to say she thought *Fiddler* was about her Irish grandmother. "We worked very hard to concentrate on universal values," Harnick has said. "Ultimately, it was a story that just happened to be about Jewish people. What *Fiddler* did was show that basically Jews are just like everybody else."

Fiddler on the Roof offered "one of the first post-Holocaust representations of pre-Holocaust Jewish life," wrote authors Roger Bennett and Josh Kun in their book *And You Shall Know Us by the Trail of Our Vinyl: The Jewish Past as Told by the Records We Have Loved and Lost*. "Philip Roth may have rightfully decried it as 'shtetl kitsch,' but the quaint feel-good romance of Old World poverty (complete with a coming-to-America happy ending) created the first true universal Fast Pass to American

Jewishness. . . . No other Jewish anything has had a never-ending after-life in Norway, Rhodesia, Finland, Mexico, Austria, Holland, and Japan as *Fiddler* has."

For producer Prince, "What the show ultimately celebrated was this melting pot called America. At the end of the show, that's where they were going. It is to America that so many of these people came. And that's the strength of this country—its identification with so many cultures and religions. It's an amazing experiment that worked."

19

The Phenomenon

F*iddler on the Roof* has probably inspired few more passionate admirers than Lin-Manuel Miranda, the man behind *In the Heights*, the 2008 Tony Award–winning musical about New York's Washington Heights. Miranda saw *Fiddler* initially in first grade, played "a generic son" in the opening number of his school's sixth-grade production, and never forgot it.

When Miranda got an assignment to interview *Fiddler*'s Joseph Stein for the Dramatists Guild Fund's "The Legacy Project," he could not have been more excited. Not only did he grow up with *Fiddler*, he told Stein, but also "*Fiddler*'s DNA is all over *In the Heights*. Almost every creative discussion about the structure of the show would come back to *Fiddler*. *Fiddler* was our blueprint."

Comparisons start with the opening number of *In the Heights,* in which composer/lyricist Miranda and librettist Quiara Alegría Hudes present their onstage community to the audience. "We start with the graffiti artist," explained Miranda. "He's our fiddler, and he introduces us to his family. Then we go to the business owners and the outliers, and by the end of the opening number, you know the town. *Fiddler*'s opening number was such a master class in how to introduce our world.

"What does 'Tradition' do incredibly well?" asked Miranda. "First of all, it makes us familiar with Tevye's world. We can relax and say, 'I know these people.' We see Golde nudge Tevye. We hear Tevye say, 'I have five daughters.' These are really human moments where we get to know and love them and be on their side. That's a way of making an audience feel taken care of."

Miranda and playwright Hudes similarly focused on their own community. "We don't have Cossacks in Upper Manhattan," said Miranda. "What we have is much harder to dramatize actually, which is gentrification. We show what gets lost and what is worth saving. Those sorts of questions are central to both our shows."

Elisa and Joseph Stein went backstage after seeing *In the Heights* so Stein could tell Miranda how much he enjoyed the show. "I hope so," Miranda responded, "because all the best stuff we took from you." Stein paused, smiled, and said, "You know, you're right."

When Miranda and his future wife, Vanessa Nadal, were planning their September 2010 wedding, he found yet another chance to revisit *Fiddler*. In Los Angeles that summer with a touring production of *In the Heights*, the actor was on the hotel's treadmill, listening to his iPod, when the *Fiddler* song "To Life" popped up. "I was getting married in three months, and I realized this was the only father-in-law, son-in-law song I ever heard. 'My daughter! My wife!' I thought, We have to surprise Vanessa with this at the wedding."

By the time the song finished, Miranda was casting it in his head with characters from his own life. Frank, his future father-in-law, would be Tevye, and his father would play the Russians. "I stopped working out and went upstairs to my hotel room to write down who would play what, and then I e-mailed everyone," said Miranda. "I called Frank first. He grew up in New York, he's an old-school crooner, and he loves singing. When he said 'I'm in,' I knew my dad would say yes. My poor Puerto Rican dad had to sing in Russian, but he's a worse ham than I am."

When he got back to New York at the beginning of August, the performer started rehearsals with the two fathers. He'd often disappear, telling his future bride that he had meetings on his next musical, *Bring It On*. Then he'd go twenty blocks to his future father-in-law's house to sing with him. The growing production number rehearsed at *In the Heights* choreographer Andy Blankenbuehler's studio—he was also doing *Bring It On* choreography, said Miranda, "so it was a good cover"—and friends from various productions of *In the Heights* helped create simplified versions of the music and dance steps.

Next Miranda got the bridal party involved, so that, by the number's conclusion, there were about thirty-five people dancing. Their friends were scattered, so most of the dance rehearsals were the week before the wedding. Miranda even scheduled a big rehearsal after his fiancée Vanessa's bridal shower since he knew everyone would be around. "I told her I had a *Bring It On* rehearsal, and her friends told her they had no time to hang out with her," said Miranda. "As the weekend went on, she told me about how all our friends are getting along so well."

Then came the big event, and his new wife was definitely surprised by it all. As more and more people joined the singing and dancing, she looked more and more astonished, laughing and covering her face. "When everyone was dancing, she asked her bridal party, 'Did you guys know this was going to happen?'" said Miranda, watching his wife's expressions on a wedding video. "They all said 'no,' and two minutes later, they were up there. I was by her side all day, and I had to just trust that everyone got their microphones. It was a lot of work to make it look effortless, but it went off without a hitch."

Miranda's nearly six-minute video, called "To Life: Vanessa's Wedding Surprise," went up on YouTube four days after the wedding, and had a million views the first week. By early 2014, it had more than 3.3 million views and had been the number one video in Israel. "There were so many comments about how we were a good Jewish couple," Miranda laughed. "I'm Puerto Rican and Mexican, my wife is Dominican and Austrian. The only religion I take seriously is musical theater."

The best-known wedding song from *Fiddler*, however, is probably still "Sunrise, Sunset." Los Angeles wedding DJ Señor Amor calls it "the traditional father/daughter dance song. People grew up listening to the original Broadway recording, and I don't strictly play it at Jewish weddings. My wife, from Lubbock, Texas, had 'Sunrise, Sunset' played at her own first wedding when she was eighteen, and she's definitely not Jewish."

"Sunrise, Sunset" got some contemporizing in late 2011, courtesy of Rev. Joshua Ellis, a former Broadway press agent who had long been a fan of the song. "We used to joke—what did people do at weddings before 1964?" asked Ellis. "Were there two and a half minutes of silence waiting for them to write 'Sunrise, Sunset'?"

But given its references to little girls and little boys, it was not so familiar at same-sex weddings. It didn't apply to gay couples, explained Reverend Ellis, an interspiritual minister who was eager to change that. He'd been officiating at same-sex weddings in New York since four days after the New York State Marriage Equality Act went into effect in the summer of 2011, and he was about to officiate at the wedding party of entertainer/singer Richard Skipper and landscape architect Daniel Sherman. So, after making sure Skipper and Sherman wanted him to use an updated version of the song, Ellis went to lyricist Sheldon Harnick.

Introduced by mutual friends, Ellis sent Harnick an e-mail with his request. The lyricist thought it was a good idea and took the question to Richard Ticktin, his late partner Jerry Bock's lawyer and friend, who agreed with him. "Jerry would have been thrilled," Ticktin said later. "It made 'Sunrise, Sunset,' which was always relevant, even more relevant in this day and age. It sounded right to me."

Soon after Harnick e-mailed new lyrics to Ellis, Ellis sent Harnick another e-mail saying he knew he was pushing his luck, but would Harnick consider doing it for lesbians, as well? Two days later, lyrics for lesbian couples arrived. About three weeks after that came a follow-up e-mail from Harnick. The then eighty-seven-year-old lyricist wrote that he'd given the matter additional thought and written two more verses for Gentiles.

The lyrics had their world premiere on October 1, 2011, when Skipper and Sherman celebrated their July marriage with a special party. The couple, among the first one hundred to get married the day same-sex marriages became legal in New York, was immortalized in the media, and so were Harnick's new lyrics, which got coverage everywhere from *The New York Times* to Brides.com and Lesbilicious.co.uk.

Skipper also provided details in his blog, where he observed that "Josh said it was a shot in the dark . . . [but] Mr. Harnick opened his heart and put pen to paper and gave my partner and myself a GIFT that will continue to give for all eternity. *Fiddler on the Roof* is about embracing tradition while accepting the changes that are also happening. What could be more appropriate than this song?"

What did Harnick write? The original lyrics, sung by Tevye at his eldest daughter Tzeitel's wedding, began: "Is this the little girl I carried?/Is this the little boy at play?" The changed lyrics for couples of two men included a new beginning of: "Is this the little boy I carried?/Is that the little boy at play?" For couples of two women, it began similarly "Is this the little girl I carried?/Is that the little girl at play?" Nobody tampered, however, with such memorable lines as Golde's "I don't remember growing older./When did they?"

While "Sunrise, Sunset" might dominate weddings, "If I Were a Rich Man" is surely a close second in popular culture. When New Yorker Isaac Sasson of Flushing, Queens, won a thirteen-million-dollar Lotto jackpot, for instance, he told a reporter that the first thing he thought of when he got the news "was Tevye from *Fiddler on the Roof* dancing around singing, 'If I Were a Rich Man.'"

"If I Were a Rich Man," too, has had a few makeovers. The first popularized redo, "Rich Girl," came courtesy of the English reggae duo Louchie Lou & Michie One in 1993, with such lyrics as "If me rich, would I take a mon offa the streets/And if me rich, would I build up a school and teach in a-it." The song has had more than half a million YouTube hits and is still played in clubs.

Gwen Stefani released her own version of "Rich Girl" in 2004 on her debut solo album, *Love. Angel. Music. Baby.* Her pirate-themed music video, which had 24 million hits (and 8,500 comments) by 2013 on YouTube, is replete with Japanese schoolgirls, rapper Eve, and lots of semi-clad Stefani footage. Among its lyrics: "Think what that money could bring/I'd buy everything/Clean out Vivienne Westwood/In my Galliano gown."

Louchie Lou, Michie One, and Gwen Stefani joined many other musicians interpreting those *Fiddler* songs. Besides cast albums in several languages, early recordings by such people as the Barry Sisters, Cannonball Adderley, and Ferrante & Teicher have been joined over the years by jazz and easy listening versions, parodies, and many a karaoke album; even St. Thomas the Apostle Children's Choir recorded songs from *Fiddler*. YouTube offers innumerable renditions by everyone from the Temptations to assorted Japanese Tevyes.

Then there are the *Fiddler* sing-alongs. At the Loft Cinema in Tucson, Arizona, *Fiddler* sing-along participants were offered a "Tequila 'Sunrise, Sunset' drink special," while Chapel Hill, North Carolina, hosted "the first annual *Fiddler on the Roof* sing-along and kosher Chinese dinner." A sing-along at the Capitol Theater in Olympia, Washington, helped collect coats and blankets for the homeless.

In Southern California, *Fiddler on the Roof* sing-alongs have become a holiday tradition since the Laemmle theater chain launched an annual Christmas Eve sing-along in 2008. Christmas Eve fell on a Friday night in 2010, and Laemmle Theatre's president Greg Laemmle began that year's screening by saying, "Welcome fellow *shabbaz* [Sabbath] violators." By 2012, *Fiddler*'s Christmas Eve sing-along had expanded to three Laemmle theaters, and, by 2013, to six.

As sing-alongs and YouTube videos have made clear, *Fiddler*'s melodies appeal to singers of all ages and nationalities—and talent. Captured on assorted videos and Internet sites are schoolchildren, college students, and everyday folk who sing on and off key to "If I Were a Rich Man," "Matchmaker, Matchmaker," "To Life," and everything else.

Some of those amateurs wind up as professionals, of course. Several prominent performers have played in *Fiddler* not only on Broadway during its long run and subsequent revivals, but also in high school, college, and community theater productions when they were younger. For instance, Josh Gad, nominated for a Tony Award for portraying Elder Cunningham in *The Book of Mormon*, has publicly thanked his high school drama teacher for the chance to play Tevye "with the worldliness and life experiences that only a fifteen-year-old could bring to that role."

Jack McBrayer, the sweet Southern lad on TV's *30 Rock*, told talk show host Conan O'Brien that he once played the rabbi's son, Mendel, in a Conyers, Georgia, production of *Fiddler*, despite an accent more Southern than Yiddish. And when the actor John C. Reilly was in school, he, too, was in *Fiddler*. "I played the Russian commissar and didn't even get to sing," Reilly complained to a reporter. "So I stood backstage every night, singing 'Sunrise, Sunset.'"

Sacha Baron Cohen recycled his Tevye experiences to snare the part of competitive singing barber Pirelli in Tim Burton's film *Sweeney Todd.* Having played Tevye when he was at Cambridge, the actor sang "If I Were a Rich Man" at his audition for the film. Producer Richard Zanuck later said on the *Sweeney Todd* special edition DVD that Cohen's "abridged version" of *Fiddler* did more than greatly amuse him and Burton. "Despite all the laughter, we realized, 'This guy's got a great voice.' He had the part right then."

After half a century of steady reinforcement, *Fiddler on the Roof* has achieved recognition far beyond the theater or movie house. People who have never seen the show or movie can often recognize not just *Fiddler*'s songs but also some of its best-known lines and jokes. Comedy writers have also found many a good sight gag in Anatevka.

Consider the blind violinist who appears onstage near the start of the musical *The Producers*. When Mel Brooks came up with the character, recalls *The Producers* director Susan Stroman, "I couldn't help but think of *Fiddler on the Roof.* It didn't work to put a violinist on a roof at the Shubert Theatre, but I did it for a scene we later had to cut from *The Producers* film. If you love the theater, you love that show and want to cross paths with it."

A spoof of "Tradition" concluded one of the first *Forbidden Broadway* satirical revues in 1982. Various actors each sang about their ambitions in the properly syllabled title song "Ambition!" said Gerard Alessandrini, creator, writer, and director of *Forbidden Broadway*. They wore such costumes as babushkas and aprons, he added, plus "we did some very watered-down Jerome Robbins choreography with arms raised and fingers snapping" in a parody *Forbidden Broadway* presented on and off for years.

"Everybody knows *Fiddler on the Roof*," said Alessandrini. "It may be the most famous musical ever, and any kind of halfway good spoof is very funny. It's also a dramatic musical, and it's more effective to make fun of a dramatic musical. There's a double advantage to the show being not only well-known but food for parody."

Fiddler is similarly a continuing source of material for Jon Stewart and *The Daily Show*. One night in the fall of 2012, Stewart lampooned his Jewish roots during a scene in which he read Philip Roth's *Portnoy's Complaint* while listening on earphones to "Sunrise, Sunset"; perhaps six weeks later, he sang a few bars of "Tradition" when discussing Middle East problems.

From *Seinfeld* and *Friends* to *Saturday Night Live* and *Mad Men*, television writers have frequently mined *Fiddler* for cultural references, plot points, and ready humor. When *The Simpsons'* Homer Simpson was trying to get money for a triple bypass, for instance, he assured the show's Rabbi Krustofski: "Now I know I haven't been the best Jew, but I have rented *Fiddler on the Roof* and I will watch it."

Among the most ambitious parodies was a January 1973 *Mad* magazine cover story called "Antenna on the Roof" featuring Alfred E. Neuman on the roof with violin in hand as Chaim Topol, Molly Picon, and the film's other lead actors clamor below. A "sing-along rendition" by artist Mort Drucker and writer Frank Jacobs reworked *Fiddler* from a musical "about the problems of people who had *nothing*" to a version "about the problems of people who have *everything*." Tevye's three oldest daughters appear as sex fanatics whose sentimental song "Matchmaker, Matchmaker" has been reworked as "Head-shrinker, Head-shrinker."

In April 2004 at the eighteenth annual Easter Bonnet Competition for Broadway Cares/Equity Fights AIDS, the top award went to the casts of *Avenue Q* and *Fiddler on the Roof* who joined forces to present a skit entitled "Avenue Jew." The resulting mashup, immortalized on YouTube, starts with a monster puppet playing the violin, then trying to eat it. In a later scene with two male puppets, one sings "Find Me a Boy, No Foreskin Attached."

Fiddler was used again to raise money to fight AIDS in 2007, the year *In the Heights* first triumphed off-Broadway. For Broadway Cares/Equity Fights AIDS' twenty-first annual Easter Bonnet Competition, actor Miranda led a number called "Tradizzle" that started with a fiddler playing those familiar opening notes. Soon young people in shorts and T-shirts filled the stage, singing out hip-hop lyrics and rapping to the tune of "Tradition."

Fiddler's Sheldon Harnick heard about "Tradizzle," and when he was called upon to present Miranda with an award a few years later, the lyricist turned his introduction into a rap-inspired rendering of the younger man's bio. Miranda called the presentation "one of the great honors of my life" and has Harnick's sheet music transcription of the introduction framed over his piano at home.

Miranda came away with another *Fiddler*-inspired memory just after he concluded his Dramatists Guild video interview with playwright Stein. Before leaving Stein's home, he returned a call and learned that he and playwright Quiara Alegría Hudes had received Pulitzer Prize nominations for *In the Heights*. He shared the news with Stein, who remarked that *Fiddler* never won the Pulitzer. Quipped Miranda: "But *Fiddler* won the hearts of millions."

EPILOGUE

20

Closing the Circle

The year 2010 was a sad one for the *Fiddler on the Roof* family. Joseph Stein passed away first, at age ninety-eight, on October 24th. Jerry Bock, who was among the dozen speakers at Stein's memorial service, died, at age eighty-one, less than two weeks later on November 3rd. Sheldon Harnick, then in his mid-eighties, became the show's sole surviving author.

Just two days before Bock's death, the composer and Harnick received lifetime achievement awards from the Dramatists Guild. Broadway marquees dimmed their theater lights in Bock's memory as they had for Stein.

At services for Stein at New York's Riverside Memorial on October 27, 2010, speakers noted how glad the librettist was to have introduced so many people to the theater through *Fiddler*. There was a piano on hand, several of his collaborators sang show tunes, and even son Harry Stein felt the mood was more celebratory than mournful. "The house was standing room only," recalled the younger Stein. "He'd have loved to have been there—though he'd have said, 'I'd have loved to be anywhere.'"

Bock's memorial was held at the American Airlines Theatre the following January, where friends and colleagues recounted many of their shows with Bock. Performers sang, writers spoke, friends wept. "When I direct a show with a traditional score, I tell the casting director to ask actors to sing a Bock and Harnick song," director Lonny Price said that day. "Always. And the reason is that the best of our humanity comes out with their material."

Also speaking at the memorial was Tony Walton, set designer on *She Loves Me* and one of *Fiddler*'s original investors. When Harold Prince was raising money for the show, said Walton, "He said he was counting on his friends. I put in two hundred dollars, it still trickles in, and it was the only sensible financial decision I ever made in my life."

It was a sensible financial decision for many other people, as well. By fall of 1968, *Fiddler*'s original 152 investors had received distributions of $4.2 million, or $11.29 for each dollar invested, *The New York Times* reported at the time, and by the end of 2013, producer Prince's office put that return at $38.84 per dollar. *Fiddler* royalties were still averaging more than $2.5 million a year in recent years, excluding Broadway but including all secondary amounts licensed by Music Theatre International, according to MTI's CFO, Peter Gerstheimer.

A few months after the Bock memorial, Harnick wrote a tribute to Bock and Stein in *The Dramatist* about his pleasure in knowing and working with them both. He ended his remarks by saying he'd received "countless messages of condolence," and he wanted to share the one "that made me smile." The actor Brad Oscar wrote: "The Lord must have serious second act trouble if he sent for both Joe Stein and Jerry Bock."

Joseph Stein had taken a shot at rekindling *Fiddler*'s magic in 1986 with a musical called *Rags*, which picked up the story of immigrant Jews once they arrived in New York. "So many people asked me to write a sequel to *Fiddler*," Stein said. "I didn't want to, in the sense of using those characters, but I thought the idea of writing about the immigrant experience was exciting."

Rags, with music by Charles Strouse and lyrics by Stephen Schwartz, received poor notices and closed after just four performances. But it was nominated for four Tony Awards, including one for Stein's libretto, and had quite a dramatic demise. When the show was scheduled to close,

Rags' actors marched from the theater to the TKTS booth in Times Square chanting "Keep *Rags* Open!!"

Rags was Stein's last Broadway musical, but he had several other pieces in progress after that. "He was working on something until his last day," said his widow, Elisa Stein. "He was working on a musical called *Heaven Can Wait*, with my daughter, his stepdaughter Jenny Lyn Bader, when he died. The last scene he wrote in the hospital was a dialogue among three angels."

Stein didn't even let hospitals get him down. About a year before he died, the playwright was in New York's Mount Sinai Hospital, expecting to be released soon. But hearing that his friend Freddie Gershon might want to visit, he gave Gershon some instructions. "I have played the *Fiddler* card to get a lot of attention," Stein told Gershon. "Everyone here knows that I wrote *Fiddler on the Roof* but nobody knows what it means to write a show or who writes what. So if the nurses begin to sing to you, 'Sunrise, Sunset,' don't say I didn't write it!"

Back at home later, Stein would sometimes sit in his study, reviewing photographs online of nonprofessionals who were appearing in *Fiddler*. One afternoon, fascinated by pictures of children performing *Fiddler* at a middle school in Namibia, he turned to his archivist, Hannah Kohl, to say, "We're everywhere. Where do you think we're playing now?"

Why guess? Kohl sent an e-mail to Music Theatre International, which licenses such productions, and MTI sent back a list of every production coming up in the next few months—a multipage, single-spaced printout. "The show was all over the world, and Joe got such a kick out of it," Kohl said. "He was still thrilled."

Around the same time, Harnick sent an e-mail to Stein, forwarding a YouTube clip of Israel's IDF Marching Band, soldiers all, performing in Moscow's Red Square for the very first time. Forty-five musicians played for nearly ten minutes, and their musical selections included both "Sunrise, Sunset" and "If I Were a Rich Man."

Stein got Harnick on the phone, and they were both watching it simultaneously. Stein was laughing and crying, watching it again and again. "There were moments of shock, pride, and happiness," recalled

Kohl. "'Do you see this?' he'd ask me. 'Do you see what's happening here? I never thought I would live to see something like this. They chased us out of Russia, and now they're cheering us.'"

Sholem Aleichem's legacy, too, continues strong. To this day, Aleichem's life and work are celebrated by family and friends in an annual ceremony. According to his great-grandson Kenneth Kaufman, the writer in his will "asked his descendants to remember him on the anniversary of his death by having his family and good friends gather together to read his will and to pick out a story, one of the really merry ones, in whatever language they understand best."

These annual memorials, or *yahrzeits*, have gone on since the first anniversary of his death, and today five generations of descendants attend the annual event. Alecheim's granddaughter Bel Kaufman has long been the centerpiece of the gatherings, held first in private homes, including Kaufman's, and more recently at the Brotherhood Synagogue on Gramercy Park South. Kenneth Kaufman, who hosted the 2011 *yahrzeit*, set the mood that year by repeating a joke from the previous year: "I have been to a great many *yahrzeits* since I was a young boy. Of all the ones our family held, this is by far the most recent."

Aleichem's legacy goes far beyond the family, of course. "The love he inspires is not the way a reader usually loves a writer," said Bel Kaufman, herself a celebrated writer for the best-selling 1965 novel *Up the Down Staircase*. "He is loved like a close member of the great global Jewish community. I gave a talk about him some years ago in Montreal, and when I finished, an old man was wheeled to the stage by a nurse. He stretched out his hand and said, 'I live in an old people's home. I'm blind, and I cannot see you, I'm deaf, and I cannot hear you, but when I learned Sholem Aleichem's granddaughter was in my city, I insisted they bring me here so I could touch your hand.'"

For former *New York Times* drama critic Frank Rich, *Fiddler*'s legacy similarly goes beyond the show itself. Director-choreographer Robbins and producer Prince, working separately and together, "redefined the musical to dramatize such weighty concerns as the street gangs of *West Side Story*, the semi-psychotic mother of *Gypsy*, and the pogroms of *Fiddler on the Roof*," said Rich. "*Fiddler*, coming last, ended the Broadway supremacy of escapist hit musicals like *Funny Girl* and *Hello, Dolly!* and many of the enduring musical classics after *Fiddler* exactly followed the Robbins/ Prince blueprint. First came *Cabaret*, with Prince taking up where Robbins left off, and then the Sondheim musicals. We remember *Fiddler* not for 'Matchmaker, Matchmaker,' but for 'Tradition' and 'Anatevka'—the serious stuff that was propelling the musical theater forward."

Will *Fiddler on the Roof* still move audiences in fifty more years? Harvey Fierstein thinks so. "I've played the show in San Francisco, Fort Worth, Atlanta, and Toronto. I've played it all over, and the reaction is the same. When I was on Broadway, I'd look out into the house, and there would be Hasidic Jews and nuns or maybe a high school cheerleading team in town for a competition, and they all sat with rapt attention watching it. They all got it. The day the boys finished writing it and put it up on the stage, it was part of our culture.

"The audience is there for that show wherever you go," summarized Fierstein. "And the reactions are the same wherever you go. It doesn't matter if you're playing a theater or an opera house or an arena. *Fiddler* goes directly to the heart. The show reaches you, no matter who you are or where you are in your life. It changes with you."

Topol felt similarly. "I think about the life I have now as a father and husband," the performer said in 2012. "When Tevye and Golde sing 'Do You Love Me?' they have been married twenty-five years. And every time I sang it, I'd think, How can I maintain *my* marriage for twenty-five years? You need a lot of good will. And then suddenly I was married twenty-five years, and then thirty, then forty, then fifty. I found myself thinking about Tevye and Golde, married only twenty-five years. They're children."

Asked if he had concerns about being so strongly identified with the role of Tevye, a part he was still playing several decades after the film, Topol responded: "There are only about five or six actors in the world who have come to represent a single role: Anthony Quinn as Zorba, Yul

Brynner as the King, Rex Harrison as Professor Higgins . . . I'm sure every actor would like to have such an opportunity. I could only wish for two such roles."

Topol also looked upon the film experience with nostalgia. "More than forty years after we shot it, it's still a film you can watch today. Most films made forty years ago, you can't watch anymore. But every Christmas or Easter, it's a family film that comes on television everywhere, from Madrid to Tel Aviv. More than one billion people have seen the film now."

Librettist Harnick was at Lincoln Center in 2011 with Norman Jewison when the film screened as part of the Film Society of Lincoln Center's retrospective for the filmmaker. "I was so moved," Harnick told the audience who had just seen the film. "As I'm sure you all know, Jerry Bock and Joe Stein died within a week and a half of each other not too long ago. As I looked at the movie, I thought, What a splendid memorial this is."

Visibly moved, Jewison replied in kind. "I must say, I was totally inspired by the lyrics and the work that was done on this play. Trying to translate it to the screen was a lot of pressure. I didn't want to screw it up."

Acknowledgments

I would first like to thank the extensive *Fiddler on the Roof* family of creators, producers, directors, actors, musicians, designers, archivists, and fans who gave me so much of their time.

While everyone I interviewed was incredibly welcoming, I should single out a few people. Lyricist Sheldon Harnick and producer Harold Prince have talked with me a great deal these last few years, always graciously. Lynn Stalmaster came to my home with extensive notes from his casting of the *Fiddler* film, while the film's director/producer Norman Jewison twice sat with me for long meetings at his Malibu home, sharing not just great stories but also his *Fiddler* contacts.

I interviewed the late composer Jerry Bock several years ago, when I was writing about *Fiddler on the Roof* for the *Los Angeles Times,* and I greatly appreciate his lawyer and friend, Richard Ticktin, familiarizing me with Bock's early years and achievements. My earlier conversations with playwright Joseph Stein were similarly augmented by his widow, Elisa Stein, son, Harry Stein, and archivist, Hannah Kohl. Guiding me through her late husband's papers, Elisa Stein found articles and scrapbooks for me to read, videos and film clips to watch, even offering to feed me as the hours swept by.

Raphael Mostel, the composer, was an invaluable source of both background and anecdote on his celebrated uncle, the late Zero Mostel. Eric

Price, assistant to Harold Prince, was never too busy to honor one more request for facts or guidance with archives and photographs.

Many *Fiddler* performers also opened their homes and offices. *Fiddler*'s original Tzeitel, Joanna Merlin, had made extensive notes of what she wanted to say, while her onstage groom, Austin Pendleton, readily reconstructed many months of rehearsals, and out-of-town tryouts. Michele Marsh, daughter Hodel in Jewison's film, not only read aloud from letters she sent home to her mother at the time but, when I wearied, even shared Xeroxing chores.

Freddie Gershon, CEO of Music Theatre International, Richard Salfas, Carol Edelson, and other MTI executives proffered background and expertise on the wonders of musical theater licensing. Norio Miyazaki at Toho Co., Ltd., in Tokyo and producer Kim Poster at Stanhope Productions Limited in London similarly shared their knowledge of international *Fiddler* productions, while composer/orchestrator/conductor Larry Blank introduced me to many of the show's original Broadway musicians.

The Getty Research Institute once again afforded me a place to research and write in glorious quiet, making available extensive study materials on the great modernist painter Marc Chagall. The GRI's Alexa Sekyra, Sabine Schlosser, Rebecca Zamora, and Aimee Calfin were enormously helpful, as were the librarians and other staff of the Beverly Hills Library, once again a great resource on art, theater, and film. Once again, too, I drew on the vast collections of the Los Angeles Public Library, where I particularly appreciate the support and reference staff of the Donald Bruce Kaufman branch.

The Margaret Herrick Library of the Academy of Motion Picture Arts and Sciences was again another invaluable resource. I am especially grateful for the assistance of archivist Barbara Hall, who acquainted me with the Herrick's diverse *Fiddler on the Roof* materials. Ned Comstock, senior library assistant at the University of Southern California's Cinematic Arts Library, was a wonderful guide to the riches of the library's film collections.

In New York, I spent several weeks at the New York Public Library for the Performing Arts, Dorothy and Lewis B. Cullman Center, at Lincoln Center, reviewing documents and other research on *Fiddler*'s creators and early productions. Not only was I able to view an early *Fiddler on the Roof* stage production at the library's Theatre on Film and Tape Archive, but again and again I delved into folders, scrapbooks, recordings, and other holdings at the Jerome Robbins Dance Division and Billy Rose Theatre Division. I cannot thank enough the patient and knowledgeable John Calhoun at Billy Rose, Charles Perrier and Jan Schmidt at Jerome Robbins, and Eydie Wiggins, one of many members of the library staff who went out of her way to make sure my research needs were met.

I am also grateful to Christopher Pennington, executive director of the Jerome Robbins Foundation/The Robbins Rights Trust, for granting me permissions and access to historical documents and other papers relevant to my book.

My great thanks to my many interview subjects, among them Lynn Ahrens, Koji Aoshika, Gerard Alessandrini, David Andrews Rogers, Lisa Jalowetz Aronson, Adrienne Barbeau, Sammy Dallas Bayes, Theodore Bikel, Ken Billington, Paul Blake, Larry Blank, Jerry Bock, Randall Buck, Glenn Casale, Gino Conforti, Judi Davidson, Carol Edelson, Rev. Joshua Ellis, Tanya Everett, Harvey Fierstein, Freddie Gershon, Paul Michael Glaser, Henry Goodman, Michael Hackett, Sheldon Harnick, Rosalind Harris, Ron Jannelli, Norman Jewison, Bel Kaufman, Sandra Kazan, Hannah Kohl, Elaine Kussack, David Leveaux, Michele Marsh, Kyle McGinley, Joanna Merlin, Lin-Manuel Miranda, Norio Miyazaki, Raphael Mostel, Austin Pendleton, Rick Pessagno, David Picker, Kim Poster, Erwin Price, Rose Tillotson Price, Harold Prince, Frank Rich, Michael Riedel, Señor Amor, Richard Salfas, Neva Small, Lynn Stalmaster, Elisa Stein, Harry Stein, Joseph Stein, Susan Stroman, Richard Ticktin, Chaim Topol, Robin Wagner, Gerri Weagraff, John Williams, David Wohl, Jerry Zaks, and Louis Zorich.

Many other people should also be acknowledged here. For their help with background, contacts, research tips, or other courtesies, I wish to thank Jean Picker Firstenberg, George Weinberg, Cari Beauchamp, Jim McHugh, Sasha Anawalt, Barbara Casey, Irene Lacher, Jean Ann Allen, Dyanne Asimow, William Batchelder, Barbara Becker, Leo Braudy, Casey Chehrenegar, Courtney Davis, Tom D'Ambrosio, Steve Edlund, Allison Engel, Hershey Felder, Sharon Ferritto, Glenna Freedman, Linda

Friedman, Bronya Galef, Helen Guditis, Matt Hessburg, Rebecca Kasilag, Linda Kaufman, Gere Kavanaugh, Terry Lee, Ron Mandelbaum, Marcia Metzger, Rick Miramontez, Benedict Nightingale, Kenji Ogino, Lee Ramer, Jamie Richardson, David Rintels, Victoria Riskin, Steve Ross, Arthur B. Rubinstein, Erica Ryan, Julie Salamon, Richard Schickel, Paul Shapiro, Abby Sher, Jonathan Steiner, Louise Steinman, Joey Stocks, Mark Swed, Brooks Tillotson, and Lawrence Weschler.

I much appreciate early assistance from the artist Lindsay Ljungkull Clark, who worked with me until her own work pulled her away, and researcher Casie Kesterson came aboard to assist in organizing reference materials, notes and other research. Katelynn Whitaker contributed greatly in helping me ready my manuscript for publication.

My agent and friend Susan Ramer has again been a great source of support, encouragement and wisdom, and I feel similarly about Michael Flamini, my wise and witty editor at St. Martin's. He was excited by this project from his initial reading of my book proposal, and his enthusiasm never diminished. His wonderful assistant Vicki Lame expressed similar sentiments as she patiently guided me through the editorial process. I would also like to express my gratitude to Steve Snider for his joyous cover, as well as to copy editor Carly Sommerstein, designer Steven Seighman, and publicist John Karle.

Sadly, my longtime friend Douglas Ring died while I was writing this book, and I must now thank him posthumously. I wish also to acknowledge the comfort and counsel of friends Angela Rinaldi, Susan Loewenberg, Cindy Miscikowski, Susan Grode, Ruth Weisberg, and Alexis Smith. Ron Rapoport deserves special thanks for his many smart suggestions as an engaged listener and generous first reader.

It truly does take a village.

Notes

Most of my interviews for this book were done between 2010 and 2012. All remarks that did not originate in my own interviews have been noted here as to source. Because so many early chapters cite archives and papers at the New York Public Library's Library of the Performing Arts, Dorothy and Lewis B. Cullman Center in Lincoln Center, New York City, I am abbreviating that institution as NYPL. In later chapters I similarly abbreviate reference materials from the Margaret Herrick Library, Academy of Motion Picture Arts and Sciences as Herrick Library.

INTRODUCTION

vii *remains among Broadway's sixteen longest-running shows ever:* The Broadway League.

vii *including fifteen in Finland alone:* Richard Altman and Mervyn Kaufman, *The Making of a Musical: Fiddler on the Roof* (New York: Crown, 1971), 151.

CHAPTER 1

4 *Aleichem's Tevye stories . . . traditions:* Sholom Aleichem, *Tevye's Daughters* (New York: Crown, 1949), x–xi.

4 *An incredibly popular writer . . . "Aleichem":* Sholom Aleichem, *Favorite Tales of Sholom Aleichem,* trans. Julius and Frances Butwin (New York: Avenel Books, 1983), xi.

4 *Few writers . . . boroughs:* "Vast Crowds Honor Sholem Aleichem," *New York Times,* May 16, 1916.

4 The "boys," . . . rights: Jerry Bock diary, Bock Papers, NYPL.

5 *Proceeding without a producer . . . "to do":* Sheldon Harnick, interview by Peter Stone, "Fiddler on the Roof," *Dramatists Guild Quarterly,* Spring 1983, 11.

5 *In his outline . . . "for today":* Otis L. Guernsey, *Best Plays of 1964–1965 (The Burns Mantle Yearbook)* (New Hampshire: Ayer Co., 1964), 118.

6 *The shtetls . . . United States:* Sholem Aleichem, *Tevye the Dairyman and the Railroad Stories,* trans. Hillel Halkin (New York: Schocken, 1987), xi–xv.

6 *Adapting that world . . . "believe it":* Gregory Bossler, "Writers & Their Work: Joseph Stein." *The Dramatist,* January/February 2006, 9.

6 *God is an . . . "my brother":* Joseph Stein, excerpt from unidentified television interview, April 26, 2004, courtesy of Elisa Stein.

6 *The playwright found . . . deal with it:* Guernsey, *Best Plays of 1964,* 119.

7 *While Stein worked . . . their fourth song:* Bock diary, Jerry Bock Papers.

7 *Then, in November . . . "sentimental":* Audiotape played at Jerry Bock Memorial, January 24, 2011.

7 *It was the music . . . "something here":* Sheldon Harnick at screening of *Fiddler on the Roof,* Film Society of Lincoln Center, May 29, 2011.

8 *In her foreword . . . "exists":* Mark Zborowski and Elizabeth Herzog, *Life Is with People: The Culture of the Shtetl* (Madison, CT: International Universities Press, 1952), 12.

8 *It almost embarrasses . . . "take from":* Harnick at Lincoln Center, 2011.

8 *Bock, however . . . "for me":* Terry Gross, *Fresh Air,* National Public Radio, "Jerry Bock and Sheldon Harnick discuss writing music for Fiddler on the Roof," June 21, 2004.

9 *As the show's . . . "the musical":* Louis Calta, "Fiddler Is Saying Hello to a Record," *New York Times,* July 21, 1971.

CHAPTER 2

10 *He told . . . "the South":* Barbara Isenberg, "Surprise—It's Tradition," *Los Angeles Times*, January 13, 2002.

10 *As Prince said . . . "do it":* Remarks at Jerry Bock Memorial, January 24, 2011.

10 *Born in New York . . . award-winning musicals:* Later the most honored producer/director in Broadway history, Prince had won twenty-one Tony Awards by 2013 and counted up more than fifty productions, among them *Cabaret, Company, Evita,* and *The Phantom of the Opera.*

11 *First of all . . . "than words":* Isenberg, *Los Angeles Times.*

11 *In the early . . . to the rescue:* Deborah Jowitt, *Jerome Robbins: His Life, His Theater, His Dance* (New York: Simon & Schuster, 2004), 341.

11 *"I think it was . . . really was":* Greg Lawrence, *Dance with Demons: The Life of Jerome Robbins* (New York: G. P. Putnam's Sons, 2001), 336.

12 *Aleichem had . . . Schwartz:* Philip Lambert, *To Broadway, To Life!: The Musical Theater of Bock and Harnick* (Oxford University Press, 2011), 139–40.

12 *There had also been . . . to Broadway:* Sam Zolotow, "Aleichem Stories Inspire a Musical," *New York Times*, August 20, 1962.

12 *They did have . . . money:* Sheldon Harnick, interview by Peter Stone, "Fiddler on the Roof," *Dramatists Guild Quarterly*, Spring 1983, 15.

12 *They played the score . . . Penn:* Jerry Bock diary, NYPL.

12 *Penn later wrote . . . "important show":* Jerry Bock, interview by Peter Stone, "Fiddler on the Roof," *Dramatists Guild Quarterly*, Spring 1983, 16.

14 *Jerome Wilson Rabinowitz . . . Anatevka:* Amanda Vaill, *Somewhere: The Life of Jerome Robbins* (New York: Broadway Books, 2006), 5–9.

14 *When Robbins . . . "background I had":* *Jerome Robbins: Something to Dance About*, American Masters, PBS, July 31, 2009.

14 *"It was a very . . . "back in Russia":* Greg Lawrence, *Dance with Demons: The Life of Jerome Robbins* (New York: G. P. Putnam's Sons, 2001), 337.

14 *So it was . . . "It's our people":* Jerome Robbins Papers, NYPL.

15 *For Prince . . . "do the same":* Hal Prince, *Contradictions: Notes on Twenty-six Years in the Theatre* (New York: Dodd, Mead, 1974), 104.

15 *The very first . . . "something deeper":* Liane Hansen, "Jerry Bock and Sheldon Harnick, who wrote the lyrics for 'Fiddler on the Roof,' discuss the show's longevity and endurance," *Weekend Edition Sunday*, National Public Radio (May 7, 2000).

16 Song lyrics courtesy of Sheldon Harnick.

16 *On Forum . . . was about:* Jowitt, *Jerome Robbins*, 344.

16 *"Tradition . . . it worked":* *Dramatists Guild Quarterly*, Spring 1983, 19.

CHAPTER 3

17 Forum's *composer/lyricist . . . "do not blacklist":* Kate Mostel et al., *170 Years of Show Business* (New York: Random House, 1978), 8.

18 *When Robbins . . . "cracked up":* Lawrence, *Dance with Demons*, 311.

18 *Not only . . . "New York theater":* Kate Mostel et al., *170 Years*, 139.

19 *When they first . . . "monologue for him":* Bossler, "Writers & Their Work," 6.

19 *Mostel may have . . . "thanks":* Kate Mostel, et al., *170 Years*, 164.

19 *But Mostel did not . . . 1963:* Jared Brown, *Zero Mostel: A Biography* (New York: Atheneum, 1989), 208–10.

19 *After Stein and Robbins . . . "something special":* Kate Mostel et al., *170 Years*, 163–65.

19 *His Eastern European . . . East Side:* Brown, *Zero Mostel*, 1–3.

20 *In his 1971 book . . . Julius La Rosa:* Altman and Kaufman, *The Making*, 71.

20 *Other auditioners . . . Bosley:* Jerome Robbins Papers, NYPL.

20 *According to Kate . . . " for it?":* Kate Mostel et al., *170 Years*, 165.

20 *Prince considered Mostel . . . much later:* Prince, *Contradictions*, 105.

20 *On October 25th . . . "Jerry Robbins":* Jerome Robbins Papers, NYPL.

21 *With Pendleton in place . . . Rabbi:* Vaill, *Somewhere*, 367.

23 *Arthur did not . . . "human being":* Bea Arthur, *Just Between Friends*, 2002, NYPL Theatre on Film and Tape.

24 *Voluminous audition . . . apiece:* Jerome Robbins Papers, NYPL.

24 *When it came to . . . ability:* Harnick, *Dramatists Guild Quarterly*, 19.

25 According to the program at Detroit's Fisher Theatre, actor Robert Berdeen performed in Detroit as Fyedka. On Broadway, he played the Russian Sasha and understudied Fyedka.

26 *Writing an appreciation . . . "illuminated it":* Leo Lerman, "Jean Rosenthal 1912–1969," *New York Times*, May 11, 1969.

26 *Costume designer . . . "Madame Butterfly":* Frank Rich, *Interview with Patricia Zipprodt*, NYPL, Theatre on Film and Tape, 1996.

27 *But Zipprodt . . . electric brushes:* Patricia Zipprodt article in Kennedy Center program, 1976.

27 *After all the . . . "reluctantly":* Prince, *Contradictions*, 107.

27 *Rich told the designer . . . "each week":* Rich, *Interview with Patricia Zipprodt*, NYPL.

27 *It must have been . . . "assignment":* Frank Rich with Lisa Aronson, *The Theatre Art of Boris Aronson* (New York: Alfred A. Knopf, 1987), 171.

28 *Fiddler on the Roof* marked the first time Aronson and Prince worked together, and it was the start of an amazing collaboration that lasted until not long before Aronson's death in 1980. Their work together after *Fiddler* included not just the musicals *Cabaret* and *Zorba*, but a roster of such Stephen Sondheim shows as *Company* (1970), *Follies* (1971), *A Little Night Music* (1973), and *Pacific Overtures* (1976), which added five Tony Awards to Aronson's three earlier wins. See idbd.com.

CHAPTER 4

29 *"You get on . . . ahead of time":* Hansen, *Weekend Edition Sunday*.

30 *His notes . . . "should be":* Jerome Robbins Papers, NYPL.

30 *Citing . . . "our job":* Ibid.

31 *Indeed, the same day . . . for the show:* Jerome Robbins Papers, NYPL.

31 *For Aronson . . . "traditions alive":* B. Aronson, *Marc Chagall* (Berlin: Razum-Verlag, 1924), 14.

31 *Robbins gave . . . "reality":* Aronson Papers, NYPL.

31 *Robbins was particularly . . . the future:* Aronson Papers, NYPL.

31 *Paul Lipson . . . "always with them":* Arthur Sainer, *Zero Dances: A Biography of Zero Mostel* (New York: Limelight Editions, 1998), 242–43.

31 *Chagall appears . . . violinist himself:* Marc Chagall, *My Life*, trans. Dorothy Williams (London: Peter Owen Publishers, 1965), 17.

32 *While the rooftop fiddler . . .* The Old Country: Jerry Bock Papers, NYPL.

33 *The director . . .* The Cantor's Son: Jerome Robbins Papers, NYPL.

33 *the set designers . . . set details:* Rich with Aronson, *The Theatre Art*, 172.

33 *Aronson's files . . . unpaved streets:* Aronson Papers, NYPL.

34 *Robbins "got so upset . . . secretly":* Rich, *Interview with Patricia Zipprodt*, NYPL.

34 *Dance scholar . . . wedding dances:* Jerome Robbins Papers, NYPL.

34 *Costume designer Zipprodt . . . were wearing:* Patricia Zipprodt article in Kennedy Center program, 1976.

35 *When the director . . . "ballet out of that!":* Lawrence, *Dance with Demons*, 284–85.

35 *The circle idea . . . "American musical theater":* Rich with Aronson, *The Theatre Art*, 172–76.

36 *With Robbins . . . "Robbins was":* Prince, *Contradictions*, 105.

CHAPTER 5

37 *On April 3rd . . . extensions or trims there:* Harold Prince Papers, NYPL.

38 *Robbins told Bock and Harnick . . . "that wail":* Jerome Robbins Papers, NYPL.

38 *Just a few days . . . to start rehearsals:* Prince, *Contradictions*, 108.

39 *Prince had previously . . . lunched alone:* Ibid., 33.

39 *Another reason . . . "of the world":* Lawrence, *Dance with Demons*, 338–39.

41 *"He would just pull . . . snake!":* Jerome Robbins: Something to Dance About, American Masters, PBS, July 31, 2009.

41 *Interviewed shortly . . . "worked it out":* Barbara Gelb, "Robbins: He Kicks Up a Storm," *New York Times*, November 1, 1964.

41 *Bock, Stein and Harnick . . . of the show:* Harnick, *Dramatists Guild Quarterly*, 18–19.

41 *With the show's new emphasis . . . "new dialogue":* Burns-Mantle, 119.

41 *The director would . . . "better the other way":* Something to Dance About, PBS.

41 *But when . . . "Matchmaker":* Dramatists Guild Quarterly, 20.

42 *Similarly . . . "Move along!":* Lyrics courtesy of Sheldon Harnick.

43 *Mostel . . . "ending of it":* Jackson Bryer and Richard Davison, eds., *The Art of the American Musical: Conversations with the Creators* (New Brunswick, NJ and London: Rutgers University Press, 2005), 90.

43 *Mostel also asked . . . "the same thing":* Brown, *Zero Mostel*, 219–20.

44 *Mostel had been injured . . . wife, Kate:* Kate Mostel et al., *170 Years*, 149.

44 *After each performance . . . "temperature":* Ibid.

45 *Then came the final night . . . "overall coolness":* Altman and Kaufman, *The Making*, 3.

CHAPTER 6

49 *Stein found . . . "out of town":* Bossler, "Writers & Their Work," 9.

49 *Designed by . . . Broadway-bound shows:* See www.broadwayindetroit.com.

50 *Librettist Stein . . . "they have a pogrom!":* Stein, *Dramatists Guild Quarterly*, 23.

50 *Robbins had some . . . "one applaud":* Harnick, *Dramatists Guild Quarterly*, 24.

50 *When Robbins decided . . . "to hear it":* Kate Baldwin, *She Loves Him: Kate Baldwin, Live at Feinstein's*, with Sheldon Harnick, P.S. Classics, compact disc.

50 *The lyricist was worried . . . "I had been":* Bryer and Davison, eds., *The Art of the American Musical*, 87.

51 *Everything was expensive . . . "pocket $75,000":* Prince, *Contradictions*, 107.

51 *In his opening . . . "Rosenthal":* Tew, *Variety*, July 28, 1964.

51 *When Tew called . . . "entire company":* Altman, *The Making*, 9.

52 *The day after . . . "anyone's while":* Jay Carr, "Review of Fiddler on the Roof," unpublished but read on radio and TV, July 28, 1964.

52 *Peter Bellamy . . . in the mid-thirties:* Peter Bellamy, "Zero Mostel Magnificent in *Fiddler on the Roof*," *The Plain Dealer*, July 31, 1964.

52 *Before they left . . . end of the show:* Stein, *Dramatists Guild Quarterly*, 14.

53 *Altman has written . . . "time off":* Altman, *The Making*, 17 and 57.

54 *The "Chava Ballet" . . . "backbreaking rehearsal":* Sainer, *Zero Dances*, 247.

54 *And Robbins had . . . "Chava's action":* Aronson Papers, NYPL.

54 *"We found that" . . . with dancing:* Stein, *Dramatists Guild Quarterly*, 23.

55 *Bock and Harnick . . . more real to him:* *Dramatists Guild Quarterly*, Spring 1983, 13–14.

55 *Harnick was walking . . . "be more careful":* Robert Berkvist, "Jerry Bock, 'Fiddler on the Roof' Composer, Dies at 81," *New York Times*, November 3, 2010.

56 *Already Fiddler . . . "almost certain hit":* Richard Christiansen, *Chicago Daily News*, August 7, 1964.

56 *One day later . . . ticket sales:* Unsigned, "Detroit Responding to 'Fiddler on Roof,'" *New York Times*, August 8, 1964.

56 *When Fiddler opened . . . almost entirely redone:* STAGE program at Fisher Theatre, 15.

56 *Sister Mary Immaculate . . . "I ever saw":* Dan Sullivan, "A Robust 'Fiddler' Approaches Its 3rd Birthday," *New York Times*, September 4, 1967.

56 *"Fiddler for us . . . something to do":* Altman and Kaufman, *The Making*, 33.

57 *The Washington Post's . . . to his readers:* Leo Sullivan, "Fiddler on Roof is a new musical to enjoy, enjoy," *Washington Post*, August 28, 1964.

57 *Washington Star . . . "without ever finding":* Harry MacArthur, "National's 'Fiddler' a Winner," *The Star*, August 28, 1964.

57 *As Rich recounts . . . "this scene!":* Frank Rich, *Ghost Light* (New York: Random House, 2000), 211–12.

58 *Lipson had been hired . . . go on anyway:* Sainer, *Zero Dances*, 243.

58 *People could say . . . "can do it!":* Sainer, *Zero Dances*, 244.

58 *"I remember . . . than that!":* Stein, *Dramatists Guild Quarterly,* 26.

59 *Then the actor . . . "of Miracles":* Altman and Kaufman, *The Making,* 51–2.

59 *Among the many . . . routine:* Ibid. 67–8.

61 *When Robbins finished . . . "goes in tonight!":* Lawrence, *Dance with Demons,* 342.

61 *That evening . . . "forgive everything":* Altman and Kaufman, *The Making,* 68.

CHAPTER 7

62 *Robbins even . . . show better:* Maurice Edwards in Jowitt, *Jerome Robbins,* 352.

63 *When it came . . . "by your painting":* Harold Prince Papers, NYPL.

64 *According to "Frank" . . . Jewish folk music:* Frank Farrell, "Frank Farrell's New York-Day by Day: The Play was the thing, Dinner's forced to wait." *New York World-Telegram and Sun,* September 23, 1964.

64 *But after performing . . . that night:* Joanne Stang, "At Home with Tevye," *New York Times,* October 4, 1964.

64 *"Fiddler on the Roof . . . might have been":* Walter Kerr, review of *Fiddler on the Roof, New York Herald Tribune,* September 23, 1964.

64 *Daily News critic . . . "and inspiring":* John Chapman, "'Fiddler on Roof' Great Musical," *Daily News,* September 23, 1964.

65 *At The New York . . . "is relative":* Howard Taubman, "Theater: Mostel as Tevye in 'Fiddler on the Roof,'" *New York Times,* September 23, 1964.

65 *By 1:00 p.m. . . . into 1965:* Sam Zolotow, "Fiddler Scores Year's First Hit," *New York Times,* September 24, 1964.

67 *"Mail orders . . . were added":* Hackensack *New Jersey Record,* September 28, 1964.

67 *In early October . . . "artful simplicity":* Brooks Atkinson, "Artful Simplicity of Sholem Aleichem Captured in Fiddler on the Roof," *New York Times,* October 6, 1964.

67 *In a letter . . . "of the show":* Joseph Stein to Brooks Atkinson, October 7, 1964, letter courtesy of Elisa Stein.

68 Billboard *writer . . . "this season"*: Mike Gross, "Mostel Most in Musical," *Billboard*, October 3, 1964.

CHAPTER 8

69 Newsweek's *drama critic . . . "for our time"*: Richard Gilman, "Hail the Conquering Zero," *Newsweek*, October 19, 1964, 94–5.

69 *with room after room . . . books about theater*: Zero Mostel, *Zero by Mostel* (New York: Horizon Press, 1965).

69 *Kate Mostel once . . . in Europe*: Kate Mostel et al., *170 Years*, 153.

70 *according to the play . . . interview*: Jim Brochu, *Zero Hour*.

70 *His first big job . . . WPA*: Kate Mostel et al., *170 Years*, 39–40.

71 *During the initial part . . . colleagues*: Brown, *Zero Mostel*, 232.

72 *Richard Altman . . . "to* me": Altman and Kaufman, *The Making*, 112.

72 *In late May . . . Astor Hotel*: Sam Zolotow, "'Fiddler,' With 10 Nominations, Heads the List for Tony Awards," *New York Times*, May 21, 1965.

73 *Each winner . . . "will thank me"*: Brown, *Zero Mostel*, 233.

73 *For the show's . . . "bar mitzvah"*: Sam Zolotow, *New York Times*, September 22, 1966.

73 *Prince expanded . . . the 1,287-seat Broadhurst*: Sam Zolotow, "2 Shows to Shift to Bigger Houses," *New York Times*, December 16, 1966.

73 *When Prince . . . Tampere*: Dan Sullivan, "A Robust Fiddler Approached Its 3rd Birthday," *New York Times*, September 4, 1967.

73 *The* New York Times *. . . "as fresh"*: Clive Barnes, "Theater Reappraisal: 1259th 'Fiddler on the Roof' Retains the Freshness of 3 Years and 6 Days Ago," *New York Times*, September 28, 1967.

75 *As part of a tribute . . . in song*: See www.timeout.com/newyork /theater/tony-clip-5-bette-midler-in-Fiddler-on-the-Roof-1968 -musicals.

75 *Maria . . . "warm blanket"*: Barnes, "Theater Reappraisal," September 28, 1967.

75 In September 1968 . . . and Canada: "2d Fiddler Going on Road," *New York Times*, July 27, 1968.

75 *In early 1969 . . . for curtain calls:* Richard Piro, *Black Fiddler* (New York: William Morrow, 1971).

77 *On Wednesday . . . various languages:* Louis Calta, "'Fiddler' Is Saying Hello to a Record," *New York Times,* July 21, 1971.

77 *According to . . . producer:* Harold Prince Papers, NYPL.

78 *At the end . . . in 1974:* "Mayor Hails 'Fiddler' At 2,845th Performance," *New York Times,* July 22, 1971.

78 *Less than a year . . . sang "Tradition":* Phillips McCandlish, "Fiddler, 3,225 Performances Old, Tops Long-Run List; Fiddler Becomes Theater's Longest-Running Hit," *New York Times,* June 18, 1972.

79 *The show was . . .* New York Times: "'Fiddler' Bows Out After 3,242d Show," *New York Times,* July 3, 1972.

79 Fiddler *held its . . . December 8, 1979:* Tom Buckley, "'Grease' Breaks a Record on Broadway," *New York Times,* December 7, 1979.

79 *However, while . . . Broadway show:* The Broadway League.

79 *As* Fiddler *. . . than $3.7 million:* Christopher Pennington, Executive Director, the Jerome Robbins Foundation/The Robbins Rights Trust.

79 *In 1987 . . . said Robbins.* Robert Greskovic, "'Fiddler' Royalties Support Dance Film Collection," *Los Angeles Times,* June 3, 1987.

CHAPTER 9

81 *"He was . . . ruin the show":* Lawrence, *Dance with Demons,* 349.

81 *Future Tevye . . . "had Golde!":* Theodore Bikel, *Theo: The Autobiography of Theodore Bikel* (Madison: University of Wisconsin Press, 1994), 323.

82 *The situation . . . "way of coping":* Bryer and Davison, eds., *The Art of the American Musical,* 91–2.

83 *Asked when . . . "were concerned":* Bock, *Dramatists Guild Quarterly,* 21.

84 *"Zero . . . two minutes":* David Cote, interview with Joseph Stein, *The Times* (London), May 14, 2007.

84 *For example . . . "hole with dirt":* Altman and Kaufman, *The Making,* 117.

84 *The producer knew . . . "the story":* Prince, *Contradictions,* 105–6.

84 *As early as . . . would be "impossible":* Harold Prince Papers, NYPL.

86 *Several established stars . . . "star equipment":* Ibid.

86 *Apprised of their . . . him the words:* Chaim Topol, *Topol by Topol.* (London: Weidenfeld and Nicolson, 1981), 3.

87 *"I had seen . . . Tevye":* Kelly Nestruck, *The Guardian,* May 18, 2007.

88 *"What Jerry did . . . that was Jerry":* Lawrence, *Dance with Demons,* 349–50.

88 *"Once in a generation . . . star overnight":* Altman and Kaufman, *The Making,* 168.

88 *Sixteen critics . . . "of the season":* Stanley Richards, ed., *Ten Great Musicals of the American Theatre* (Radnor, PA: Chilton Book Co., 1973), 743.

89 *Topol's description . . . "the next best thing":* Topol, *Topol,* 116.

89 *The London production . . . again in 1994:* See www.atthemusicals .com.

CHAPTER 10

93 *Also in Fiddler's Broadway audience . . . unlikely:* Walter Mirisch, *I Thought We Were Making Movies, Not History* (Madison: University of Wisconsin Press, 2008), 303.

93 *"I tried . . . willing to wait":* Altman and Kaufman, *The Making,* 181.

93 *By the time . . . months:* A. H. Weiler, "United Artists Reported Close to Acquiring 'Fiddler on Roof,'" *New York Times,* January 26, 1966.

94 *United Artists purchased . . . a while:* Prince, *Contradictions,* 109.

94 *The next question was . . . Robbins and Wise:* Turner Classic Movies Classic Film Festival screening of *West Side Story,* May 1, 2011.

94 *when* West Side Story *. . . for directing:* See www.oscars.org.

96 *Actor George . . . "do something":* TCM screening, 2011.

98 *As he did all that . . . and Romania:* Norman Jewison, *This Terrible Business Has Been Good to Me* (New York: Thomas Dunne Books/ St. Martin's Press, 2005), 177.

98 *At one point . . . "to insure the film":* Q&A after screening of *Fiddler on the Roof,* Norman Jewison retrospective, Film Society of Lincoln Center, Walter Reade Theater, New York, May 29, 2011.

98 *The army wasn't . . . "were removed":* Fiddler on the Roof movie souve-

nir program, 1971, Cinematic Arts Library, University of Southern California.

99 *"In trying to . . . must have":* Herb A. Lightman, "On Location with 'Fiddler on the Roof,'" *American Cinematographer*, December 1970, 1222, Herrick Library.

99 *They did extensive . . . "anything else":* Robert Boyle and George E. Turner, *An Oral History* (Margaret Herrick Library, Academy of Motion Picture Arts and Sciences, Oral History Program, 1998), 236

99 *In Israel . . . "period details":* Hannah Brown, "Topol pays his debt to Tevye," *Jerusalem Post*, December 16, 2004.

99 *The director wanted to . . . immediate surroundings:* Jewison, *This Terrible Business*, 178–80.

100 *But while . . . "plot points":* Altman and Kaufman, *The Making*, 187.

CHAPTER 11

101 *"I didn't like . . . immediately":* Film Society of Lincoln Center screening, May 29, 2011.

101 *"I think the casting . . . century":* Scott Simon, *Weekend Edition*, National Public Radio, October 13, 2001.

102 *Among the performers . . . Burton:* Altman and Kaufman, *The Making*, 184.

102 *The creative team . . . an old man:* United Artists press release, Herrick Library.

103 *He saw Topol's . . . "imagination had":* Jewison, *This Terrible Business*, 179.

103 *"Chaim Topol . . . life into Tevye":* Lincoln Center, May 29, 2011.

103 *Topol had joked . . . "blame him?":* Topol, *Topol*, 147.

103 *His biographer . . . "talk about it":* Brown, *Zero Mostel*, 277–78.

104 *Mostel's son . . . "Topol's son!":* People, March 7, 1988, Herrick Library.

104 *Jewison and his . . . then seventy-two:* Fiddler on the Roof souvenir program, 1971, Cinematic Arts Library, University of Southern California.

105 *Maria Karniolva . . . also considered:* Mirisch, *I Thought*, 308.

105 *entering a field . . . got the part:* Altman and Kaufman, *The Making*, 185.

105 *"There was something . . . from Norma":* Lincoln Center, May 29, 2011. Jewison notes in his book *This Terrible Business Has Been Good to Me* that Crane was undergoing treatment for breast cancer while the movie was being made but kept her illness private, except for telling Jewison and a few others. She died in September 1973, at age forty-four.

106 *Altman explained . . . "Tzeitel-like quality":* Altman and Kaufman, *The Making*, 191.

108 *Leonard Frey . . . Boys* in the Band: Altman and Kaufman, *The Making*, 190.

108 During fall 2013 and early 2014, actor Glaser toured the U.K. as Tevye in a stage production of *Fiddler on the Roof.* Reviewers praised his charisma, humor, and Russian accent.

109 *Lovelock was . . . English father:* Souvenir program, Cinematic Arts Library, USC.

CHAPTER 12

110 *The director was . . . Putney Heath:* Jewison, *This Terrible Business*, 175–77.

110 *At Pinewood . . . and others: The Players and the Film-Makers,* Cinematic Arts Library, USC.

111 *Abbott, who had . . . "starting fresh":* Altman and Kaufman, 182 and 195.

112 *Jewison turned . . . "ask him":* Lincoln Center, May 29, 2011.

113 *When the director . . . "it was wonderful":* Ibid.

CHAPTER 13

117 *The Yugoslavian village . . . synagogue:* Altman and Kaufman, *The Making*, 199.

117 *Boyle worried . . . "in Poland":* Boyle and Turner, *An Oral History*, 236–38.

118 *Boyle also found . . . he observed: Fiddler on the Roof* (2-Disc Collector's Edition) DVD 2006.

118 *The production . . . Anatevka:* Boyle and Turner, *An Oral History,* 237.

118 *When writer . . . "the shooting":* Herb A. Lightman, "On Location with 'Fiddler on the Roof,'" *American Cinematographer,* December 1970, 1204–11, Herrick Library.

118 *Morris had . . . "should look!":* Oswald Morris and Geoffrey Bull, *Huston, We Have a Problem: A Kaleidoscope of Filmmaking Memories* (Lanham, MD: Scarecrow Press, 2006), 242–45.

119 *most of the actors . . . exchange:* Hotel Esplanade Inter-Continental brochure, 1971.

119 *Actress Molly Picon . . . "the parks":* Picon letter, September 2, 1970, Howard W. Fleming Collection, Herrick Library.

120 *Before filming . . . "Shave their pits!":* Warren Clements, "Extra! Extra! Extra!" *Globe and Mail,* January 26, 2007.

120 *Transportation was . . . just for him:* Morris and Bull, *Huston, We Have,* 243.

121 *Asked what was his greatest . . . sunshine: Fiddler on the Roof* (2-Disc Collector's Edition).

121 *Even if snow . . . very cold outside:* Morris and Bull, *Huston, We Have,* 247–48.

122 *Topol, in turn . . . "my heart":* Topol, *Topol,* 155.

123 *"Look at these faces . . . anywhere else":* Lightman, "On Location with," 1244.

123 *Yugoslavian residents . . . grow out:* Randy Haberkamp, *Fiddler on the Roof,* Great to Be Nominated program, Academy of Motion Picture Arts and Sciences, July 24, 2006.

123 *"Our experience . . . look Jewish":* Topol, *Topol,* 156.

125 *A documentary . . . wiping away tears: Fiddler on the Roof* (2-Disc Collector's Edition).

125 *While it worked . . . humidity inside:* Morris and Bull, *Huston, We Have,* 245.

126 *Within the huge . . . back in London:* Boyle and Turner, *An Oral History,* 238–39.

126 *They were fortunately . . . "the hills":* Morris and Bull, *Huston, We Have*, 247.

126 *The cinematographer . . . "into their faces":* *Weekend Edition*, October 13, 2001.

126 *By fall . . . bottle dance there:* Morris and Bull, *Huston, We Have*, 246.

126 *Writing to a friend . . . "whiskey":* Picon letter, Herrick Library.

127 *Later, in London . . . "been destroyed":* Bernard Weinraub, "Tevye's Suffering Enacted for Movie," *New York Times*, January 5, 1971.

127 *Back at Pinewood . . . dream sequence:* Morris and Bull, *Huston, We Have*, 249

127 *Jewison wrote a friend . . . "great snow":* Hal Ashby Collection, Herrick Library.

CHAPTER 14

128 *The evening . . . "personalities":* Mirisch, *I Thought We Were Making Movies*, 310.

128 *It concluded . . . John Lindsay:* Jerry Bock Papers, NYPL.

128 *Opening night . . . film and supper:* Bernadine Morris, "After Fiddler, a Benefit Fete, and Another, and Another," *New York Times*, November 5, 1971.

129 *The major critics . . . "film ever":* Ernest Parmentier, ed., *filmfacts:* a publication of the American Film Institute, March 15, 1972.

129 *Writing in . . . "ever made":* Pauline Kael, "A Bagel with a Bite Out of It," *The New Yorker*, November 13, 1971.

129 *Vincent Canby . . . "life out of it":* Vincent Canby, "Fiddler on a Grand Scale: Life-style of the Aleichem Characters Is Missing Amid Production's Grandeur," *New York Times*, November 4, 1971.

130 *Variety critic . . . "box office":* Land., "Fiddler on the Roof," *Variety*, November 1, 1971.

130 *Argentina . . . Finland:* See www.imdb.com.

131 *In Israel . . . wipe away a tear:* Jimy Tallal, "Director Norman Jewison tells tales of *Fiddler on the Roof*," *Malibu Times*, May 5, 2010.

132 *The 44th Academy Awards . . . Courage:* Herrick Library.

132 *Cinematographer . . . silk stocking:* Ibid.

132 *"It was entirely . . . experiences"*: Morris, *Huston, We Have a Problem*, 250.

133 *Topol won a Golden Globe . . . "solid gold"*: Topol, *Topol*, 103.

133 *A disappointed . . . and others*: Jewison's film *The Hurricane*, which starred Denzel Washington as boxer Rubin "Hurricane" Carter, was released later that year, garnering critical praise. See www.oscars.org.

133 *By 1999 . . . Oscars*: Ibid.

133 *While the . . . "movement"*: Mirisch, *I Thought We Were Making Movies*, 310–12.

134 *Around the time . . . "Christianson"*: Film Society of Lincoln Center, May 29, 2011.

CHAPTER 15

138 *One after another . . . pass up*: Louis Calta, *New York Times*, December 7, 1971.

138 *Adler, who made . . . on Broadway*: Wolfgang Saxon, obituary for Luther Adler, *New York Times*, December 9, 1984.

138 *By the time . . . "one thousand times"*: John Corry, "The 17 Years of 'Fiddler' Tradition," *New York Times*, July 20, 1981.

138 *Paul Lipson returned . . . death in 1996*: Mel Gussow, obituary for Paul Lipson, *New York Times*, January 5, 1996.

141 *When Luther Adler . . . "examined"*: "Luther Adler Tour in 'Fiddler' Planned," *New York Times*, January 27, 1966.

141 *Consider John Preece . . . "this part"*: James D. Watts, Jr., "Actor hits 1,900th performance as Tevye in 'Fiddler on the Roof,'" *Tulsa World*, May 6, 2012.

141 *By late 2011 . . . "what we do"*: Bruce R. Miller, "Tradition: Actor Holds Record for 'Fiddler' performances," *Sioux City Journal*, November 11, 2011.

142 *Playing the Edinburgh . . . on the part!"*: Gillian Ferguson, "Topol Meets His Match," *The Sunday Times* (London), September 4, 1994.

142 *Zero Mostel came back . . . "because of Zero"*: Brown, *Zero Mostel*, 289.

144 *Producers of . . . across the stage:* See www.youtube.com/watch?v=ah
    AOU1HZXlc.

144 *In 1976 . . . until June 1977:* Kate Mostel et al., *170 Years*, 170.

145 *Mostel brought with . . . paid for it:* Brown, *Zero Mostel*, 292.

145 *The tour did very . . . "every few seasons":* Zero Mostel Papers, NYPL.

145 *By the time. . . . "beautifully":* David Richards, "Fiddler Is Still In
    Tune," *Washington Post*, December 29, 1976.

145 *Jerome Robbins. . . . "prayer shawl":* Mel Gussow, *New York Times*,
    December 30, 1976.

146 Fiddler *played . . . "other one stayed":* Brown, *Zero Mostel*, 294–96.

147 *Not long after . . . sixty-two years of age:* Kate Mostel et al., *170 Years*,
    171–74.

147 *Mostel . . . "theatergoer's actor":* Robert D. McFadden, *New York Times*,
    September 9, 1977.

147 *Robbins got involved . . . "and direct":* John Corry, "The 17 Years of
    'Fiddler' Tradition," *New York Times*, July 20, 1981.

147 *"It's a good enough . . . out of that":* Dan Sullivan, "A Robust Fiddler
    Approached Its 3rd Birthday," *New York Times*, September 4, 1967.

148 *Fiddler hadn't changed . . . "masterpiece?":* John Corry, "The 17 Years
    of Fiddler Tradition," *New York Times*, July 20, 1981.

148 *"I saw this Fiddler . . . aren't that good":* John Corry, "The Other Star
    of 'Fiddler,'" *New York Times*, December 31, 1973.

148 *It was back . . . "respectful replications":* David Richards, "Tried and
    Trusty Fiddler; At National Theatre, Familiar Tunes," *Washington
    Post*, March 24, 1990.

CHAPTER 16

151 *Molina didn't seem . . . "it's irrelevant":* Joe Dziemianowicz, "He
    raises a new 'roof,'" New York *Daily News*, February 6, 2004.

151 *At the start . . . original production:* Desmond Ryan, "Déjà vu on Broad-
    way: 7 revivals in the wings," *Philadelphia Inquirer*, February 22, 2004.

152 *Given that expectation . . . "'Matchmaker'":* Matthew Gurewitsch,
    "Tradition? The Delicate Task of Retuning 'Fiddler,'" *New York Times*,
    February 26, 2004.

152 *Writing the song . . . "same pressure":* Ibid.

152 *Yet Bock conceded . . . into rehearsal:* Terry Gross, *Fresh Air*, National Public Radio, June 21, 2004.

153 *Given their . . . "separated":* Ibid.

155 *Various reporters . . . "not injured":* Jason Zinoman, "On Stage and Off," *New York Times*, March 5, 2004. In a profile of Riedel for *New York* on May 21, 2005, Meryl Gordon recalled the incident, quoting a headline from the *New York Post*'s "Page Six," which read " 'ROOF' DIRECTOR FLOORS POST."

155 *by the novelist . . . "Jewish soul":* See Thane Rosenbaum, "Playing to Everyone," *Los Angeles Times*, February 15, 2004.

155 *Cultural critic . . . "pure Broadway":* Ruth Franklin, "Shtetl Shtick," *New York Times*, February 29, 2004.

155 *Writer Philip Roth . . . "shtetl kitsch":* Philip Roth, "Rereading Saul Bellow," *The New Yorker*, October 9, 2000.

155 *For Ozick . . . "he repudiated":* Cynthia Ozick, "Sholem Aleichem's Revolution," *The New Yorker*, March 28, 1988.

155 *In a review . . . "that it did":* Ben Brantley, "A Cozy Little McShtetl," *New York Times*, February 27, 2004.

156 Washington Post *critic . . . Verandah:* Peter Marks, "A Fiddler on the Roof Hopelessly Out of Tune," *Washington Post*, February 27, 2004.

156 *More positive was . . . "baseless":* John Simon, *New York*, March 8, 2004.

156 *And at the . . . "poetic momentum":* John Lahr, "Bittersweet," *The New Yorker*, March 8, 2004.

156 Time's *Richard Zoglin . . . "for everybody":* Richard Zoglin, "Theater: Getting Beyond Zero," *Time*, March 8, 2004.

156 *Concluded* Variety *. . . "on the Roof":* Christopher Isherwood, "Fiddler's Somber Tune," *Variety*, March 1, 2004.

157 *"My world exploded . . . Jewish, too":* Harvey Fierstein, Artsbeat blog, *New York Times*, November 5, 2010.

158 *In a* New York Times *review . . . "of one":* Ben Brantley, "An Exotic Tevye in Old Anatevka," *New York Times*, January 21, 2005.

158 *Countered . . . "enchanted":* Clive Barnes, *New York Post,* January 21, 2005.

158 *Then came . . . "strike twice":* Jesse McKinley, "Shaking Things Up in Broadway's Shtetl," *New York Times,* August 8, 2005.

158 *Brantley . . . "is saying":* Ben Brantley, "Tevye Takes a New Wife, and This One Is TV Famous," *New York Times,* October 14, 2005.

CHAPTER 17

163 *As the* New York Times' *. . . "until he dies":* Brantley, "A Cozy Little McShtetl."

CHAPTER 18

169 Fiddler on the Roof *. . . four weeks:* David Benedict, *Variety,* July 16–22, 2007.

169 *The* Daily Express *. . . "West End":* See www.thisistheatre.com.

170 *A reporter was . . . "play him":* "*Fiddler on the Roof* Opens in Germany to Warm Applause," *New York Times,* February 2, 1968.

171 *A production in Prague . . . "last night":* Thomas Quinn Curtiss, "Paris Welcomes 'Fiddler' at Last," *New York Times,* November 16, 1969.

171 *Nearly two decades . . . "Soviet Union":* Andrew Rosenthal, Associated Press, *The Globe and Mail,* December 26, 1983.

170 *Fiddler played Warsaw . . . "cities and towns":* Matthew C. Vita, Associated Press, *The Globe and Mail,* April 16, 1985.

171 *"I get a lot of joy . . . each time"* Unidentified video interview, April 26, 2004.

172 *The first production . . . Bayes:* Robert Trumbull, "Japanese 'Fiddler on the Roof' Welcomed by Tokyo Audience," *New York Times,* September 7, 1967

172 *Violinist Isaac Stern . . . "a few men":* Isaac Stern with Chaim Potok, *My First 79 Years* (New York: Alfred A. Knopf, 1999), 105.

173 *Morishige was . . . "good friend":* Tomoya Iwasaki, *The Daily Yomiuri,* Tokyo, December 5, 1998.

173 *It was when . . . "turbulence":* Joseph Stein as told to Kelly Nestruck, *The Guardian*, May 18, 2007.

174 By December 2012, a rehearsal video of "Tradition" in Japanese had 578,000 hits on YouTube. See www.youtube.com/watch?v=e GoRo-nPLOM.

175 *With its timeless . . . "toothless":* Joseph Stein, Jerry Bock and Sheldon Harnick, *Fiddler on the Roof* (New York: Crown, 1964), 105.

175 *The better the play . . . "not to follow traditions":* Barbara Isenberg, "Surprise—It's Tradition," *Los Angeles Times*, January 13, 2002.

175 *"We worked . . . everybody else":* Thane Rosenbaum, "Playing to Everyone," *Los Angeles Times*, January 15, 2004.

175 Fiddler on the Roof . . . *"as* Fiddler *has":* Roger Bennett and Josh Kun, *And You Shall Know Us by the Trail of our Vinyl: The Jewish Past as Told by the Records We Have Loved and Lost* (New York: Crown, 2008), 144–45.

176 *"What the show . . . experiment that worked":* Barbara Isenberg, "Surprise—It's Tradition," *Los Angeles Times*, January 13, 2002.

CHAPTER 19

177 *When Miranda got . . . "our blueprint":* Unedited footage, *The Legacy Project*, Dramatists Guild Fund, courtesy of Elisa Stein.

179 *Miranda's nearly six-minute video . . . the number one video in Israel:* See www.youtube.com/watch?v=KgZ4ZTTfKO8.

180 *The lyrics had . . . "than this song?":* richardskipper.blogspot.com, October 4, 2011.

181 *The original lyrics . . . "at play":* Erik Piepenburg, "Miracle of Miracles: 'Sunrise, Sunset' Gets a Gay Makeover," *New York Times*, October 3, 2011.

181 *When New Yorker . . . 'a Rich Man'":* John Mazor, "Lotto's Luckiest Seven," *New York Post*, September 22, 2007.

181 *The first popularized . . . in clubs:* See www.youtube.com/watch?v=z 432Pwci0-Y.

181 *Gwen Stefani . . . "gown":* See www.youtube.com/watch?v=9rlNp WYQunY.

181 *Besides cast albums . . . Tevyes:* See *And You Shall Know Us by the Trail of our Vinyl: The Jewish Past as Told by the Records We Have Loved and Lost* by Roger Bennett and Josh Kun.

182 *For instance . . . "to that role":* "The Book of Mormon's Josh Gad recalls life as a teenage Tevye," www.broadway.com, September 8, 2011.

182 *And when . . . "'Sunrise, Sunset'":* Jason Solomons, *The Observer,* December 4, 2004.

183 *Sacha Baron Cohen . . . for the film:* John Hiscock, *The Telegraph,* December 21, 2007.

183 *Producer . . . "right then":* Larry Getlen, *New York Post,* March 30, 2008.

184 The Simpsons . . . *"watch it":* See simpsonswiki.com/wiki/Homer's_Triple_Bypass/Quotes.

184 In April 2004 . . . *"Attached":* See www.youtube.com/watch?v=_dprUZL-QvQ.

184 Fiddler *was used . . . of "Tradition":* Jeannie Lieberman, www.theaterscene.net, April 24, 2007.

185 In 2012, Miranda's cowriter, Quiara Alegría Hudes, did win the Pulitzer Prize, for "a distinguished play by an American author." Her play, *Water by the Spoonful,* recounted life after Iraq for a returning war veteran.

CHAPTER 20

190 *Also speaking . . . "in my life":* Bock Memorial, January 24, 2011.

190 *By fall . . . at the time: New York Times,* September 3, 1968.

190 *A few months . . . "Jerry Bock": The Dramatist,* March/April 2011. Brad Oscar, a Tony Award nominee for creating the role of Franz Liebkind in *The Producers,* did a turn as Tevye in the summer of 2012 at the Barrington Stage Company.

190 *Joseph Stein . . . "was exciting":* Gregory Bossler, "Writers & Their Work," 9.

190 *Rags. . . . "open!!":* Kenneth Jones, www.playbill.com, November 10, 1999.

191 *Around the same time... "Rich Man"*: Amir Mizroch and Yaakov Katz, *Jerusalem Post*, September 4, 2009.

193 *Asked if he had concerns... "two such roles"*: Cathie James, "Topol—The Once and Future Fiddler," *Toronto Star*, July 31, 1990.

194 *Librettist Harnick... "screw it up"*: Lincoln Center screening, May 29, 2011.

Selected Bibliography

Aleichem, Sholom. *Favorite Tales of Sholom Aleichem*. Trans. Julius and Frances Butwin. New York: Avenel Books, 1983.

————. *Old Country Tales*. Trans. Curt Leviant. New York: Putnam, 1966.

————. *Tevye's Daughters*. New York: Crown, 1949.

————. *Wandering Stars*. New York: Crown, 1952.

Altman, Richard, and Mervyn Kaufman. *The Making of a Musical: Fiddler on the Roof*. New York: Crown, 1971.

Atkinson, Brooks. "Artful Simplicity of Sholem Aleichem Captured in 'Fiddler on the Roof.'" *New York Times*, October 6, 1964.

Bennett, Roger, and Josh Kun. *And You Shall Know Us by the Trail of Our Vinyl: The Jewish Past as Told by the Records We Have Loved and Lost*. New York: Crown, 2008.

Bikel, Theodore. *Theo: An Autobiography of Theodore Bikel*. Madison: University of Wisconsin Press, 2002.

Bock, Jerry, Sheldon Harnick, and Joseph Stein. Interview by Peter Stone. "Fiddler on the Roof." *Dramatists Guild Quarterly*, Spring 1983.

Bordman, Gerald. *American Musical Theatre: A Chronicle*. London: Oxford University Press, 1978.

Bossler, Gregory. "Writers & Their Work: Joseph Stein." *The Dramatist*, January/February 2006.

Boyle, Robert F. and George E. Turner. *An Oral History with Robert F. Boyle*. Beverly Hills, CA: Academy of Motion Picture Arts and Sciences, Oral History Program, 1998.

Brown, Jared. *Zero Mostel: A Biography*. New York: Atheneum, 1989.

Bryer, Jackson, and Richard Davison, eds., *The Art of the American Musical: Conversations with the Creators*. New Brunswick, NJ and London: Rutgers University Press, 2005.

Calta, Louis. "Fiddler Is Saying Hello to a Record." *New York Times*, July 21, 1971.

Chagall, Marc. *My Life*. Trans. Dorothy Williams. London: Peter Owen, 1965.

Corry, John. "The 17 Years of 'Fiddler' Tradition." *New York Times*, July 20, 1981.

Fiddler on the Roof (2-Disc Collector's Edition) DVD. Directed by Norman Jewison. Metro-Goldwyn-Mayer, 2006.

Great to be Nominated 3: Fiddler on the Roof DVD. The Academy of Motion Picture Arts and Sciences, 2006.

Gilman, Richard. "Hail the Conquering Zero." *Newsweek*, October 19, 1964.

Greskovic, Robert. *Los Angeles Times*, June 3, 1987.

Guernsey, Otis L. *The Best Plays of 1964–1965 (The Burns Mantle Theater Yearbook)*. New York: Dodd Mead, 1965.

Hansen, Liane. "Jerry Bock and Sheldon Harnick discuss writing music for Fiddler on the Roof." *Fresh Air*. National Public Radio. June 21, 2004.

Isenberg, Barbara. "Surprise—It's Tradition," *Los Angeles Times*, January 13, 2002.

Jewison, Norman. *This Terrible Business Has Been Good to Me*. New York: Thomas Dunne Books/St. Martin's Press, 2005.

Jowitt, Deborah. *Jerome Robbins: His Life, His Theater, His Dance*. New York: Simon & Schuster, 2004.

Kael, Pauline. "A Bagel with a Bite Out of It." *Deeper Into Movies*. Boston and Toronto: Atlantic Monthly Press Book/Little, Brown, 1973.

Lambert, Philip. *To Broadway, To Life!: The Musical Theater of Bock and Harnick*. New York: Oxford University Press, 2010.

Lawrence, Greg. *Dance with Demons: The Life of Jerome Robbins.* New York: G. P. Putnam's Sons, 2001.

Lightman, Herb A. "On Location with 'Fiddler on the Roof.'" *American Cinematographer*, December 1970.

"Mayor Hails 'Fiddler' at 2,845th Performance." *New York Times*, July 22, 1971.

McFadden, Robert D. "Zero Mostel Dies of Heart Failure at 62; Star of 'Fiddler' Was Trying Out New Play." *New York Times*, September 9, 1977.

Mirisch, Walter. *I Thought We Were Making Movies, Not History.* Madison: University of Wisconsin Press, 2008.

Morris, Bernadine. "After 'Fiddler' a Benefit Fete, and Another, and Another." *New York Times*, November 5, 1971.

Morris, Oswald, with Geoffrey Bull. *Huston, We Have a Problem: A Kaleidoscope of Filmmaking Memories.* Lanham, MD: Scarecrow Press, 2006.

Mostel, Kate and Madeline Gilford with Jack Gilford and Zero Mostel. *170 Years of Show Business.* New York: Random House, 1978.

Mostel, Zero. *Zero by Mostel.* New York: Horizon Press, 1965.

Piro, Richard. *Black Fiddler.* New York: William Morrow, 1971.

Prince, Hal. *Contradictions: Notes on Twenty-six Years in the Theatre.* New York: Dodd, Mead, 1974.

Rich, Frank. *Ghost Light: A Memoir.* Random House, 2000.

Rich, Frank with Lisa Aronson. *The Theatre Art of Boris Aronson.* New York: Alfred A. Knopf, 1987.

Sainer, Arthur. *Zero Dances: A Biography of Zero Mostel.* New York: Limelight Editions, 1998.

Stage: The Program for the Fisher Theatre. Detroit, 1964.

Stein, Joseph and Jerry Bock and Sheldon Harnick. *Fiddler on the Roof.* New York: Crown, 1964.

Stern, Isaac with Chaim Potok. *My First 79 Years.* New York: Alfred A. Knopf, 1999.

Topol, Chaim. *Topol by Topol.* London: Weidenfeld and Nicolson, 1981.

Vaill, Amanda. *Jerome Robbins: Something to Dance About.* American Masters, PBS, July 31, 2009.

————. *Somewhere: The Life of Jerome Robbins*. New York: Broadway Books, 2006.

Vishniac, Roman. *Polish Jews: A Pictorial Record*. New York: Schocken Books, 1947.

Vogel, Frederick G. *Hollywood Musicals Nominated for Best Picture*. Jefferson, NC and London: McFarland, 2003.

Zborowski, Mark and Elizabeth Herzog. *Life Is with People: The Culture of the Shtetl*. Foreword by Margaret Mead. Madison, CT: International Universities Press, 1952.

Zolotow, Sam. "Aleichem Stories Inspire a Musical." *New York Times*, August 20, 1962.

————. "'Fiddler' Scores Year's First Hit: 300 Line Up for Tickets to Musical with Mostel." *New York Times*, September 24, 1964.

Index